America at Risk

CONTEMPORARY POLITICAL AND SOCIAL ISSUES

Alan Wolfe, Series Editor

Contemporary Political and Social Issues provides a forum in which social scientists and seasoned observers of the political scene use their expertise to comment on issues of contemporary importance in American politics, including immigration, affirmative action, religious conflict, gay rights, welfare reform, and globalization.

Putting Faith in Partnerships:Welfare-to-Work in Four Cities
   Stephen V. Monsma

The New Imperial Presidency: Renewing Presidential Power after Watergate
   Andrew Rudalevige

Self-Financed Candidates in Congressional Elections
   Jennifer A. Steen

Trust beyond Borders: Immigration, the Welfare State, and Identity in Modern Societies
   Markus M. L. Crepaz

America Beyond Black and White: How Immigrants and Fusions Are Helping Us Overcome the Racial Divide
   Ronald Fernandez

America at Risk: Threats to Liberal Self-Government in an Age of Uncertainty
   Robert Faulkner and Susan Shell, Editors

America at Risk

Threats to Liberal Self-Government in an Age of Uncertainty

Edited by

Robert Faulkner and Susan Shell

With the Assistance of Thomas E. Schneider

THE UNIVERSITY OF MICHIGAN PRESS

ANN ARBOR

Copyright © by the University of Michigan 2009

All rights reserved

Published in the United States of America by

The University of Michigan Press

Manufactured in the United States of America

☉ Printed on acid-free paper

2012 2011 2010 2009   4 3 2 1

A CIP catalog record for this book is available from the British Library.

Library of Congress Cataloging-in-Publication Data

America at risk : threats to liberal self-government in an age of
uncertainty / edited by Robert Faulkner and Susan Shell ; with the
Assistance of Thomas E. Schneider.
     p.   cm. — (Contemporary political and social issues)
    Includes bibliographical references and index.
    ISBN-13: 978-0-472-11668-3 (cloth : alk. paper)
    ISBN-10: 0-472-11668-1 (cloth : alk. paper)
    1. Liberalism—United States.   2. Democracy—United States.
3. United States—Politics and government—2001–   I. Faulkner, Robert
K., 1934–   II. Shell, Susan Meld, 1948–   III. Schneider, Thomas E., 1963–

JC574.2.U6A45   2009
320.973—dc22

2008022949

Acknowledgments

This book was supported by a grant from the John M. Olin Foundation. Indeed, the book is a commemoration, now that the Olin Foundation has closed its doors, of generosity that began in 1997. The Olin grant enabled Boston College's Department of Political Science to sponsor many stimulating talks and debates, of which the opinions and differences expressed here are some indication. We particularly thank the foundation's agile representatives, William Voegeli and James Piereson.

The editors are grateful to Marc Landy, Dennis Hale, R. Shep Melnick, and Alan Wolfe for good counsel in the planning and in arranging publication. We owe special thanks to Thomas E. Schneider, who prepared the essays for publication, and to Jeffrey Bacon, who put together the index.

We are grateful above all to our authors for the quality of their contributions.

Robert Faulkner and Susan Shell

Contents

Part Four: Dilemmas of Self-Government

America at Risk

Introduction

The purpose of this book can be simply stated: to set forth and examine the most important dangers confronting America today. With that aim the editors sought out political analysts whom we had reason to think first-rate. Then we encouraged each to select a problem that he or she thought particularly serious. The result is this volume of essays. While plural in spirit, there is a central theme: the corrosion of the liberal constitutional order that has for so long guided the country at home and abroad.

Why such a volume now? By most accounts America is for the foreseeable future the most powerful nation in the world. That power, however, is hardly accompanied by a spirit of triumphalism. As we write, a troubled war in Iraq remains of doubtful outcome. Both major political parties are in a state of some intellectual and moral disarray. The country remains hopelessly dependent for the time being on foreign resources, both mineral and monetary. And the rising economic and military powers to the East remind us that no nation remains supreme forever. Our best efforts to prevent the spread of nuclear weapons to irresponsible regimes seem to be stymied. And world opinion of the United States appears to be at an all-time low.

To be sure, American democracy retains enviable strengths. Its economy has been an engine of growth and power. Its military power is unrivaled. The authority of our Constitution and the legitimacy of our basic institutions are taken for granted by the vast majority of citizens. We enjoy extraordinary freedom, prosperity, and security. And the spirit of the nation remains remarkably unbowed. Americans seem willing to do more to meet the challenges that the country faces than has so far been asked of them. Nevertheless, one of the luxuries of strength is the opportunity for thoughtful reflection on the dangers ahead.

Among the authors in this book the reader will not find visionary reformers, philosophic dreamers, angry revolutionaries, or gloomy reactionaries. The work is not a forum for the extreme or impracticable, however desirable in another land, time, or world, nor is it a partisan tract. Amid the variety of political outlooks in the United States we looked to those from different camps who wished to preserve the country and, if to reform it, to do so without giving up its fundamental liberal, democratic, and capitalist arrangements. We looked above all for authors who, rising above the narrowness of political sect and party, might also rise above conventional narrownesses of issue, "cause," and doctrine. Also, unlike other volumes of similar title, this one is not limited to a particular aspect of the American order, be it democratic fairness, homeland security, or K–12 education. It aims instead to sketch a broad picture, composed through the wide-ranging reflections of a diverse group of authors. A number of concerns, to be sure, such as race and specific problems of the poor, are not adequately or directly addressed. And there are, no doubt, many important voices and points of view not here included. Within such limits, the volume attempts nevertheless to foster a conversation that speaks directly and productively, without the jargon and zeal of methodologies, schools, or narrow creeds, to major challenges of the years ahead. Such a conversation, we think, is long overdue. It is our good fortune as a nation to have the time and resources to think past the present. It would be a shame if, in the pressure of the moment and of academic "business as usual," such an opportunity were missed.

Amid the variety, the essays that follow sound several persistent themes: political ideas matter and are in a troubled state; domestic and foreign affairs cannot be neatly separated; and democracy and liberal self-government, for all their strengths, presently suffer from peculiar weaknesses that we ignore at our peril.

In Part 1, "Wages of Empire," two critical but sympathetic foreign voices address American foreign policy with a penetration that reaches to issues of domestic character and weakness. They bring out, to begin with, the general reluctance of America to assume the imperial role that past "superpowers" have often adopted. Pierre Manent, in "The Transatlantic Predicament," encourages the reluctance and discourages the imperialism. He sketches with foreboding the widening gap in outlook between the United States and Europe in particular. The United States, victorious in its great wars, thinking itself innocent in its devotion to human rights and self-government, prides itself in being *the* model of humane and democratic ways. In fact, it has edged aside European colonialism only to take on itself an implicitly imperial role, worldwide, and a "colonial" disdain, not least for its European allies in particular. This is not simply George W. Bush's doing. It is a development long in the making, Manent relates, and the American conduct of the Iraq war—which under the guise of a war on terrorism sought "a huge, an unheard-of reformation of the Muslim world"—was the not unpredictable effect. American identification of enlightened progress with its own aggrandizing self-interest galls the Europeans. According to Manent, however, the Europeans are in a worse way, a way that weakens them before American assertiveness. Consumed with guilt over the Holocaust and the world wars, they are half-engaged in giving up their old countries in favor of a humane but transnational Europe. They bank on a humanitarian hope for the future that remains without effectual governance or decisive loyalty. Indeed, the Europeans long for a progressive and humane order without the old politics of power and particularity. Their model is Doctors Without Borders. A distressing asymmetry appears, according to Manent. Europe suffers from an inability to impose spatial and political limits on itself and within itself; the United States acts as if among the nations of the earth only one had full legitimacy. The answer to this impossibly divided outlook lies in greater "self-restraint" on both sides, but most of all, on the side with greater strength. Still, a deeper uneasiness shows itself in Manent's account. He seems to worry over not only America's hubris, and Europe's apolitical humanitarianism, but also the spiritual "shallowness" of the contemporary modern Western civilization that both share: this "machine for happiness and pleasure."

Niall Ferguson ("American Democracy: The Perils of Imperialism?") also discerns weakness and foolish innocence—but in America itself and its imperial governance rather than in the imperial temptation. He cautions against hopes for a liberal nation self-limited by respect for other self-determining nations—by the supposition, that is, that "we're not an imperial power, we're a liberating power." Instead Ferguson appraises the United States as a liberal empire with the peculiar virtues and demands of such an empire. Indeed, for Ferguson the United States is the direct descendent of the British Empire, however much Americans may resist that notion. Yet it is a "dysfunctional" descendant. The trouble lies not in America acting as an empire, without due regard for the rights and claims of other nations, but in our not being willing fully to shoulder its burdens. There is a "chronic lack of imperial stamina," with potentially dire consequences both for the United States and for world order generally. Ferguson outlines four imperial "deficits": lack of manpower, lack of economic investment (owing mainly to high foreign debt), lack of resolve over the long term (the crucial defect), and growing lack of international legitimacy (owing especially to the cruelties, blindness, and exaggerations connected with the Iraq war). In calling attention to this fourth problem, does not Ferguson's argument converge with some of the concerns for self-restraint and liberal principle broached by Manent? Imperial or not, the liberal United States, in Ferguson's view, should not needlessly deprive itself of the moral and political high ground, and, in the end, cannot do so with impunity.

Part 2, "Creeds and Parties," turns to issues of domestic partisanship and political creeds, broadly construed. What is first and foremost are controversies over the fundamentals of liberalism itself, especially among the intellectuals who carry on and protect the creed. In "Defending Liberty: Liberal Democracy and the Limits of Public Power," William Galston would recover an intellectual rationale for the old and crucial liberal doctrine of limited government. Galston finds limited government endangered by threats practical and theoretical, popular as well as patriotic, from the Left as well as the Right. There are everyday political pressures for ever more equality and prosperity and for ever more security and unity. There are also fashionable doctrines antithetical to the old liberal distinction between government and society; Galston singles out feminism and socialism, as well as theories urging the priority of democratic community or of authentic political decision. Still, Galston's most striking step is not the diagnosis but the response. He seeks a rationale bridging the usual divide between Left and Right. He would supplement or even replace the old principles of toleration, property rights, and free expression, the principles devised by classic liberals (such as John Locke) and revised by progressive liberals (such as John Stuart Mill). Galston defends limited government not by the teachings of Locke or Mill, both of which he criticizes, but chiefly by a position that he calls "political pluralism." This involves a recognition of "multiple and competing sources" of authority and allegiance that cannot be reduced to a single hierarchy. Liberalism needs to respect persons for the dignity of their claims and especially the most deserving claims, especially those that concern themselves with the quest for truth, religious or otherwise. In bringing the vocabulary, if not the full attitude and method, of the later John Rawls to bear in this way, Galston tries to show how a cause generally left to the Right can be made of renewed interest to the Left. He would give reasons to adherents of a variety of intellectual perspectives to defend a liberalism that is both politically sensible and morally inspiring.

If Galston is at ease with a public sphere without a single authoritative moral standpoint—at least a standpoint that makes "plenary" claims—James Ceaser is not. Indeed, Ceaser thinks the postmodern "nonfoundationalism" that Galston engages to be "the greatest danger" to America: it undermines the priority of the rights and constitutionalism at the core of liberalism. Nonfoundationalism is a deep relativism, and it grows in influence. Having been advocated by Rawls, Rorty, Derrida, Habermas, and others of the "most celebrated thinkers of our time," the deconstruction of foundations, especially liberal foundations, has become a dominant intellectual and moral force in the academy and beyond. Unlike Galston's "political pluralism," which makes room for the possibility of absolute, nonplenary standards, "political nonfoundationalism" denies in principle all fundamental principles. Its adherents insist instead that a skeptical "reasonableness," a detached "irony" about any "story," are what fit a maturely democratic people. Why not take lightly, then, equal rights and constitutional government? The deconstructing that Galston would tease toward a politically sound direction is itself for Ceaser a profound danger. "People may sacrifice for a truth, but in what measure will they do so for a 'narrative'?" Nonfoundationalism is not the friend of liberalism it appears to be, nor is it the fruit of a fully justified philosophic skepticism that it claims to be. Tracing the provenance of this position to a decayed belief in the progress of reason, Ceaser urges acknowledgment of both its political radicalism and its intellectual deficiency.

While postmodernism is in this country largely the province of liberated liberals (although Ceaser claims some "traditionalist" precursors), the final essay of Part 2 maintains that contemporary conservativism has also lost its principles, albeit out of ambition, not intellectual undermining. Alan Wolfe finds especially dangerous "compassionate conservatism," not conservatism as such. In "The Dangers of Conservative Populism" he charges conservatives themselves with abandoning devotion to limited government, balanced budgets, and cautious foreign policies. On issues ranging from judicial activism to executive power and Iraq, conservatives have jettisoned their traditional commitment to institutional restraint and the containment of momentary political enthusiasms. The cause is hunger for office. Having turned populist to win elections, conservatives now appeal to a populism at odds with their own best instincts and highest virtues. "Conscience is what conservatives do best." Now they are not doing it at all. They respond instead to the majority who vote and the minority who pay. Liberals, Wolfe observes, had displayed a similar hubris (albeit one that involved pushing their principles too far). Beguiled by the New Deal's success, and by their experience with civil rights, liberals lost touch with popular moral opinion and insisted instead upon a progressive and universal "autonomy." Now conservatives have also lost touch, but with their own original mission of educating and refining democratic energies. In short, Wolfe alleges a Faustian bargain by which conservatives and Republicans bought much of their recent political good fortune. If one adds Wolfe's concerns to Galston's and Ceaser's, the sum seems to be this: a variety of pressures and doctrines, right as well as left, pragmatically political as well as intellectual, erode the individualistic and constitutionalist duties and limits that made American democracy a liberal democracy.

Part 3 ("A Divided People?") addresses four specific areas of domestic politics and policy: the weakening of the nuclear family, growing economic inequality, an unprecedented influx of illegal immigrants, and a growing antagonism between secularizing intellectuals and those adhering to religious tradition. These are practical problems, and yet the disputes over principle just sketched play a considerable role in their creation. In the first of these essays Susan Shell argues that the liberal family becomes less and less able to perform the civic role once thought reasonable and necessary: namely, producing and raising liberal citizens. In the last James Q. Wilson contends that the American separation of church and state is becoming unstuck, due less now to the religious than to a novel liberal zeal, of the kind that Wolfe also speaks of, among America's enlightened secularists. The two middle essays argue, however, that what some consider grave dangers are not really so, at least in the form usually feared by partisans left and right. However one might regret the injustice of growing economic inequality, Kay Schlozman and Traci Burch find that it has not led to a measurable decline in the poor's political "voice." And whatever one might think of the special problems posed by illegal immigration, the real crisis has to do with the assimilation of immigrants generally, according to Peter Skerry, not with illegals as such.

In "The Future of the Liberal Family" Shell confronts bad news about demographics and upbringing, in American society and also in liberal democracies generally. Can such systems sustain themselves in light of declining birthrates and the current tendencies toward diminished investment in the next generation? While Shell finds a variety of sources for the problem, she concentrates on a cause lying deep within the inner development of the country's own liberal creed. Locke's original version had sharply distinguished between political and parental power—thereby allowing for a robust wall of separation between the public and the private spheres. The same wall of private rights that enhances the power of the family vis-à-vis the state, however, also diminishes the family's authority over the individual. The current crisis of the liberal family, Shell claims, embodies both the original liberal emancipation from traditional fatherly authority *and* later corrections aiming for ever more individual satisfaction. Having thrown off much husbandly and paternal authority, later patrons of the liberal family were inclined to throw off restraints necessary for sustaining a liberal society. More precisely: both Rousseau's sentimentalization of marriage, and Kant's attempt to reinvest it with transcendent meaning, have resulted in an emphasis on subjective satisfaction and autonomous individual choice that is at odds with crucial civic purposes. Hence, for example, the large number of families without fathers that constitute, in her words, "a kind of civic scandal." A partial remedy, Shell argues, lies in recognizing the need that gave rise to the original liberal plan. In particular, it means openly acknowledging the civic importance of the nuclear family and, in particular, the crucial role of liberal fathers in educating their children about an appropriate balance between freedom and civic responsibility.

Schlozman and Burch focus on the problem of achieving democratic political equality. They grant and demonstrate that economic inequality is not only greater in America than in most liberal democracies but also on the rise. Neither our affluence, our redistributions, nor our social mobility blunts the general conclusion that material rewards are flowing in diminishing proportion to all but the most affluent. Still, their specifically political findings are paradoxical. The authors are social scientists who seek to examine in quantitative ways the political effect of the growing economic inequality, especially the effect on electoral outcomes and public policy. They examine in particular differentials in political "voice," understood as measurable participation, sorted by social class, in various lobbying and activist voluntary associations. Here the conventional wisdom, which points to a growing disparity in political clout, proves surprisingly doubtful. That one's economic class makes a decided difference in one's voice so defined is common knowledge, but their evidence makes it doubtful that such disparities have risen in the recent past. Nevertheless, the authors close by noting other changes that should speak against complacency on the issue, changes such as the declining importance of labor unions, the rise of corporate political activism, and the rise of liberal voluntary associations focused less on labor and the poor than on gays, the disabled, women, and the environment.

Peter Skerry ("The Real Immigration Crisis") contends that while illegal immigration is noised about as a crisis, and is, indeed, a problem, the graver concern is something that neither restrictionists nor expansionists face up to: integrating the flood of legal immigrants. Much public posturing about illegals is really directed against the strains and burdens brought by what may be the largest influx of legal immigrants in our history. There is truth in the ordinary citizen's apprehensions as to the effects on jobs, wage levels, taxes, neighborhoods, and crime. On this fiery issue, Skerry advises, officials should work to satisfy the reasonable demands of public sentiment, which are not essentially racist or hysterical. He hints at the possibility of moderate restrictions on quantity and quality of immigration. His essay, however, is chiefly about a failure of principle and of courage on the part of American public leaders, both conservative and liberal. We have to make clear to the immigrants what is necessarily expected of them, which compassionate liberals are reluctant to do, and we have also to extend a helping hand, which laissez-faire conservatives are reluctant to do. A certain dogmatic abstractness afflicts both sides of the public debate. Neither side adopts the standpoint of liberal democratic *citizens* who wish to make their actual political and social life go well. There is thus "a lack of moral leadership, as well as of political imagination." One result is a major "opinion gap" between the public and its leaders, perhaps the largest gap, Skerry claims, on any major issue. Withal, leaders cannot simply ignore the rise in immigrant numbers, legal and otherwise. There may be no immediate crisis in "cohesion"; with respect to immigration itself we may muddle along. But there will be subtler effects. There is likely to emerge a new underclass, largely Hispanic and mostly Mexican. This untended sore may supply another reason for the visible disaffection of ordinary citizens from their institutions, a process of disillusionment that also concerns James Q. Wilson and Hugh Heclo.

Wilson argues that religious polarization is high in historic terms and growing, and that this degree of antagonism endangers both our civic culture and our capacity for common endeavors such as national defense. But the type of division is also new, and this too reflects a certain change in opinion, especially contemporary liberal opinion. While the past saw inter-denominational tensions, the current struggle is chiefly between religious believers and a secularism that increasingly understands itself in quasi-religious terms. In Wilson's view the latter misconstrues the religious character of America, which on the whole neither "threatens politics, restricts human freedom, [nor] seeks theocratic rule." The peculiar benignity of American religiosity is partly traceable, he maintains, to the lack of an established church associated with autocratic rule and to the general silence of the federal government on religious matters. These constraints of "culture and constitution" have encouraged evangelical enthusiasms and have sometimes favored more demanding sects over laxer ones. But they have also helped to sustain American religion's unusually tolerant and democratic character. While conservative religious movements have become especially adept at using democratic institutions for their own policy purposes, Wilson shows, they do not represent the united political front that secularist critics fear. Prominent divinity schools that were once hotbeds of evangelical fervor, for example, are now "barely able to endorse Christianity." Wilson dwells too on the civic contribution of religion: it tends to foster strong families, law-abidingness, and other desirable civic qualities. In light of such considerations Wilson urges greater understanding and tolerance on the part of both sides of the cultural debate, but especially upon his fellow intellectuals and his colleagues in the academy.

Part 4, "Dilemmas of Self-Government," explores difficulties in how Americans rule themselves and are in turn ruled: by law and government in the usual sense, yes, but also through the economy and through a distinctively modern intellectual project of progress.

Peter Rodriguez suggests that we are undergoing an unprecedented failure of economic self-government, a failure that threatens both our economic strength and our capacity for political self-government. The United States may be way ahead in the race for prosperity and power, but it cannot keep the lead so long as it allows itself to become increasingly dependent upon foreign creditors and suppliers. What our mothers told us was right: if we spend more than we earn, in the long run it will hurt us. Private consumers are overspending, with an unprecedented and increasing private debt load, and the national government is typically in deficit, with an immense and increasing public debt. Ferguson noted the problem; Rodriguez expands upon it. In about two decades the country has slid from saving 10 percent of its disposable income to what, as of all of 2006, is a negative rate.

Yes, some economic dangers seem more obvious, such as the trade deficit, a grave competitive disadvantage with China, the Social Security deficit, the reduced value of the dollar. But at the root of them all, according to Rodriguez, is the easy street of excessive consumption, public and private. It must be acknowledged that capital investment, a key to a dynamic modern economy, has kept up. How can that be, in the absence of domestic savings? The answer, of course, is through immense foreign loans and large foreign purchases of such American assets as stocks, bonds, banks, corporations, and real estate. The country falls into debt and sells off its capital, all for short-term consumption. We indulge in a public home equity loan, so to speak, and for the public's immediate pleasures and needs. But won't China, India, the Saudis, and other such up-and-coming lenders put fewer eggs in the American basket? One cannot blame them for uneasiness at American prospects—and for a search for greater profits elsewhere. If so, can one expect Americans to stop their self-indulgence in order to invest themselves or pay off their debts? If not, an economic crisis is at least likely, whether sudden or drawn out, and then independence and prosperity are at stake, as well as preeminence. Rodriguez refrains from definite predictions of doom, but he concludes definitively: whatever the uncertain future, we by our own actions have unnecessarily put America at risk. We have put our future and our strength at the beck and call of others; and we have done so in good part for consumables that a comfortable middle class, and a very cosseted upper class, might well have done without.

Harvey Mansfield opens up a darker danger, albeit under cover of automatic toilet flushers and an Italian comedy. Does the very governing idea of modern civilization, that of progress by rational control of nature and man, foster an enervating human passivity? Ceaser called for defense of America's foundational principles; Mansfield, like Shell, discerns an inherent danger even there. Ferguson, Rodriguez, and Galston too feared the everyday impulse to the easy life; Mansfield concentrates on the protective systems that insidiously nurture and sustain that impulse.

In his compressed way Mansfield updates Tocqueville's fear of a new kind of democratic despotism: "a network of small, complicated, painstaking, uniform rules" that does not thwart citizens—it promises to satisfy them—but nevertheless "extinguishes their spirits and enervates their souls." Mansfield, however, locates the source not in a historically developing social equality, but in the original modern plan to overcome nature, especially the irrationality of human nature. The enlightenment projectors would make reason powerful by making it an instrument of basic desires such as health and security (as well as the sexual pleasure promised in Machiavelli's *Mandragola*). This move to instrumental reason requires liberation from superstition and moral scruple—the seminal deconstruction—but for the sake of rational institutions that promise effectual satisfaction—the seminal construction. Modern liberation and liberty is then calculated and supervised; when progressives foster liberation, they can never keep "hands off the person being liberated." But the modern "controllers" don't rule; they induce and represent. The leading devices are rational bureaucracy, an insistently tolerant pluralism, the free enterprise economy with its economic science, and, the fundamental device, a representative government that gives us what we would ask for if we were rational, while allowing us to think we asked for it. Nevertheless, Mansfield, like Tocqueville, urges less a return to premodern practices and habits than a greater appreciation for institutions in our midst that encourage self-government and a self-respect born of initiative. One such subordinate institution is conservatism. Conservatives can defend the "traditional" prejudices that help counteract the dominant progressive tendency to continual innovation and ever extended effectual power. Mansfield advises progressives to be more tolerant of conservatives, at least of a conservatism not scolding, but "suitably restrained, in touch with human nature, and still in love with virtue."

In a final, deeply pessimistic essay, Hugh Heclo suggests that American liberal democratic institutions are already subject to a potentially fatal separation of the people from their government. Manent lamented such separation in the weakened European nation-states; Heclo thinks the decay of representative government is well established in the United States. His thesis bears on most of the others in this volume. Galston thinks that limited government needs a new defense; Schlozman and Burch worry about the advantages of money and the political weakness of the less privileged; Skerry fears that the political class is oblivious to reasonable popular concerns and to popular disaffection from government; Mansfield worries that the gospel of progress itself encourages popular passivity before progressive leaders and systems. Heclo's is a comprehensive thesis: a systemic manipulation by leaders of the led has replaced the old reciprocal relation of represented and representative. The corruption is not the small potatoes of graft. A manipulative "system of democratic leadership" has replaced the old deliberative transaction. Heclo confesses ignorance of the source and even of an adequate characterization. But he details the parts: a professionalization of political communication (including polling and campaign management); the new media (TV and the Internet) that emphasize visual images and tailor messages to personal interests; an openness in courts, Congress, and the executive to immediate demands of the people and of policy activists; and the increasing commercialization of political transactions, such as policy-making, lobbying, and communication, in which money formerly played a smaller role. Politicians now, to an unprecedented degree, can avoid serious public arguments over policy, including arguments directed at voters. For most people now politics is increasingly something that is "done to them." A kind of "lumpen-citizenry" develops, Heclo argues, which develops its own reactions, such as distrust, cynicism, and withdrawal into comfort zones of personal bias. Subject to such forces of political dissolution, both citizens and their erstwhile leaders tend to lose touch with each other and with the real problems confronting us as a whole. The great American experiment in popular government, Heclo concludes, is headed toward a major crisis.

In sum: the following essays supply a broad picture of pressing dangers that America now faces. The authors seek to place peculiar challenges to democratic self-government in the context of America's overall strengths and weaknesses. In this sense, the book addresses the direction of the country as a whole. When many among the governing classes no longer accept tenets long taken for granted (e.g., the importance of the Atlantic Alliance, of avoiding a runaway increase in foreign debt, or even of foundational liberal and conservative principles), it is time to reassess the so-called conventional wisdom. This volume aims to contribute to that endeavor.

PART ONE

Wages of Empire

The Transatlantic Predicament

Pierre Manent

The current lull in the transatlantic shouting match is a good time to survey the situation on the Western front, although relief at our renewed comity risks blinding us to the huge continental drift that has already taken place. The dispute about Iraq brought to light a profound divergence about the world, and what we are supposed to do in the world, between Europeans and Americans, which the provisional convergence about Iran has not removed. We need to take stock of where we are before a new crisis renews our reciprocal disappointment, suspicion, and animosity. To begin with, I will briefly revisit the run-up to the Iraqi war, not to rub salt in fresh wounds, but to stress how much the American government and opinion misjudged the European scene. I am aware that we Europeans are equally and reciprocally prone to misjudge American dispositions. This is precisely the point: are our perspectives on the world and our respective roles in it amenable to some sort of unity, at least compatibility and concert?

Back to the Iraqi quarrel. Among the innumerable sound bites we were treated to, Secretary Rumsfeld's one about "old Europe" deserting America's good cause and "new Europe" joining it deserves pride of place. It was certainly a smart rhetorical move. The problem was that the administration did not heed Dick Morris's rule and began to believe its own spin. My purpose here is not to discuss for the umpteenth time the pros and cons of the American action in Iraq, only to stress the following: whatever the merits of the case, the fact is that, across the whole of Europe, public opinion was overwhelmingly against the war. In this respect, I am sorry to report, however grating their stridency to many European, including French, ears, Chirac and Villepin were the self-appointed but accurate spokesmen for European opinion. Now, it is true that a number of European governments officially supported the American position. But much more significant is how little political capital they were ready to spend on it. It was a purely governmental thing, which moreover took on paradoxically "private" traits since the most explicit European support for the United States came in the form of an "open letter" in the newspapers—a letter initiated by an American lobbyist. Such was the European support. The only statesman who spent political capital was of course Tony Blair, and it is not unrelated that the United Kingdom is the sole country effectively helping the Americans in Iraq. Today the thin European battalions, or most of them, have left Iraq, or are on their way out, or are even thinner. Let us face it: the United States did not receive any help to speak of from the countries of continental Europe in the Iraqi campaign.

In Spain, the gap between the government position and the feelings of the citizenry grew to a perilous extreme. That was not lost on the terrorists who unleashed carnage in a Madrid station. A few days later, the Aznar government, which had been poised to win handily, was beaten at the polls. Every sensible person will agree that the concatenation of events was particularly distressing: for the first time, a terrorist action dictated the electoral results, and thus so to speak appointed the government, in a democratic country. But the condescending or openly contemptuous commentaries on the Spaniards "caving in to terrorism" were unwarranted. Here was a government that had led Spain onto a path that the Spanish citizens were clearly loath to follow, without trying much to persuade them of its validity. When, as a consequence of this policy, a terrible attack was visited upon the Madrid population, the same government frantically tried to deflect the attention away from international, Islamic terrorism toward the domestic, Basque brand. The circumstances were admittedly traumatic, and I am not alleging bad faith or cover-up. But why extract from the Security Council a public condemnation of ETA terrorism as the inquiry was just beginning and indications pointing toward Islamic terrorism were already coming in? Such being the circumstances, how to reproach the Spanish electorate for losing faith in their government and cashiering it?

I have dwelt at some length on these events in Spain to illustrate how actions that were deeply offensive in American eyes were proper and sound, at the very least understandable, in the Spanish context. I am not suggesting that it all depends on the point of view and that all points of views are equally serious and wise. Far from it! But it is a big part of the American problem that the American view—at least a view not yet seriously challenged in the United States—on recent events and the response they call for is not widely shared in the rest of the world and specially in Europe. To wax indignant at European supineness will only make things worse. It does not mean that European views should go unchallenged. As will be apparent soon, I do not sympathize with the current mood in Europe.

Now, let us try to get a hold on what I have called the continental drift. When it comes to dressing up the contrast between Europe and America, it seems that everything has been said or written. The language tends to be overwhelmingly "psychological," or "cultural." These kinds of parallel portraits are fun to read, and they are sometimes enlightening. I will take a more strictly political tack. I am afraid the conclusions will be dispiriting to many, inasmuch as the chasm between Europe and the United States will appear to derive from the fundamentals of their respective political situations and makeup. Neither cultural sensitivity courses for Americans, nor boot camps or bodybuilding for Europeans will do the trick.

It has been rightly remarked that disagreements about what is right, what should be done, are often rooted in different perceptions of what *can* be done, and that the latter in turn are often rooted in different evaluations of what *the agent* is or feels capable of doing. This idea is much less cynical than it sounds. In truth, you can only *will* what you feel able to do—some conditions being given—what can come to be a part of a *doable* plan of action. Otherwise, it is not will, but a vague desire—a *velléité*. At any rate, this general proposition bears nicely upon the current differences of approach between Europe and the United States. The Americans think that they can do much—that is, much good—in a world that is susceptible to big, even dramatic changes, while the Europeans are loath to join a world where changes are incremental, and mostly beyond our control. It strikes me that the "fall of Communism" elicited very different—even opposite—reactions in Europe and America. For the Europeans, it was the defeat of the most radical project for changing the world, a project that had been nurtured on European soil. For the Americans, it was proof that the world could change swiftly, even dramatically, and for the better if only you are willing to rise up to the challenges. Thus spoke President Reagan: "Mr. Gorbachev, tear down this wall!" How has Europe, how has the continent of revolutions come to be the most conservative place on earth? It is of course a long and complicated story. I can only pick up a few points.

For centuries, the prodigious vitality of Europe has derived in good part from the rivalry between European nations. A plurality of largely similar polities, mostly sharing the same principles of human conduct, none being strong enough to subjugate the rest and transform Europe into a mind-stultifying "Asiatic" empire: that was the recipe for the unique flourishing of the European genius. There is no need to recount how, at some juncture, the national rivalries intensified to the point of bringing devastation and dishonor upon Europe. It is not clear by the way that a serious account of modern European history would lay the blame wholly on the "European nation-state" as such. After all, the ineptitude of the Habsburg and czarist empires played a decisive role in triggering the Great War, not to speak of the anti-Semitism to the political uses of which Hitler was introduced in the witches' cauldron that was "multinational" Vienna. However that may be, after the Second World War, the nations of the European continent, first of all France and Germany, very understandably decided in their soul and body that they would never again embark upon the same path, and in order to make good on their oath, they launched the European enterprise, the "European construction."

This enterprise is of peculiar interest to us here, because it gave rise to something I would call "domestic foreign policy." Between each European nation participating in the enterprise and the rest of the world a third element interposed itself, an element that was neither national nor international, where everything was peaceful and predictable: the European association. These nations, not long ago, so to speak ruled the world, at least big chunks of it. Thus coalesced an impressive quantity of human resources. Whatever discontents arose, year after year this third element grew, and with it the promise of a new order of politics or society, of a new "governance." At some point, this movement came loose from its origins in national decisions and interpreted itself as the embryonic form of a new humanity built on "institutional mechanisms and values." "Europe" threw itself headlong into an indefinite extension, an extension that had no reason to stop at the borders, geographically or otherwise defined, of Europe, since the "mechanisms" as well as the "values" were self-evidently open to the whole of mankind.

These developments brought great benefits to the European peoples. At the same time, they progressively drained of its meaning the political, indeed human question par excellence: what is to be done? As in Woody Allen's joke, we came to always know the answer even when we had no clear idea of the question. The answer was always: Europe, by Jove, more of Europe! In this sense, I would say that Europeans conscientiously helped each other to turn their backs on the world. Beside commercial exchanges, the only meaningful relation to the world for us is the humanitarian, the compassionate one. We approach the world from the standpoint of Doctors Without Borders. It is certainly legitimate, even honorable, but politically defective. And even the humanitarian impulse is weakening as political interest in the world abates.

As a consequence each nation, except *perhaps* for reunified Germany, tends to be stuck, immobilized in the condition in which it found itself at the end of the brilliant period of development after the war—what the French call *les trente glorieuses*—before the "European construction" broke off from its political, national roots. The great, successful common European enterprises—Airbus, Ariane, and so forth—date back to this period when the nations—especially, again, France and Germany—and not the supranational institutions were in the driver's seat. Our lives still take place mostly in the national framework, but the higher political legitimacy has emigrated to "Europe." Thus we are becalmed between our respective nations that we still love but whose continuing relevance we doubt, and an abstract, formless, indefinite "Europe" that nobody knows how to bring into political existence.

This separation from the world induces a separation from oneself that in its turn aggravates the former. The higher legitimacy of Europe has been built on the delegitimation of nations. The main root of the latter, I have already noticed, lies in the disasters of the first half of the twentieth century that motivated the European enterprise in the first place. The national past tends to be morally rejected—most of it was nationalism, religious fanaticism and intolerance, inequality, sexism, homophobia, and so forth—but, somewhat bizarrely, it is painstakingly preserved or restored in its material vestiges. Our cities transform themselves into museums even for their inhabitants, who become tourists in their own birthplaces. Europe is petrified around a past whose letter it preserves or restores with as much passion as it rejects its spirit.

I have dwelt at length on the role played by the "European construction" in the immobilization of Europe. Another factor I cannot leave unmentioned. It is of course the rapid aging of the European population. It is a general phenomenon in the developed world, but some European nations—especially Germany, Spain, and Italy—face bleak prospects on this score. What future for countries that are growing old at the same clip so to speak as individual human beings? Having deliberately cut themselves off from their past, obscurely wondering whether they have any future at all, the European nations are glued to their comfortable present. From what motives could spring meaningful actions? Great ambitions end in huge catastrophes—that sums up our whole wisdom. Thus we have decided that doing something, even something good, is too risky. Our remaining ambition is to keep the innocence that, we feel, we have just regained.

The American reader, who has been kind enough to follow me this far, will think that the case is now settled, that according to my own arguments, Europe cannot hold its own in its running debate with the United States—and that I should probably apply for a green card. Alas, Europe's vices do not translate into as many American virtues.

To begin with, the retraction of European nations has had rather deleterious effects on American self-awareness. With the Europeans withdrawing from a world they had recently ruled, the United States found itself in the position of the sole world-power. For quite a long time, it had not realized that it was the natural and legitimate heir to the European empires. (The competition with "the other superpower" contributed to obscuring the situation. But in the great scheme of things, the war-induced condominium with the Soviets takes on a rather anecdotal character.) However desirous to disentangle itself from Europe and however ideologically hostile to Europe's colonial empires, the United States developed its preeminence as a participant in the European domination of the world. Coming on the heels of the French or the British, Americans pushed them aside in Indochina, Iran, Egypt, you name it. In brief, America's matchless influence came as the counterweight to, but also the complement of and the replacement for, European domination. In recent years quite a few Americans have been willing to acknowledge as much, even to boast of it, and they have asked their countrymen to resolutely shoulder the burden that was rightfully theirs. These views are not limited to the in-your-face utterances of a few strident columnists. It is a fact, I think, that Americans have now evolved a clearly "colonial" perspective on the world. The adjective *colonial* has this advantage over the more common *imperial* of acknowledging the filiation between European colonial empires and the present American preeminence. I am aware that the word will be felt by many to be very offensive. In any case, I am not writing with an "anticolonialist" animus or intent.

Through its mighty contributions to the allied victories in the two world wars, through the decisive role it played in the elaboration of a new and better international order in the immediate aftermath of the Second World War, the United States became what I would like to call an instrument of government for the whole world. That was an admirable achievement, through the soundness of the perspectives and the staying power of the institutions then put into place. And now? Rather than bringing it out of nothing, the current administration, confronting unexpected circumstances, suddenly precipitated a development long in the making. To cut a long story short, and at the risk of exaggerating the change, it was a matter of transforming this mainly indirect power into a direct, "imperial" or "colonial" power. Suddenly, allegiance pure and simple was exacted if not always rewarded; those who disagreed were mocked and stigmatized, and marked for "punishment"; there was no longer a legitimate diversity of perspectives on the world—a diversity deriving from the various physiognomies and histories of the allied nations, and for which previous presidents, including Nixon-Kissinger and Ronald Reagan, had generally shown a rather generous understanding. It is legitimate to ask whether this high-handedness has not already been mollified by the less than complete success in Iraq. Perhaps Condoleezza Rice has already shown herself to be a worthy successor to Henry Kissinger, and President Bush's good sense has prevailed upon imprudent counselors. These questions will be better answered by American commentators. I for one would not be willing to exaggerate the novelty of the course embarked upon by the current administration. In any case, for the time being, it has not yet been effectively challenged by the American people and their representatives.

As I have already said, these innovations did not come out of the blue. I was much struck during Bill Clinton's tenure by the bizarre militarization of the American posture toward the rest of the world—all the more bizarre since the world then was mostly at peace and military spending declining fast everywhere, including in the United States. The world, as I gathered from the newspapers, had been divided up into "regional commands," at the head of which a general officer, abundantly furnished with the wherewithal for his unprecedented task, played a diplomatic, more generally a political role as a part of his duties. It was difficult not to think that the American government had taken to employing proconsuls. Of course this militarization of the American outlook was lately for everybody to see in the frequent briefings of Secretary Rumsfeld, who was kind enough to share with all of us his considered, at times even his extemporaneous, views of everything.

The militarization of the American outlook has nothing to do with "militarism." It derives from the fact that the moral physiognomy of the United States was largely forged through a succession of victorious wars, the greatest of them, civil or foreign, waged for the sake of liberty and equality. The long shadow cast by the only war ever lost—that in Vietnam—was finally dissipated by the victory over Communism, in which the Americans are prompt to see, not without reason, the direct result of their policy more than the consequence of the self-decomposition of the regime. Always victorious in the good fights, America was moreover immune from the twin poisons of the twentieth century, Nazism and Communism. Today it sees itself as supremely powerful and exceptionally innocent at the same time, in contradistinction to Europe, which mainly groups nations vanquished and impure even in their own eyes. Here of course, we need to stress the growing role that the memory of the Holocaust has played in America's estrangement from Europe.

In the aftermath of the Second World War, Europe appeared to be mainly composed of victims, that is, of nations that had variously suffered from the Nazi rampage, and variously participated, often against all the odds, in the war or resistance against the Nazis. Nazi Germany had *attacked* them all! And Germany itself would soon be called to participate in the West's struggle against Communism. Today, in American eyes, Europe often appears to be mainly composed of former willing perpetrators, who variously participated in what should be considered as the common crime of the continent, the Holocaust. Each nation is accordingly handed its specific bill of collective indictment. In some measure, this American condemnation of Europe only parallels and reinforces the self-examination and sometimes the self-condemnation that has been carried on in several countries of Europe since the magnitude of the crime was assessed and confronted and that I have already noticed. A troubling circumstance is that not rarely the American condemnation extends to the new association—the European Union—which the Europeans have precisely devised in order to protect themselves against their tainted national histories. So that it seems that the Americans here are condemning not only the malady but also the remedy.

Uniquely victorious, uniquely innocent, the Americans were uniquely aggrieved on September 11, 2001. Most foreigners, including many Europeans, despite their sincere outrage and sympathy, have certainly failed to appreciate the impact of these attacks on the American soul. The United States underwent a transformation whose depth is difficult to fathom, especially for foreigners, however sympathetic. It is fair to say, I think, that an understandable but dangerous feeling of power, innocence, and vulnerability fused together has taken hold of the American soul and pushed this nation onto its present course. The risk is that with it comes a kind of spiritual retraction, involving a disquieting inability to take into account what the world looks like in *other* people's eyes. President Bush's "Let us fight them in Baghdad rather than in our cities" is worth our attention less because of the obvious flimsiness of the strategic rationale than because of the success it had with the American public, even the informed one. We are not very far from "*pereat mundus*, if only we *feel* safer."

One cannot but be struck by the spreading self-definition of the United States as the only country that is simultaneously democratic and Christian. Certainly 9/11 has prompted Americans to express their feelings more vividly. This aspect of American life is upsetting to Europeans, even to those who belong to a Christian church. Watching CNN at the beginning of the operations in Iraq, I was startled to see and hear General Tommy Franks— an impressive man—taking leave of the journalists and viewers by saying: "God's grace be upon each of you." I felt as if I had stumbled amid a party of Ironsides departing to Connemara.

I do not underestimate the strength found in these collective religious feelings. However grating, the incessant reference to God in the American civil discourse seems to me to be "more natural" than the systematic eschewing of the feared monosyllable in the public discourse of my home country. At the same time, this national religious affect needs to be prudently governed, as the experience of all times and all places attests. In particular, it seems to me to be especially imprudent to weld it onto a strategic idea as fragile as that of the "war on terrorism."

Although I readily admit that statesmen need big ideas and catchy phrases to feed and conduct the civic debate, I think that this notion of a war on terrorism is hopelessly flawed. President Bush blurted out the truth when he said that the war on terrorism could not be won. It cannot be won because it cannot be defined in political or even military terms. It is just a group of words strung together to call up moral indignation. But the most justified indignation is no substitute for clear strategic and political aims. While the evil of Nazism was well beyond moral indignation, the unconditional surrender of Germany was a political and military aim perfectly defined. There is no equivalent to this objective in the present posture summarized under the title of "war on terrorism."

The "war on terrorism" is not a war on terrorism: it is not a war on terrorism in the Basque country, or in Sri Lanka, or in Nepal. It is a war on Muslim activists who, impelled by limitless anger and resentment, are trying to hurt as grievously as possible the Americans and their allies in the Muslim world, and more generally all those they consider as enemies of their brand of Islam. These terrorists—they have certainly earned the title—are born from the convulsions that have arisen on the indefinite border between the Islamic and the Western world, and on the for us mysterious fault lines within the Islamic world. To cut a long story short—a story moreover that is not too familiar to me—they are born from a "political pathology" proper to this immense thing, the Islamic world. As much as thwarting and killing the terrorists is urgent, there is no end in sight to the enterprise except through the reformation of this same Muslim world.

This is precisely the considered purpose of the current administration! I can hear the rejoinder and it is not without merit. The only rational purpose of the action in Iraq is to weigh in at the center of the Arab-Muslim world in order to bring about the necessary changes. But then "war on terrorism" is a misnomer. The war in Iraq is a war for the reformation of the Arab and Muslim world. President Bush has repeatedly said as much in speaking of the necessary efforts to build democratic regimes and societies in these regions. *Democracy* is a too pleasant-sounding, a meretricious word. The purported reformation is a democratization indeed, but conversely the purported democratization involves a reformation. The effectual truth of the "war on terrorism" is *a war for a huge, an unheard-of reformation of the Muslim world.* Do we really think that the reformation of the Muslim world can be brought about in the wake of a war waged by a Christian armada? The Muslims cannot fail to notice that they are on the receiving end of incessant and innumerable bombing runs that are intended to help them to see the light. Nobody likes to be converted in this way.

One cannot but agree with the *ultimate* aim of this administration in Iraq and beyond. But the democratization of the Muslim world, as far as *we* are concerned, can only be a mainly indirect process in which the use of force is a last resort—at times inevitable, as in Afghanistan. In the Iraqi affair, overwhelming force, "shock and awe," has been put front and center, in a way that does not permit an easy disengagement, and even portends an extension of its use. Force, overwhelming force, tends to become *the* American way of dealing with the difficult problems of the world. The same dispositions are accordingly encouraged in America's closest allies.

How does Europe enter the picture? As the innocent, or the cynical, or the cheering, or the jeering bystander? As the sleeping-partner? As the dumb gawker? Europe's morose passivity is as dependent on America's propensity to sometimes imprudent hyperactivity as America's position of sole superpower is dependent on Europe's former domination.

Let us have a look at the Security Council, the Chamber of our recent Discontents. American commentators and representatives have readily underlined the fact that, because of its current makeup, France wields a disproportionate diplomatic power that her diminished circumstances do not warrant. I agree with this criticism. But it is the whole system of the Security Council that is lopsided to the advantage of the Western powers, including the United States. A fair "representation of the world" would make room for India, for Japan, for Brazil, and would find a slot, I suppose, for the billion of Muslims.

The system is replicated and aggravated in the Nuclear Non-Proliferation Treaty, which gives exorbitant privileges to the five nuclear-weapon states: Britain, China, France, Russia, and the United States. It is reasonable to think that the augmentation of the number of states possessing nuclear weapons would augment the risks of some terrible mishap—not necessarily the risks of nuclear war proper since the "dissuasive" character of those arms does not seem to depend on the number of players—at least the risks of their "falling into the wrong hands." At the same time, there is no doubt that the architecture of the treaty is based on the undiluted right of the stronger. To assuage legitimate grievances, the five states committed themselves to reducing and ultimately phasing out their nuclear armaments—a pledge on which they tranquilly reneged, particularly, but not exclusively, the United States, which, after being the first country to sign the Test Ban Treaty, has withdrawn its support, and has embarked on the development of new "generations" of nuclear armaments. Moreover, India and Pakistan have been subjected to no serious punishment for going nuclear (and in the case of Pakistan for being the proliferator-in-chief and the wet nurse of all the rogue states). Nor was Israel. And to complete the transformation of the Non-Proliferation Treaty into a charade, the United States has just promised to help develop India's nuclear industry, on the condition that India opens to verifications the plants and laboratories she feels like opening—while keeping the others off limits. In brief, the meaning of the treaty is what the authors and prime beneficiaries of the treaty say it is.

These well-known facts have acute relevance for the Western policy about Iran's nuclear ambitions. For the time being, there is a nice, indeed a rare agreement and an unprecedented division of labor between Europe—the "Big Three"—and the United States. There could not be any dispute about what is simply desirable: it is greatly desirable that Iran does not acquire military nuclear capabilities. At the same time, the effort to secure this result is made under the banner of a treaty that nobody can defend in conscience, which has been flouted by three very important players, and which its five beneficiaries do not fully respect. One cannot help thinking that the rare Western comity derives from the United States and Europe being equally keen on upholding as long as possible the nuclear status quo, the oligarchic, unequal, lopsided, indeed "colonial" system. The latter adjective again is not a flourish. Some American diplomats have been brazen enough to explain that Iran has no need at all of a *peaceful* nuclear industry since it has so much oil and gas. It is baffling to see intelligent and well-meaning people deprive at one stroke, without noticing it I suppose, whole nations of the elementary right to evaluate their needs and develop the means for meeting them. As a matter of fact, it would make perfect sense for the Iranians to develop a peaceful nuclear industry (I am not saying that it is their only or even principal objective): in a period of ever tighter oil supplies, it would be good husbandry for a country of nearly 70 million inhabitants (and counting) to prepare for the use of other sources of energy. At the time of this writing, the American diplomacy seems more willing to grant the Iranians their rights under the treaty, and to admit that it is a matter of allowing the development of a peaceful nuclear industry while preventing its diversion toward military misuses: a tall order indeed, but a just program, and as far as I am aware a purpose in accordance with the letter and spirit of this less than satisfactory Treaty. It is to be feared that the resentment and perverse calculations of the government of the Islamic Republic will prevent this happy prospect from becoming reality. In this case, I am not sure that the agreement between Europe and the United States will hold. And it will be the Iraqi dispute all over again.

Both Europe and the United States are the beneficiaries of a batch of "unequal treaties." The difference is that the Europeans feel some qualms about it, and would prefer that the situation was not made too visible through the frequent exercise of force, or threat of it. Admittedly it is a less than straightforward attitude. The Americans are more candid in their explicit desire to keep the outsiders out and keep them down. I am afraid they get the real situation wrong. The "fall of Communism" notwithstanding, the balance of forces has not tilted in favor of the West, and especially the United States, as much as we would like to believe. There is a first of all demographic, but also political and even economic, pressure of huge countries and immense civilizations that we cannot seriously hope to beat back for long through the regular exercise of "hard power" or the threat of it.

These remarks, one will object, do not take into account the opportunities offered by the "democratization" of these non-Western parts. Well, even if some countries soon progressed toward democracy by leaps and bounds—and some have indeed—huge chunks of mankind would continue to live according to different political and social mores, if not always principles. Some countries that recently raised much hope, like Putin's Russia, are slipping back toward a tyranny of sorts, coupled with the intimidation of neighbors and the oppression of despised minorities. And by the way, are we sure that a democratic China would be less keen to absorb Taiwan than the current China is? Certainly we have the right to defend ourselves and perhaps also the duty to nudge others toward adopting better ways. But trying to high-handedly preserve, indeed restore, the Western imperial domination is a supremely dangerous fantasy.

The drift of my remarks should be clear by now. They are not motivated by a starry-eyed devotion to the "wretched of the earth" nor by a willful disregard of the fact that, through their flawed regimes, the latter are often the first authors of their own misery. Even less are they prompted by any measure of "self-hate" or contempt for the West's accomplishments. As human trajectory, the West seems to me to offer the richest and most varied human achievements. And we are allowed to think that the West's long domination has been somewhat related to these achievements and finds therein its justification. At the same time, through America's growing separation from Europe and through Europe's growing alienation from its own past, our accomplishments have tended to become more and more shallow. With this shallowness has grown our complacency. As its heart and soul are more and more hollowed out, Europe fancies itself as the matrix of a new humanity. As for the United States, its explicit purpose of building an absolute and definitive superiority over the rest of the world is less expressive of a renewed self-confidence than of a growing and disturbing spiritual autarchy. While on both sides of the Atlantic we indulge in orgies of differently accented but equally fervid self-righteousness, our achievements have become more and more mechanical, predicated on the common assumption that through the application of the right means, through organization and investments, we will make ourselves and others the happy inhabitants of the earth. On both shores of the pond, we have built, in Rousseau's felicitous phrase, "enormous machines for happiness and pleasure," whose functioning and advertising exercise on the rest of mankind a very powerful mixture of attraction and repulsion. We cannot cover, much less repair the dislocation we bring about by simply extolling "democracy," and implying that everything we are and everything we do is legitimized simply by being "democratic."

This analysis does not lead to a neat conclusion. I will not affect to have one. I have aired my apprehension that our transatlantic disputes hide in our own eyes the deterioration of the situation of the West to which we both belong. Neither the conviction of Europe that everything will be fine if only we do nothing (except, that is, for "building Europe"), nor the conviction of the United States that everything will be fine if only we follow the American lead, seems to me to be conducive to durable success. I would plead for gently blunting the abrasiveness of our respective brands of "democracy," which measure their successes by the mere *extension* of their respective empires. Europe is unable and unwilling to give itself the limits without which a political body has neither physiognomy nor soul. The United States seems unable and unwilling to circumscribe the validity of its writ, as if among the nations of the earth one only had full sovereignty. I will not have succeeded in conveying my meaning if the reader gathered the impression that I thought that "there is not much we can do." It is a matter of bringing the United States and Europe closer to each other, and Europe closer to her spiritual sources, thereby bringing the rest of the world closer to the West: I do not think that I am guilty of timidity or defeatism with this program. However weak my voice, I am pleading for great acts of *self-restraint*, knowing all the while with Montesquieu that "it is always easier to follow one's strength than to hold it back."

The United States and Europe are two very important but circumscribed parts of mankind, which together make up "the West," a standard but mysterious appellation for this immense movement of human things through which our species has incessantly striven to better understand itself. The self-restraint I am here advocating is a necessary condition for this self-understanding.

American Democracy: The Perils of Imperialism?

Niall Ferguson

I

Is the United States an empire? For roughly a hundred years, radical critics of American foreign policy have regarded this question as otiose, a little like the question "Is the pope a Catholic?" In September 2006 the Venezuelan president Hugo Chávez brandished a copy of Noam Chomsky's *Hegemony or Survival: The Imperialist Strategy of the United States,* and declared, "The hegemonic pretensions of the American empire are placing at risk the very survival of the human species." He characterized President George W. Bush as the "spokesman of imperialism," whose goal was "to try to preserve the current pattern of domination, exploitation and pillage of the peoples of the world." "The American empire," Chávez argued, "is doing all it can to consolidate its system of domination"—its "imperialist, fascist, assassin [*sic*], genocidal . . . world dictatorship."[1] Not only is the United States obviously an empire, in other words, it is equally obviously an evil empire, bent not on the spread of democracy—as its leaders claim—but on the exploitation of the rest of the world.

Such allegations have a long history inside as well as outside the United States, dating back as far as the Anti-Imperialist League, which was formed in 1898 to oppose the American annexation of the Philippines. During the Cold War, of course, both the Soviet Union and the People's Republic of China harped incessantly on the old Leninist theme of Yankee imperialism, as did many Western European, Middle Eastern, and Asian writers, not all of them Marxists. Not so very different were the homegrown American critiques of late-nineteenth- and early-twentieth-century overseas expansion, whether populist, progressive, or socialist.[2] In the 1960s these critiques fused to produce a new and influential historiography of American foreign policy usually referred to as "revisionism."[3] Historians like Gabriel and

Joyce Kolko argued that the Cold War was the result not of Russian but of American aggression after 1945, an argument made all the more attractive to a generation of students by the contemporaneous war in Vietnam—proof, as it seemed, of the neocolonial thrust of American foreign policy.[4] The revival of American military power under Ronald Reagan prompted fresh warnings against the "imperial temptation."[5]

This tradition of radical criticism of American foreign policy shows no sign of fading away. Its distinctive anguished tone continues to emanate from writers like Chalmers Johnson,[6] echoing the strictures of an earlier generation of anti-imperialists (some of whom are themselves still faintly audible).[7] To Noam Chomsky, the Bush administration is intent on establishing "permanent hegemony," even at the risk of precipitating global catastrophe. The American empire claims to stand for democracy, but in reality it is profoundly undemocratic ("a system of elite decision-making and public ratification").[8] In the eyes of Gore Vidal, the tragedy of the Roman Republic is repeating itself as farce, with the "national-security state" relentlessly encroaching on the prerogatives of the patrician elite to which Vidal himself belongs.[9] Meanwhile, far to the right, Pat Buchanan fulminates in the now somewhat archaic isolationist idiom against East Coast internationalists intent on entangling the United States—against the express wishes of the Founding Fathers—in the quarrels and conflicts of the Old World. In Buchanan's eyes, America is following not the example of Rome but that of Britain, whose empire the United States once repudiated but now imitates.[10] Other, more mainstream conservatives—notably Clyde Prestowitz—have also heaped scorn on "the imperial project of the so-called neo-conservatives."[11]

In the past six years, however, a growing number of commentators have begun to use the term *American empire* less pejoratively, if still ambivalently,[12] and in some cases with genuine enthusiasm. Speaking at a conference in Atlanta in November 2000, Richard Haass—who went on to serve in the Bush administration as director of policy planning in the State Department—argued that Americans needed to "re-conceive their global role from one of traditional nation-state to an imperial power," calling openly for an "informal" American empire.[13] As Thomas Donnelly, deputy executive director of the Project for the New American Century, told the *Washington Post* in August 2001: "There's not all that many people who will talk about it [empire] openly. It's discomforting to a lot of Americans. So they use code phrases like 'America is the sole superpower.'"[14] Such inhibitions seemed to fall away in the aftermath of the terrorist attacks of September 11, 2001. In a trenchant article for the *Weekly Standard*—published just a month after the destruction of the World Trade Center—Max Boot explicitly made "The Case for an American Empire."[15] When his history of America's "small wars" appeared the following year, its title was taken from Rudyard Kipling's notorious poem "The White Man's Burden"—written in 1899 as an exhortation to the United States to turn the Philippines into an American colony.[16] The journalist Robert Kaplan also took up the imperial theme in his book *Warrior Politics,* arguing that "future historians will look back on the twenty-first-century United States as an empire as well as a republic."[17] "There's a positive side to empire," Kaplan argued in an interview: "It's in some ways the most benign form of order."[18] Charles Krauthammer, another conservative columnist, detected the change of mood. "People," he told the *New York Times,* were "now coming out of the closet on the word 'empire.'"[19] "America has become an empire," agreed Dinesh D'Souza, a fellow at the Hoover Institution, in the *Christian Science Monitor;* but happily it is "the most magnanimous imperial power ever." His conclusion: "Let us have more of it."[20] Writing in *Foreign Affairs* in 2002, the journalist Sebastian Mallaby proposed American "neoimperialism" as the best remedy for the "chaos" engendered by "failed states" around the world.[21] At times, Michael Ignatieff's complaint about American "nation-building" efforts in Bosnia, Kosovo, and Afghanistan seemed to be their lack of imperial rigor.[22]

While Mallaby and Ignatieff are perhaps best described as liberal interventionists—proponents of what Eric Hobsbawm has sneeringly dismissed as "the imperialism of human rights"—the majority of the new imperialists are neoconservatives, and it was their views that came to the fore during and after the invasion of Iraq in 2003. "Today there is only one empire," wrote James Kurth in a special "Empire" issue of the *National Interest,* "the global empire of the United States. The U.S. military . . . are the true heirs of the legendary civil officials, and not just the dedicated military officers, of the British Empire."[23] Speaking on Fox News in April 2003, the editor of the *Weekly Standard,* William Kristol, declared: "We need to err on the side of being strong. And if people want to say we're an imperial power, fine."[24] That same month, the *Wall Street Journal* suggested that the British naval campaign against the slave trade in the mid-nineteenth century might provide a model for American policy against nuclear proliferation.[25] Max Boot even called for the United States to establish a Colonial Office, the better to administer its new possessions in the Middle East and Asia.[26]

Officially, to be sure, the United States remains an empire in denial.[27] As Richard Nixon insisted in his memoirs, the United States is "the only great power without a history of imperialistic claims on neighboring countries,"[28] a view echoed by policymakers throughout the past two decades. In the words of Samuel R. "Sandy" Berger, President Bill Clinton's national security adviser, "We are the first global power in history that is not an imperial power."[29] While campaigning to succeed Clinton, George W. Bush echoed both Nixon and Berger: "America has never been an empire. We may be the only great power in history that had the chance, and refused— preferring greatness to power, and justice to glory."[30] He has reverted to this theme on several occasions since entering the White House. In a speech he made at the American Enterprise Institute, shortly before the invasion of Iraq, Bush stated:

> The U.S. has no intention of determining the precise form of Iraq's new government. That choice belongs to the Iraqi people. . . . We will remain in Iraq as long as necessary and not a day more. America has made and kept this kind of commitment before in the peace that followed a world war. After defeating enemies, we did not leave behind occupying armies, we left constitutions and parliaments.[31]

He reiterated this lack of imperial intent in a television address to the Iraqi people on April 10, 2003, when he declared: "We will help you build a peaceful and representative government that protects the rights of all citizens. And then our military forces will leave. Iraq will go forward as a unified, independent and sovereign nation."[32] Speaking on board the aircraft carrier *Abraham Lincoln* on May 1, the president rammed the point home: "Other nations in history have fought in foreign lands and remained to occupy and exploit. Americans, following a battle, want nothing more than to return home."[33] The same line was taken by Defense secretary Donald Rumsfeld in an interview with the television station *Al Jazeera* shortly before the Iraq war. "Would it worry you," Rumsfeld was asked, "if you go by force into Iraq that this might create the impression that the United States is becoming an imperial, colonial power?" Rumsfeld replied:

> Well I'm sure that some people would say that, but it can't be true because we're not a colonial power. We've never been a colonial power. We don't take our force and go around the world and try to take other people's real estate or other

people's resources, their oil. That's just not what the United States does. We never have and we never will. That's not how democracies behave. That's how an empire-building Soviet Union behaved but that's not how the United States behaves.[34]

Indeed, this appears to have been one of the few issues about which he and Secretary of State Colin Powell agreed. Speaking at the George Washington University in September 2003, Powell insisted: "The United States does not seek a territorial empire. We have never been imperialists. We seek a world in which liberty, prosperity and peace can become the heritage of all peoples, and not just the exclusive privilege of a few."[35] "If we were a true empire," argued Vice President Dick Cheney in January 2004, "we would currently preside over a much greater piece of the earth's surface than we currently do."[36]

Few Americans would dissent from this. Revealingly, four out of five Americans polled by the Pew Global Attitudes survey in 2003 agreed that it was "good that American ideas and customs were spreading around the world."[37] But were the same people to be asked if they considered this a consequence of American imperialism, hardly any would assent. Admittedly, Americans are not wholly oblivious to the imperial role their country plays in the world. But they generally dislike it. "I think we're trying to run the business of the world too much," a Kansas farmer told the British author Timothy Garton Ash in 2003, "like the Romans used to."[38] To such feelings of unease, American politicians respond with a categorical reassurance. "We're not an imperial power," declared President Bush in April 2004, "We're a liberating power."[39] This contrast between imperial rule and liberation has become a central leitmotif of presidential rhetoric since the invasion of Iraq. On November 6, 2003, in his speech to mark the twentieth anniversary of the National Endowment for Democracy, Bush set out a vision of "a new policy, a forward strategy of freedom in the Middle East":

> The establishment of a free Iraq at the heart of the Middle East [he argued] will be a watershed event in the global democratic revolution. . . . The advance of freedom is the calling of our time; it is the calling of our country. . . . We believe that liberty is the design of nature; we believe that liberty is the direction of history. We believe that human fulfillment and excellence come in the responsible exercise of liberty. And we believe that freedom—the freedom we prize—is not for us alone, it is the right and the capacity of all mankind.[40]

He restated this messianic credo in his speech to the Republican National Convention in September 2004:

> The story of America is the story of expanding liberty: an ever-widening circle, constantly growing to reach further and include more. . . . In our world . . . we will extend the frontiers of freedom. . . . We are working to advance liberty in the broader Middle East because freedom will bring a future of hope and the peace we all want. . . . Freedom is on the march. I believe in the transformational power of liberty: The wisest use of American strength is to advance freedom.[41]

In his mind, clearly, there is no contradiction between the ends of global democratization and the means of American military power. The democratizing mission of the United States is distinct from the ambitions of past empires because it is fundamentally altruistic.

The difficulty is, of course, that President Bush's ideal of freedom means, on close inspection, the American model of democracy and capitalism. When American neoconservatives speak of nation building, they actually mean state replicating, in the sense that they want to build political and economic institutions that are fundamentally similar to their own.[42] They may not aspire to rule; but they do aspire to have others rule themselves in the American way. Moreover, the very act of imposing "freedom" simultaneously subverts it. Just as the Victorians seemed hypocrites when they spread "civilization" with the Maxim gun, so there is something suspect about those who would democratize Fallujah with the Abrams tank. President Bush's distinction between conquest and liberation would have been entirely familiar to the liberal imperialists of the early 1900s, who likewise saw Britain's far-flung legions as agents of emancipation (not least in the Middle East during and after World War I). No less familiar to that earlier generation would have been the impatience of American officials to hand over sovereignty to an Iraqi government sooner rather than later. Indirect rule—which installed nominally independent native rulers while leaving British civilian administrators and military forces in practical control of financial matters and military security—was the preferred model for British colonial expansion in many parts of Asia, Africa, and the Middle East. Iraq itself was an example of indirect rule after the Hashemite dynasty was established there in the 1920s.

Freud defined denial as a primitive psychological defense mechanism against trauma. It is characteristic of this condition that under analysis the

sufferer may drop the defense. Significantly, little more than a month before the attacks of 9/11, the Office of the Secretary of Defense commis-
sioned a Summer Study at the Naval War College, Newport, to "explore
strategic approaches to sustain [U.S. predominance] for the long term
(~50 years)," which explicitly drew comparisons between the United States
and the Roman, Chinese, Ottoman, and British empires.[43] Such parallels
clearly did not seem outlandish to some senior American military personnel. In 2000 General Anthony Zinni, then commander in chief of U.S.
Central Command, told the journalist Dana Priest that he "had become a
modern-day proconsul, descendant of the warrior-statesman who ruled
the Roman Empire's outlying territory, bringing order and ideals from a
legalistic Rome."[44] Civilian officials, too, have been known to drop their
guard. In 2003 Vice President Cheney's Christmas card asked, "And if a
sparrow cannot fall to the ground without His notice, is it probable that an
empire can rise without His aid?" Journalist Ron Suskind reports that in an
interview in 2002, an unidentified "senior adviser to [President] Bush" said
to him that

> guys like me [Suskind] were "in what we call the reality-based community,"
> which he defined as people who "believe that solutions emerge from your judi-
> cious study of discernible reality." I nodded and murmured something about
> enlightenment principles and empiricism. He cut me off. "That's not the way
> the world really works anymore," he continued. "We're an empire now, and
> when we act, we create our own reality. And while you're studying that reality—
> judiciously, as you will—we'll act again, creating other new realities, which you
> can study too, and that's how things will sort out. We're history's actors . . . and
> you, all of you, will be left to just study what we do."[45]

II

What exactly is an empire? In the words of one of the few modern historians to attempt a genuinely comparative study of empires, it is

> first and foremost, a very great power that has left its mark on the international
> relations of an era . . . a polity that rules over wide territories and many peoples,
> since the management of space and multi-ethnicity is one of the great perennial
> dilemmas of empire. . . . An empire is by definition . . . not a polity ruled with
> the explicit consent of its peoples. . . . [But] by a process of assimilation of peo-
> ples and democratization of institutions empires can transform themselves into
> multi-national federations or even nation states.[46]

It is possible to be still more precise than this. In table 1, I have attempted a simple typology intended to capture the diversity of forms that can be subsumed under the heading "empire." Note that the table should be read as a menu rather than as a grid. For example, an empire could be an oligarchy at home, aiming to acquire raw materials from abroad, thereby increasing international trade, using mainly military methods, imposing a market economy, serving the interests of its ruling elite, and fostering a hierarchical social character. Another empire might be a democracy at home, aiming to ensure security, providing peace as a public good, ruling mainly through firms and NGOs, promoting a mixed economy, serving the interests of all inhabitants, and exhibiting an assimilative social character.

The first column reminds us that imperial power can be acquired by more than one type of political system. There is no reason why an empire should be a tyranny; there have been aristocratic, oligarchic, and even democratic empires. The self-interested objectives of imperial expansion (second column) range from the fundamental need to ensure the security of the metropolis by imposing order on enemies at its (initial) borders, to the collection of rents and taxation from subject peoples, to say nothing of the more obvious prizes of new land for settlement, raw materials, treasure, and manpower—all of which, it should be emphasized, would need to be available at prices lower than those established in free exchange with independent peoples if the cost of conquest and colonization were to be justified.[47] At the same time, an empire may provide "public goods"—that is, intended or unintended benefits of imperial rule flowing not to the rulers but to the ruled and beyond to third parties: less conflict, more trade

TABLE 1.   An Imperial Typology

Metropolitan system	Self-interested objectives	Public goods	Methods of rule	Economic system	Cui bono?	Social character
Tyranny	Security	Peace	Military	Plantation	Ruling elite	Genocidal
Aristocracy	Communications	Trade	Bureaucratic	Feudal	Metropolitan populace	Hierarchical
Oligarchy	Land	Investment	Settlement	Mercantilist	Settlers	Converting
Democracy	Raw materials	Law	NGOs	Market	Local elites	Assimilative
	Treasure	Governance	Firms	Mixed	All inhabitants	
	Manpower	Education	Delegation to local elites	Planned		
	Rents	Conversion				
	Taxation	Health				

or investment, improved justice or governance, better education (which may or may not be associated with religious conversion, something we would not nowadays regard as a public good), or improved material conditions.[48] The fourth column tells us that imperial rule can be implemented by more than one kind of functionary: soldiers, civil servants, settlers, voluntary associations, firms, and local elites can in different ways impose the will of the center on the periphery. There are almost as many varieties of imperial economic systems, ranging from slavery to laissez-faire, from one form of serfdom (feudalism) to another (the planned economy). Nor is it by any means a given that the benefits of empire should flow simply to the metropolitan society. It may be only the elite of that society (or colonists drawn from lower-income groups in the metropole, or subject peoples, or the elites within subject societies) that reaps the benefits of empire. Finally, the social character of an empire—to be precise, the attitudes of the rulers toward the ruled—may vary. At one extreme lies the genocidal empire of National Socialist Germany, intent on the annihilation of specific ethnic groups and the deliberate degradation of others. At the other extreme lies the Roman model of empire, in which citizenship was obtainable under certain conditions regardless of ethnicity. In the middle lies the Victorian model, in which inequalities of economic wealth, social status, and racial hierarchy were mitigated by a general (though certainly not unqualified) principle of equality before the law. The precise combination of all these variables determines, among other things, the geographical extent—and of course the duration—of an empire.

All told, there have been no more than seventy empires in history, if the *Times Atlas of World History* is to be believed. Applying the typology set out in the table, it is not difficult to characterize the United States as one of them. It goes without saying that it is a liberal democracy and market economy, though its polity has some illiberal characteristics and its economy a higher level of state intervention than is often assumed. In its imperial undertakings, it is primarily concerned with its own security and maintaining international communications and, secondarily, with ensuring access to raw materials, though it prefers to achieve the latter goal through trade rather than forcible extraction. It is also in the business of providing a number of important public goods: peace, by intervening against some bellicose regimes and in some civil wars; freedom of the seas and skies for trade; some formal and informal standardization of business practices; and a distinctive form of conversion usually called Americanization, which is carried out less by old-style Christian missionaries than by the exporters of American consumer goods and entertainment. Its methods of formal rule are primarily military in character; its methods of informal rule rely heavily on corporations and nongovernmental organizations and, in some cases, local elites. Note that most empires aspire to more than just military dominance along a broad strategic frontier,[49] and not all empires engage in long-term direct rule over large tracts of foreign territory. Fundamentally, however, all empires are in some measure concerned to export their institutions and culture to foreign peoples, using force if necessary.[50]

Who benefits from this empire? Some would argue, with Chomsky, that only its wealthy elite does—specifically, according to the economist and journalist Paul Krugman, that part of its wealthy elite associated with the Republican Party and the oil industry.[51] The conventional wisdom on the left is that successive administrations have used their power, wittingly or unwittingly, to shore up the position of American corporations and the regimes (usually corrupt and authoritarian) that are willing to do the same.[52] The losers have been and remain the impoverished majority of people in the developing world. Others would argue that many millions of people around the world have benefited in some way from the existence of America's empire (not least the Western Europeans, Japanese, and South Koreans who were able to prosper during the Cold War under the protection of the American "empire by invitation")[53] and that the economic losers of the post–Cold War era, particularly in sub-Saharan Africa, are victims not of American power, but of its absence.

How different is the American empire from previous empires? Like the ancient Egyptian empire, it erects towering edifices in its heartland, though these house the living rather than the dead. Like the Athenian empire, it has proved itself adept at leading alliances against rival powers. Like the empire of Alexander, it has staggering geographical range. Like the Chinese empire that arose in the Chi'in era and reached its zenith under the Ming dynasty, it has united the lands and peoples of a vast territory, and forged them into a nation. Like the Roman Empire, it has a system of citizenship that is remarkably open: Purple Hearts and U.S. citizenship have been conferred simultaneously on foreign-born soldiers serving in Iraq, just as service in the legions was once a route to becoming a *civis romanus*. Indeed, with the classical architecture of its capital and the republican structure of its Constitution, the United States is perhaps more like Rome than any previous empire—albeit a Rome in which the Senate has thus far retained its grip on would-be emperors. Yet in its capacity for spreading its own language and culture—at once monotheistic and mathematical—the United States also shares features of the Abassid caliphate established by the heirs of Mohammed. And it also has certain traits in common with the great land empires of Central and Eastern Europe. Certainly, its political structures are sometimes more reminiscent of Vienna or Berlin than they are of The Hague, capital of the last great imperial republic, or of London, hub of the first Anglophone empire.

Nevertheless, it is the British Empire of a hundred years ago that the American empire today most closely resembles: in its fundamentally liberal mission; in its global reach; in its economic dominance; in the relatively small number of troops it deploys in foreign lands; in the particular challenges it faces. American politicians may deny that they are behaving as imperialists. Their denials cut little ice in Baghdad or Kabul, where American troops on patrol look unmistakably like the "imperial grunts" of our time. Perhaps, on reflection, that is precisely what Americans find so hard to accept: that they are the redcoats now.

III

In my book *Colossus,* I set out to show that the United States is an empire; that this might not be wholly a bad thing; but that Americans might find the mantle of the last Anglophone empire a surprisingly uncomfortable garment.[54] Here, in a simplified form, is what the book argues:

1. that the United States has always been, functionally if not self-consciously, an empire;
2. that a self-conscious American imperialism might well be preferable to the available alternatives;
3. but that financial, human, and cultural constraints make such self-consciousness highly unlikely;
4. and that therefore the American empire, insofar as it continues to exist, will remain a somewhat dysfunctional entity.

By self-conscious imperialism, please note, I did not mean that the United States should unabashedly proclaim itself an empire and its president an emperor. I merely meant that Americans need to recognize the imperial characteristics of their own power today and, if possible, to learn from the achievements and failures of past empires. In other words, it is no longer sensible to maintain the fiction that there is something wholly unique about the foreign relations of the United States that sets it apart from all previous great powers. The dilemmas that America faces today plainly have more in common with those of the later Victorians than with those of the Founding Fathers.[55]

The problem facing this "empire in denial," I suggested, was that it was afflicted with three deficits. The first was a financial deficit, arising from the combination of tax cuts and increased expenditure on both domestic and foreign programs, of which nation building accounted for only a part. More generally, I suggested, the U.S. current account deficit and the attendant dependence of the American economy on foreign capital contrasted strikingly with the high levels of net capital export that characterized the British economy a hundred years ago. It was hard to see how the world's biggest borrower could exert the same leverage over foreign countries as the world's biggest lender did a century ago. Second, the United States suffered from a manpower deficit. Not only did it have a relatively small proportion of its military manpower available for overseas duty. It also lacked colonists, in the sense of Americans willing to resettle and spend the rest of their lives helping to build an American-style civil society in hot, poor countries. Finally, as a democracy, the United States was afflicted by an attention deficit disorder. Because of the pressure of the two- to four-year electoral cycle, administrations were under intense pressure to deliver results in a tighter time-frame than was realistic.

This analysis has stood up well to the test of subsequent events. The manpower deficit is now apparent for all to see in Iraq and Afghanistan, not because the United States lacks young men—it has at least seven times as many as Iraq—but because it chooses, for a variety of reasons, to employ only a tiny proportion of its population (less than 1 percent) in its armed forces, and to deploy only a fraction of these in overseas conflict zones. In 1920, to illustrate the difficulty, when British forces quelled a major insurgency in Iraq, they numbered around 135,000. Coincidentally, that is very close to the number of American military personnel currently in that same country. The trouble is that the population of Iraq was just over 3 million in 1920, whereas today it is around 24 million. Thus the ratio of Iraqis to foreign forces in 1920 was, at most, 23 to 1.[56] Today it is around 160 to 1. To arrive at a ratio of 23 to 1, roughly one million American troops would be needed. Reinforcements on that scale are, needless to say, inconceivable.

This is the reality of what Michael Ignatieff has called "Empire Lite." In theory, the American military is a lean and mean fighting machine. In practice, however, downsizing has left it with too few combat effectives to make a success of imperial policing—a labor-intensive task that renders redundant much of its high-tech hardware, while rendering vulnerable a highly trained soldiery. Each time the newspaper reports the tragedy of another death in action, I am reminded of the lines of Rudyard Kipling, the greatest of the British Empire's poets:

A scrimmage in a Border Station—
    A canter down some dark defile—
Two thousand pounds of education
    Drops to a ten-rupee jezail—
The Crammer's boast, the Squadron's pride,
Shot like a rabbit in a ride!

The financial deficit remains a real source of weakness too. True, the costs of the war in Iraq—though perhaps as much as an order of magnitude larger than the administration forecast at $290 billion since the invasion in 2003—do not amount to much in relation to the size of the U.S. economy: around 1.3 percent of gross domestic product. On the other hand, relatively little of this expenditure has gone into the reconstruction of the Iraqi economy; certainly not enough to achieve the swift recovery that might have averted today's incipient civil war. Nor is it likely that significantly more money will be available for this purpose in the future. The gross federal debt now exceeds $8.3 trillion, and, if the Congressional Budget Office's forecast turns out to be correct, we are just a decade away from a $12.8 trillion debt—more than double the burden President Bush inherited from his predecessor.[57] Moreover, the officially stated borrowings of the federal government are only a small part of the U.S. debt problem. Ordinary American households, too, have gone on a borrowing spree of unprecedented magnitude. U.S. household credit market debt has risen from just above 45 percent of GDP in the early 1980s to above 70 percent in recent years.[58] The remarkable resilience of American consumer spending in the past fifteen years has been based partly on a collapse in the personal savings rate from around 7.5 percent of income to below zero. For demographic reasons Americans need to be saving much more than this. According to the United Nations' intermediate projections, male life expectancy in the United States will rise from seventy-five to eighty between now and 2050. The share of the

American population that is aged sixty-five or over will rise from 12 percent to nearly 21 percent. By 2050 the elderly dependency ratio (the ratio of the population aged sixty-five years or over to the population aged fifteen to sixty-four) could double.[59] But the evidence is that only a minority of Americans have made adequate private provision for their retirement. That implies that most new retirees in the years ahead will depend to some extent on the systems of Social Security, Medicare, and Medicaid. Already, the average retiree receives benefits totaling $21,000 a year from these programs. Multiply this by 36 million (the current number of elderly Americans) and you can see why these programs already consume half of federal tax revenues. That proportion is bound to rise in the years ahead. All this means that the federal government has much larger unfunded liabilities than official data suggest. If one compares the present value of all projected future government expenditures—including debt service payments—with the present value of all projected future government receipts, the gap is around $66 trillion, according to calculations by economists Jagadeesh Gokhale and Kent Smetters.[60]

Americans are not just borrowing from one another and, in effect, from the next generation. They are also, to a vast extent, borrowing from foreigners. In nearly every year since 1992, the gap between the amount of goods and services the United States exports and the amount it imports has grown wider. In 2007 the current account deficit—which is largely a trade deficit—rose above 6 percent of GDP, nearly double its peak in the mid-1980s. The result has been a remarkable accumulation of foreign debt. Estimates of the net international investment position of the United States— the difference between the overseas assets owned by Americans and the American assets owned by foreigners—have declined from a modest positive balance of around 5 percent of GDP in the mid-1980s to a huge net debt of minus 20 percent today. In other words, foreigners are accumulating large claims on the future output of the United States. Foreign ownership of the U.S. federal debt passed the halfway mark in June 2004.[61] Around a third of corporate bonds are now in foreign hands, and more than 13 percent of the U.S. stock market.[62] These are largely hidden weaknesses at present. Yet it cannot be a sign of Western strength that the bill for Social Security ($555 billion) is now larger—to the tune of $43 billion—than the bill for national security ($512 billion).[63] And it cannot be a sign of imperial vigor that the United States needs to rely so heavily on foreign investors—including Asian central banks and Middle Eastern sovereign wealth funds—to help finance a foreign policy that, as we shall see below, currently enjoys minimal international support.

True, the United States benefits significantly from the status of the dollar as the world's principal reserve currency; it is one reason why foreign investors are prepared to hold such large volumes of dollar-denominated assets. But reserve-currency status is not divinely ordained; it could be undermined if international markets take fright at the magnitude of America's still latent fiscal crisis.[64] A further decline in the dollar would certainly hurt foreign holders of U.S. currency more than it would hurt Americans. But a shift in international expectations about U.S. finances might also bring about a sharp increase in long-term interest rates, which would have immediate and negative feedback effects on the federal deficit by pushing up the cost of debt service.[65]

Finally, and just as important, there is what I have called the American attention deficit disorder. Past empires had little difficulty in sustaining public support for protracted conflicts. The United States, by contrast, has become markedly worse at this. It took barely eighteen months for a majority of American voters to start telling pollsters at Gallup that they regarded the invasion of Iraq as a mistake. Comparable levels of disillusionment with the Vietnam War did not set in until August 1968, three years after U.S. forces had arrived en masse, by which time the total number of Americans killed in action was approaching thirty thousand.

IV

Is the very concept of empire an anachronism? A number of critics have argued that imperialism was a discrete historical phenomenon that reached its apogee in the late nineteenth century and has been defunct since the 1950s. "The Age of Empire is passed," declared one journalist in July 2004:

> The experience of Iraq has demonstrated . . . that when America does not disguise its imperial force, when a proconsul leads an "occupying power," it is liable to find itself in an untenable position quickly enough. There are three reasons: the people being governed do not accept such a form of rule, the rest of the world does not accept it and Americans themselves do not accept it.[66]

In supporting the claim that empire is defunct, one reviewer of *Colossus* cited nationalism as "a much more powerful force now than it was during the heyday of the Victorian era."[67] Another cited "the tectonic changes wrought by independence movements and ethnic and religious politics in the years since the end of World War II."[68]

Such arguments betray a touching naïveté about both the past and the present. First, empire was no temporary condition of the Victorian age. Empires, as we have seen, can be traced as far back as recorded history goes; indeed, most history is the history of empires precisely because empires are so good at recording, replicating, and transmitting their own words and deeds. It is the nation-state—an essentially nineteenth-century ideal—that is the historical novelty and may yet prove to be the more ephemeral entity. Given the ethnic heterogeneity and restless mobility of mankind, this should not surprise us. On close inspection, many of the most successful nation-states started life as empires. What is the modern United Kingdom of Great Britain and Northern Ireland if not the legatee of an earlier English imperialism? Second, it is a fantasy that the age of empire came to an end in a global springtime of the peoples after 1945. On the contrary, World War II merely saw the defeat of three would-be empires (the German, Japanese, and Italian) by an alliance between the old Western European empires (principally the British, since the others were so swiftly beaten) and the newer empires of the Soviet Union and the United States. Certainly, the Soviet Union was and remained, until its precipitous decline and fall, unmistakably a Russian empire. Moreover, the other great Communist power to emerge from the 1940s, the People's Republic of China, remains in many respects a Han Chinese empire to this day. Its three most extensive provinces—Inner Mongolia, Xinjiang, and Tibet—were all acquired as a result of imperial expansion, and China continues to lay claim to Taiwan as well as numerous smaller islands, to say nothing of some territory in Russian Siberia and Kazakhstan.

Empires, in short, are like the poor: always with us. Meanwhile, it is not immediately obvious why the modern media should threaten their longevity. The growth of the popular press did nothing to weaken the British Empire in the late nineteenth and early twentieth centuries; on the contrary, the mass-circulation newspapers tended to enhance the popular legitimacy of the empire. Anyone who watched how American television networks covered the invasion of Iraq ought to understand that the mass media are not necessarily solvents of imperial power. As for nationalism, it is something of a myth that this was what brought down the old empires of Western Europe. Far more lethal to their longevity were the costs of fighting rival empires—empires that were still more contemptuous of the principle of self-determination.[69]

Nevertheless, there is no denying that the American empire today is being weakened by a fourth deficit—one which I overlooked in *Colossus*. That is its legitimacy deficit. Consider only the decline in popularity of the United States in the eyes of the populations of its long-standing European allies. In 1999–2000, 83 percent of British people surveyed by the State Department Office of Research said they had a "favorable opinion" of the United States. By 2006, according to the Pew Global Attitudes Project, that proportion had fallen to 56 percent. In Germany the decline over the same period was from 78 percent to just 37 percent. In Indonesia it was from 75 to 30 percent; in Turkey from 52 to 12 percent. British respondents to the Pew surveys now give higher favorability ratings to Germany (75 percent) and Japan (69 percent) than to the United States—a remarkable transformation in attitudes in a country that has tended to cherish the memory of World War II. It is also remarkable that Britons polled by Pew regard the U.S. presence in Iraq as a bigger threat to world peace than Iran or North Korea—a view shared by respondents in France, Spain, Russia, India, China, and throughout the Middle East. Two-thirds of Americans believe their country's foreign policy considers the interests of others, an opinion shared by only 38 percent of Germans, 32 percent of Britons, 21 percent of Russians, 19 percent of Canadians and Spaniards, 14 percent of Turks, and 13 percent of Poles. More than two-thirds of Turks and Germans surveyed in 2004 believed that American leaders lied about Saddam Hussein's weapons of mass destruction prior to the previous year's invasion. In France the proportion rose to 82 percent. More than half of French respondents regarded America's true motives as being "to control Mideast oil" and "to dominate the world." Even in Britain a third and a quarter of respondents, respectively, expressed those views.[70] These are remarkable figures, testifying to a steep decline in the international standing of the United States in the space of less than a decade.

There are, it should be noted, some sources of consolation in recent surveys of international opinion. Very few Europeans, for example, would welcome it if China were to become a serious military rival to the United States (ranging from just 8 percent of Poles to 27 percent of French respondents). Outside the Middle East, there is overwhelming international opposition to Iran's acquiring nuclear weapons.[71] Nevertheless, there is no doubt that something has gone wrong. The temptation is to conclude, with Francis

Fukuyama, that the neoconservative/crypto-imperial project was fatally flawed from the outset: that "benign hegemony" was a fantasy, unilateralism a blunder, preemption impracticable, and democratization of the Middle East a delusion.[72] Yet other and perhaps more profound explanations for the collapse of American legitimacy also suggest themselves. They go to the heart of the fundamental tension that appears to exist between democracy and empire.

The first seed of future troubles was the administration's decision to treat suspected al-Qaeda personnel captured in Afghanistan and elsewhere as "unlawful enemy combatants" beyond both American and international law. Prisoners were held incommunicado and indefinitely at Guantánamo Bay. As the rules governing interrogation were chopped and changed, many of these prisoners were subjected to forms of mental and physical intimidation that in some cases amounted to torture.[73] Indeed, Justice Department memoranda were written to rationalize the use of torture as a matter for presidential discretion in times of war. Evidently, some members of the administration felt that extreme measures were justified by the shadowy nature of the foe they faced, as well as by the public appetite for retribution after the terrorist attacks of September 11, 2001. All of this the Supreme Court rightly denounced in its stinging judgment, delivered in June 2004. As the justices put it, not even the imperatives of resisting "an assault by the forces of tyranny" could justify the use by an American president of "the tools of tyrants." Yet power corrupts, and even small amounts of power can corrupt a very great deal. It may not have been official policy to flout the Geneva Conventions in Iraq, but not enough was done by senior officers to protect prisoners held at Abu Ghraib from gratuitous abuse—what the inquiry chaired by James Schlesinger called "freelance activities on the part of the night shift."[74] The photographic evidence of these activities did more than anything else to discredit the claim of the United States and its allies to stand not merely for an abstract liberty but also for the effective rule of law.

Second, it was more than mere exaggeration on the part of Vice President Cheney, the former CIA chief George Tenet, and, ultimately, President Bush himself—to say nothing of Prime Minister Tony Blair—to claim they knew *for certain* that Saddam Hussein possessed weapons of mass destruction. This, we now know, went far beyond what the available intelligence indicated. What they could legitimately have said was this: "After all his evasions, we simply can't be sure whether or not Saddam Hussein has got any WMD. So, on the precautionary principle, we just can't leave him in power indefinitely. Better safe than sorry." But that was not enough for Cheney, who felt compelled to make the bald assertion that "Saddam Hussein possesses weapons of mass destruction." Bush himself had doubts, but was reassured by Tenet that it was a "slam-dunk case."[75] Other doubters soon fell into line. Still more misleading was the administration's allegation that Saddam was "teaming up" with al-Qaeda. Sketchy evidence of contact between the two was used to insinuate Iraqi complicity in the 9/11 attacks, for which not a shred of proof has yet been found.

Third, it was a near disaster that responsibility for the postwar occupation of Iraq was seized by the Defense Department, intoxicated as its principals became in the heat of their blitzkrieg. The State Department had spent long hours preparing a plan for the aftermath of a successful invasion. That plan was simply junked by Secretary Rumsfeld and his close advisers, who were convinced that once Saddam had gone, Iraq would magically reconstruct itself after a period of suitably ecstatic celebration at the advent of freedom. As one official told the *Financial Times,* Under Secretary Douglas Feith led

> a group in the Pentagon who all along felt that this was going to be not just a cakewalk, it was going to be 60–90 days, a flip-over and hand-off, a lateral or whatever to . . . the INC [Iraqi National Congress]. The DoD [Department of Defense] could then wash its hands of the whole affair and depart quickly, smoothly and swiftly. And there would be a democratic Iraq that was amenable to our wishes and desires left in its wake. And that's all there was to it.[76]

When General Eric Shinseki, the army chief of staff, stated in late February 2003 that "something of the order of several hundred thousand soldiers" would be required to stabilize postwar Iraq, he was brusquely put down by Deputy Secretary Wolfowitz as "wildly off the mark." Wolfowitz professed himself "reasonably certain" that the Iraqi people would "greet us as liberators." Such illusions were not, it should be remembered, confined to neoconservatives in the Pentagon. Even General Tommy Franks was under the impression that it would be possible to reduce troop levels to just fifty thousand after eighteen months. It was left to Colin Powell to point out to the president that "regime change" had serious—not to say imperial—implications. The Pottery Barn rule, he suggested to Bush, was bound to be applicable to Iraq: "You break it, you own it."[77]

Fourth, American diplomacy in 2003 was like the two-headed Pushmepullyou in *Doctor Doolittle:* it pointed in opposite directions. On one side was Cheney, dismissing the United Nations as a negligible factor. On the other was Powell, insisting that any action would require some form of UN authorization to be legitimate. It is possible that one of these approaches might have worked. It was, however, hopeless to try to apply both. Europe was in fact coming around as a consequence of some fairly successful diplomatic browbeating. It is often forgotten today that no fewer than eighteen European governments signed letters expressing support of the impending war against Saddam. Yet the decision to seek a second UN resolution—on the ground that the language of Resolution 1441 was not strong enough to justify all-out war—was a blunder that allowed the French government to regain the initiative by virtue of its permanent seat on the Security Council. Despite the fact that more than forty countries declared their support for the invasion of Iraq and that three (Britain, Australia, and Poland) sent troops, the threat of a French veto, delivered with a Gallic flourish, created the indelible impression that the United States was acting unilaterally—and even illegally.[78]

V

All these mistakes had one thing in common: they sprang from a failure to learn from history. It was said that President Bush was reading Edward Morris's *Theodore Rex* as the war in Iraq was being planned; presumably he had not got to the part where the American occupation sparked off a Filipino insurrection. Before the invasion of Iraq, deputy national security adviser Stephen Hadley was heard to refer to a purely unilateral American invasion as "the imperial option." Did no one else grasp that occupying and trying to transform Iraq (with or without allies) was indeed a quintessentially imperial undertaking—one that could not only encounter stiff local resistance but also, consequently, take many years to succeed?

Had policymakers troubled to consider what befell the last Anglophone occupation of Iraq, they might have been less surprised by the persistent resistance they encountered in the central provinces of the country since 2004. For in May 1920 there was a major anti-British revolt there. This happened six months after a referendum (in practice, a round of consultations with tribal leaders) on the country's future, and just after the announcement that Iraq would become a League of Nations "mandate" under British trusteeship rather than continue under colonial rule. Strikingly, neither consultation with Iraqis nor the promise of internationalization sufficed to avert an uprising.[79] In 1920, as in 2004, the insurrection had religious origins and leaders, but it managed to transcend the country's ancient ethnic and sectarian divisions. The first anti-British demonstrations were in the mosques of Baghdad, but the violence quickly spread to the Shiite holy city of Karbalā, where British rule was denounced by Ayatollah Muhammad Taqi al-Shirazi, the historical counterpart of today's Shiite firebrand, Moktada al-Sadr. At its height, the revolt stretched as far north as the Kurdish city of Kirkuk and as far south as Samawah. Then, as in 2004, much of the violence was more symbolic than strategically significant—British bodies were mutilated, much as American bodies were at Fallujah. But there was a real threat to the British position. The rebels systematically sought to disrupt the occupiers' infrastructure, attacking railways and telegraph lines. In some places, British troops and civilians were cut off and besieged. By August 1920 the situation in Iraq was so desperate that the general in charge appealed to London not only for reinforcements but also for chemical weapons (mustard gas bombs or shells), though, contrary to historical legend, these turned out to be unavailable and so were never used.[80]

The British eventually ended the rebellion through a combination of aerial bombardments and punitive village-burning expeditions. Even Winston Churchill, then the minister responsible for the Royal Air Force, was shocked by the actions of some trigger-happy pilots and vengeful ground troops. And despite their overwhelming technological superiority, British forces still suffered more than two thousand dead and wounded. Moreover, the British had to keep troops in Iraq long after the country was granted "full sovereignty." Although Iraq was declared formally independent in 1932, British troops remained there until 1955, thirty-eight years after their initial arrival in Baghdad and General F. S. Maude's famous proclamation: "Our armies do not come into your cities and lands as conquerors or enemies, but as liberators . . . It is [not] the wish of [our] government to impose upon you alien institutions."

Is it conceivable that the United States will succeed in defeating the Iraqi insurgency as decisively as their British predecessors in 1920? Is it conceivable that American troops will still be in Iraq in 2041? To each question, the answer is almost certainly no. As I sought to show in *Colossus*, most American occupations of foreign countries have been of relatively short duration, which may well account for their relative lack of success in fundamentally altering the political institutions of the countries in question. Leaving aside American Samoa, Guam, the Northern Mariana Islands, Puerto Rico, and the Virgin Islands, which remain American dependencies, the United States occupied Panama for seventy-six years, the Philippines for forty-eight, Palau for forty-seven, Micronesia and the Marshall Islands for thirty-nine, Haiti for nineteen, and the Dominican Republic for eight. The formal postwar occupations of West Germany and Japan continued for, respectively, ten and seven years, though U.S. forces still remain in those countries, as well as in South Korea. Troops were also deployed in large numbers in South Vietnam from 1965, though by 1973 they were gone. It seems likely that the U.S. presence in Afghanistan and Iraq will be at the shorter end of this scale.

Pace Chávez and Chomsky, this is the real problem—not the "hegemonic pretensions" of the United States, but its chronic lack of imperial stamina. Far from being bent on world domination and the exploitation of less developed economies, the United States has, over a hundred years, evinced a profound ambivalence toward the temptations and tribulations of empire. This is perhaps not so surprising. History suggests that empires will come into existence and endure so long as the benefits of exerting power over foreign peoples exceed the costs of doing so in the eyes of the imperialists; and so long as the benefits of accepting dominance by a foreign people exceed the costs of resistance in the eyes of the subjects. (Such calculations must implicitly take account of the potential costs of relinquishing power to another empire.) At the moment, in these terms, the costs of running countries like Iraq and Afghanistan look too high to most Americans, especially given the federal government's latent fiscal crisis and the country's mounting foreign indebtedness; the benefits of doing so seem at best nebulous; and no rival empire seems able or willing to do a better (or worse) job.

Yet it is important to remember that variables do vary, and so all these things could change. In our ever more populous world, where certain natural resources are destined to become more scarce, the old mainsprings of imperial rivalry remain. Look only at China's recent vigorous pursuit of privileged relationships with major commodity producers in Africa and elsewhere. Consider the irony that American intervention in Iraq seems principally to have benefited Iran, another country with a long and illustrious imperial history. Or ask how long a neoisolationist America would remain disengaged from the Greater Middle East in the face of new terrorist attacks devised in that region.

Empire today, it is true, is generally both unstated and unwanted. But history strongly suggests that the calculus of power could quite easily swing back in its favor tomorrow.

NOTES

1. For a translation of Chávez's speech, see http://www.newsmax.com/archives/arti cles/2006/9/20/123752.shtml (accessed March 12, 2008).

2. See, e.g., Scott Nearing, *The American Empire* (New York: Rand School of Social Science, 1921); Joseph Freeman and Scott Nearing, *Dollar Diplomacy: A Study in American Imperialism* (New York: B. W. Huebsch and the Viking Press, 1925).

3. For an early example, see William Appleman Williams, *The Tragedy of American Diplomacy* (Cleveland: World Publishing, 1959).

4. See, e.g., Gabriel and Joyce Kolko, *The Limits of Power: The World and United States Foreign Policy, 1945–1954* (New York: Harper and Row, 1972).

5. Robert W. Tucker and David C. Hendrickson, *The Imperial Temptation: The New World Order and America's Purpose* (New York: Council on Foreign Relations Press, 1992), 53, 211.

6. Chalmers Johnson, *Blowback: The Costs and Consequences of American Empire* (London: Little, Brown, 2000).

7. See, e.g., Eric Hobsbawm, "America's Imperial Delusion," *Guardian*, June 14, 2003.

8. Noam Chomsky, *Hegemony or Survival: America's Quest for Global Dominance* (New York: Metropolitan Books, 2003), 3–5. According to Chomsky, "Neoliberal initiatives of the past thirty years have been designed to restrict [the public arena], leaving basic decision-making within largely unaccountable private tyrannies, linked closely to one another and to a few powerful states."

9. Gore Vidal, *The Decline and Fall of the American Empire* (Berkeley, Calif.: Odonian Press, 1992).

10. Patrick J. Buchanan, *A Republic, Not an Empire* (Washington, D.C.: Regnery, 1999), 6.

11. Clyde Prestowitz, *Rogue Nation: American Unilateralism and the Failure of Good Intentions* (New York: Basic Books, 2003).

12. See, e.g., Andrew Bacevich, *American Empire: The Realities and Consequences of U.S. Diplomacy* (Cambridge: Harvard University Press, 2002), 243: "Although the U.S. has not created an empire in any formal sense . . . it has most definitely acquired an imperial problem. . . . Like it or not, America today *is* Rome, committed irreversibly to the maintenance and, where feasible, expansion of an empire that differs from every other empire in history. This is hardly a matter for celebration; but neither is there any purpose served by denying the facts."

13. Quoted in Bacevich, *American Empire*, 219.

14. Thomas E. Ricks, "Empire or Not? A Quiet Debate over U.S. Role," *Washington Post*, August 21, 2001.

15. Max Boot, "The Case for an American Empire," *Weekly Standard*, October 15, 2001.

16. Max Boot, *The Savage Wars of Peace: Small Wars and the Rise of American Power* (New York: Basic Books, 2002), xx.

17. Robert D. Kaplan, *Warrior Politics: Why Leadership Demands a Pagan Ethos* (New York: Random House, 2001), 151.

18. Emily Eakin, "It Takes an Empire," *New York Times,* April 2, 2002.

19. Eakin, "It Takes an Empire."

20. Dinesh D'Souza, "In Praise of an American Empire," *Christian Science Monitor,* April 26, 2002.

21. Sebastian Mallaby, "The Reluctant Imperialist: Terrorism, Failed States, and the Case for American Empire," *Foreign Affairs,* March–April 2002, 6.

22. Michael Ignatieff, *Empire Lite: Nation-Building in Bosnia, Kosovo and Afghanistan* (London: Vintage, 2003), 3, 22, 90, 115, 126. See, however, Ignatieff, "Why Are We in Iraq? (And Liberia? And Afghanistan?)," *New York Times Magazine,* September 6, 2003.

23. James Kurth, "Migration and the Dynamics of Empire," *National Interest,* Spring 2003, 5.

24. James Atlas, "A Classicist's Legacy: New Empire Builders," *New York Times,* May 4, 2003.

25. "Interdicting North Korea," *Wall Street Journal,* April 28, 2003.

26. Max Boot, "Washington Needs a Colonial Office," *Financial Times,* July 3, 2003.

27. Niall Ferguson, *Empire: The Rise and Demise of the British World Order and the Lessons for Global Power* (New York: Basic Books, 2003), 370.

28. Quoted in Walter Russell Mead, *Special Providence: American Foreign Policy and How It Changed the World* (New York: Alfred A. Knopf, 2001), 6.

29. Speech at the Council on Foreign Relations, 1999, quoted in the *Washington Post,* August 21, 2001.

30. Quoted in Bacevich, *American Empire,* 201.

31. "Transcript of President Bush's Speech," *New York Times,* February 26, 2003.

32. Transcript from the Office of International Information Programs, U.S. Department of State.

33. "Transcript of President Bush's Remarks on the End of Major Combat in Iraq," *New York Times,* May 2, 2003.

34. Secretary of Defense Donald Rumsfeld, interview with Al Jazeera TV, February 27, 2003, press release, Department of Defense.

35. Colin L. Powell, "Remarks at The Elliott School of International Affairs, George Washington University," September 5, 2003, http://www.state.gov/secretary/former/powell/remarks/2003/23836.htm.

36. Quoted in Andrew Roberts, *A History of the English-Speaking Peoples since 1900* (London: Weidenfeld and Nicolson, 2006), 626.

37. Minxin Pei, "The Paradoxes of American Nationalism," *Foreign Policy,* May–June 2003, 32.

38. Timothy Garton Ash, *Free World: Why a Crisis of the West Reveals the Opportunity of Our Time* (London: Penguin, 2004), 102.

39. "Transcript of Bush's Remarks on Iraq: 'We Will Finish the Work of the Fallen,'" *New York Times,* April 14, 2004.

40. "Remarks by the President at the 20th Anniversary of the National Endowment for Democracy," November 6, 2003, http://www.whitehouse.gov/news/releases/2003/11/20031106-2.html (accessed March 12, 2008).

41. "President's Remarks at the 2004 Republican National Convention," September 2, 2004, http://www.whitehouse.gov/news/releases/2004/09/20040902-2.html (accessed March 12, 2008).

42. See Francis Fukuyama, *State-Building: Governance and World Order in the 21st Century* (Ithaca, N.Y.: Cornell University Press, 2004).

43. "Strategies for Maintaining U.S. Predominance," Office of Net Assessment, Office of the Secretary of Defense, Summer Study, August 1, 2001, esp. p. 22.

44. Dana Priest, *The Mission: Waging War and Keeping Peace with America's Military* (New York: W. W. Norton, 2003), 70.

45. Ron Suskind, "Without a Doubt," *New York Times Magazine*, October 17, 2004.

46. Dominic Lieven, *Empire: The Russian Empire and Its Rivals* (New Haven: Yale Nota Bene, 2002), xiv.

47. For an attempt at a formal economic theory of empire, see Herschel I. Grossman and Juan Mendoza, "Annexation or Conquest? The Economics of Empire Building," NBER Working Paper no. 8109 (February 2001).

48. See Deepak Lal, *In Praise of Empires: Globalization and Order* (New York: Palgrave Macmillan, 2004).

49. On the significance of the frontier in imperial history, see Charles S. Maier, *Among Empires: American Ascendancy and Its Predecessors* (Cambridge: Harvard University Press, 2006).

50. See David Rieff, *At the Point of a Gun: Democratic Dreams and Armed Intervention* (New York: Simon and Schuster, 2005).

51. Paul Krugman, *The Great Unraveling: Losing Our Way in the New Century* (New York: W. W. Norton, 2003).

52. For recent diatribes see Michael Mann, *Incoherent Empire* (London: Verso, 2003); Chalmers Johnson, *The Sorrows of Empire: Militarism, Secrecy, and the End of the Republic* (New York: Metropolitan Books, 2004); and Ivan Eland, *The Empire Has No Clothes: U.S. Foreign Policy Exposed* (Oakland, Calif.: Independent Institute, 2004).

53. Geir Lundestad, *The American "Empire" and Other Studies of US Foreign Policy in a Comparative Perspective* (Oxford: Oxford University Press, 1990).

54. Niall Ferguson, *Colossus: The Rise and Fall of the American Empire* (New York: Penguin, 2004).

55. It is symptomatic that John Lewis Gaddis interprets the present predicament of the United States with reference to John Quincy Adams: John Lewis Gaddis, *Surprise, Security, and the American Experience* (Cambridge: Harvard University Press, 2004).

56. Calculated from figures in Lieutenant-General Sir Aylmer L. Haldane, *The Insurrection in Mesopotamia, 1920* (Edinburgh: W. Blackwood and Sons, 1922).

57. Current Budget Projections, March 3, 2006, http://www.cbo.gov/budget/budproj.pdf.

58. My own calculations based on data provided by the Federal Reserve Bank of St. Louis.

59. Niall Ferguson and Laurence J. Kotlikoff, "Benefits without Bankruptcy: The New New Deal," *New Republic,* August 15, 2005.

60. Jagadeesh Gokhale and Kent Smetters, "Fiscal and Generational Imbalances: An Update," in *Tax Policy and the Economy,* vol. 20, ed. James Poterba (Cambridge: MIT Press, 2006). See also Peter G. Peterson, *Running on Empty: How the Democratic and Republican Parties Are Bankrupting Our Future and What Americans Can Do about It* (New York: Farrar, Straus and Giroux, 2004). According to the April 2004 report of the Medicare trustees, the system's obligations to future retirees are underfunded by $62 trillion; see Joe Lieberman, "America Needs Honest Fiscal Accounting," *Financial Times,* May 25, 2004.

61. Treasury Bulletin, June 2004, http://www.fms.treas.gov/bulletin/.

62. Ray Dalio, "My Ruminations," *Bridgewater Daily Observations,* November 21, 2006.

63. *Economic Report of the President 2006,* http://www.whitehouse.gov/cea/erp06.pdf, Table B-80, p. 377.

64. Niall Ferguson, "A Dollar Crash? Euro Trashing," *New Republic,* June 21, 2004.

65. See Paul Krugman, "Questions of Interest," *New York Times,* April 20, 2004.

66. Roger Cohen, " 'Imperial America' Retreats from Iraq," *New York Times,* July 4, 2004.

67. Daniel Drezner, "Bestriding the World, Sort of," *Wall Street Journal,* June 17, 2004.

68. Michiko Kakutani, "Attention Deficit Disorder in a Most Peculiar Empire," *New York Times,* May 21, 2004.

69. See Niall Ferguson, *The War of the World: Twentieth-Century Conflict and the Descent of the West* (New York: Penguin, 2006).

70. Pew Global Attitudes Project, June 13, 2006, http://www.people-press.org/.

71. Pew Global Attitudes Project.

72. Francis Fukuyama, *America at the Crossroads: Democracy, Power, and the Neoconservative Legacy* (New Haven: Yale University Press, 2006).

73. By the end of August 2004, there had been around 300 allegations of mistreatment of detainees; 155 had so far been investigated, of which 66 had been substantiated. *Wall Street Journal,* August 26, 2004.

74. *Wall Street Journal,* August 26, 2004.

75. Bob Woodward, *Plan of Attack* (New York: Simon and Schuster, 2004), 249.

76. "The Best-laid Plans?" *Financial Times,* August 3, 2003.

77. Woodward, *Plan of Attack,* 150, 270.

78. See the remarks of UN secretary general Kofi Annan in an interview with the BBC in September 2004, http://news.bbc.co.uk/2/hi/middle_east/3661640.stm (accessed March 12, 2008).

79. See Toby Dodge, *Inventing Iraq: The Failure of Nation-Building and a History Denied* (New York: Columbia University Press, 2003).

80. Daniel Barnard, "The Great Iraqi Revolt: The 1919–20 Insurrections against the British in Mesopotamia," paper presented at the Harvard Graduate Student Conference in International History, April 23, 2004, http://www.fas.harvard.edu/~conih/ab stracts/Barnard_article.doc (accessed March 12, 2008).

PART TWO

Creeds and Parties

Defending Liberty: Liberal Democracy and the Limits of Public Power

William A. Galston

The defense of liberty is the distinctive aim of liberal democracy. By monopolizing force and respecting the rule of law, even autocracies can protect individuals' lives and security. In modern circumstances, however, only liberal democracies have given sustained and effective attention to the preservation of liberty. They do so in two different ways, reflecting the distinction between liberty's public and private dimensions.

From the liberal democratic perspective, *public* liberty is collective self-government, the antithesis of which is tyranny. Given the less admirable side of human nature, tyranny is the near-certain result of concentrating political power in a single individual or institution. To minimize the possibility of tyranny, liberal democracy disperses power among a variety of entities, defined functionally or geographically. Often but not always, written constitutions formalize the dispersion of power. This strategy gives rise to a number of familiar topics and challenges, among them the separation of powers, the relation among legislative, executive, and judicial functions, and federalism.

Private liberty consists in the ability of individuals to act in ways that are not determined by collective decisions. This is not to say that the public sphere is irrelevant to private liberty. On the contrary; without appropriately designed public institutions and suitably motivated public officials, individuals cannot be secure in the exercise of private liberty. Even though liberal democracy stands or falls with the distinction between the public and private spheres, students of liberal democracy tend not to consider deeply enough how the distinction between public and private is to be understood. This oddly neglected question is the subject of my essay.

Liberal Democracy and the Public/Private Distinction

There are three key dimensions of decisions that claim to be authoritative—structure, substance, and scope. *Structure* denotes the institutional and procedural arrangements through which decisions are made—by the one, the few, or the many, with equal or unequal participation, directly or through representatives, and so forth. It is, in my judgment, an open question whether decision-making structures must fall within a certain range for their decisions to be deemed acceptable, as many democratic theorists insist. *Substance* encompasses the outcomes of decision-making processes, assessed in a host of familiar terms—just or unjust, promoting the common good or special interests, consistent with the rule of law or constituting the arbitrary use of power, among others.

Scope (the principal focus of this essay) points to the range within which the authority-bearer is entitled to decide. At the heart of liberalism is the idea that political authority cannot rightly dominate the full range of human life. All rightful government is limited government. No matter how much we prize a particular structure of political decision-making, such as democracy, its exercise becomes illegitimate when it breaches this limit. As Leo Strauss puts it, "Liberalism stands and falls by the distinction between state and society or by the recognition of a private sphere, protected by the law but impervious to the law."[1] Liberal democracy, then, is *limited* democracy. Its antonym is not conservative democracy (whatever that might be), but rather *plenary* or *total* democracy.

Practical Challenges to Limited Democracy

In a volume devoted to dangers facing the United States, it may seem odd to identify liberal democracy itself as threatened. At first glance, the basic institutions and practices of liberal democracy would appear to be virtually unchallenged. But appearances are deceptive, or so I shall argue. Today, practical challenges to liberal democracy have emerged on four different fronts. None of these is novel; each has roots, and analogues, through American history.

The first challenge arises from the desire for *security;* more precisely, from the sense that security is threatened. In the wake of September 11, 2001, many Americans have become more willing to compromise liberties and invade privacies they would have defended in other circumstances. As

Alexander Hamilton, no foe of energetic government, remarked in *Federalist* 8, "Safety from external danger is the most powerful director of national conduct. Even the ardent love of liberty will, after a time, give way to its dictates. The violent destruction of life and property incident to war, the continual effort and alarm attendant on a state of continual danger, will compel nations the most attached to liberty to resort for repose and security to institutions which have a tendency to destroy their civil and political rights. To be more safe, they at length become willing to run the risk of being less free."

The second threat to limited government stems from an excessive desire for *prosperity*. In many circumstances, for example, an individual's property claims will stand opposed to policies that promise to increase the aggregate wealth of a community. One need not believe that the liberty to use one's property as one sees fit is absolute (it is not) to see that liberty is diminished if ownership may be set aside simply in the name of an aggregative calculus. But as of 2005, that understanding has been enshrined in our constitutional jurisprudence. In the case of *Kelo v. New London*,[2] the Supreme Court allowed the city of New London, Connecticut, to displace long-established homeowners to facilitate the development of property for use by office buildings, a new hotel, and research facilities of the Pfizer pharmaceutical corporation. It was not only a small but hardy band of libertarians who objected to this decision; many liberals were forced to face the fact that the activist economic principles they had long endorsed led step by step to a disregard for individual claims that they now saw as excessive. Indeed, given the key post–New Deal precedents on property rights, a strong case can be made that the Court had little choice but to reach a conclusion that a majority of Americans saw as a reductio ad absurdum.

The third threat to limited government comes from the drive toward *equality*. Let me offer an example. Since Plato's *Republic* the logic has been clear: the more one cares about meritocracy (in contemporary terms, equality of opportunity), the more one will see family autonomy as an obstacle. Not only do children differ in natural endowments; parents differ in the resources they can devote to developing their children's talents and in their inclination to do so. The resulting inequalities may become self-reinforcing and self-perpetuating. It is reasonable for governments to create institutions and opportunities that lean against these family-based inequalities. To "break the cycle of disadvantage," public authorities will be tempted to go farther—to restrict the liberty of parents in order to promote the "best interests of the child." Within limits, it is proper for them to do so. The difficulty is that in itself, the logic of equality does not acknowledge those limits. Liberty and equality are not opposed in every respect; indeed, the most ardent lovers of liberty will affirm the moral necessity of equal liberty. But these two great principles part company when the claims of either are pressed to the hilt. A government determined to eradicate inequality will inevitably expand its power and transgress against liberties rightly regarded as fundamental.

Finally, limited government is eroded by the desire for civic *unity*. As Madison argued in *Federalist* 10, liberty and social diversity are twinned. But especially in times of insecurity, social differences—of religion, language, educational and civil institutions—are experienced as threats. In the wake of the First World War, public authorities sought to repress German language instruction and to outlaw Catholic parochial schools. Today, reputable scholars talk darkly of the danger Spanish-speaking immigrants pose to the integrity of our polity and culture. And while the government's desire to interdict the flow of funds to Islamist extremists is understandable, there is a growing danger that legitimate charities will be caught in the antiterrorist dragnet.

Theoretical Objections to Limited Democracy

Liberal democracy is exposed, not only to practical challenges, but to theoretical objections as well. First, it may be argued that the consequences of limiting governmental authority and of immunizing a private sphere are unacceptable. In contending that liberal privacy has been used to shield intrafamilial injustice and violence from public scrutiny and redress, contemporary feminists are only the latest in a long line of objectors. Marx and his followers offered much the same critique of "private" property. As Strauss observes, "[G]iven this—the necessary existence of such a private sphere—the liberal society necessarily makes possible, permits, and fosters what is called by many people 'discrimination.'" Yet the remedy for these ills, he continues, would be worse than the disease: "The prohibition against every 'discrimination' would mean the abolition of the private sphere, the denial of the difference between the state and society, in a word, the destruction of liberal society; and therefore, it is not a sensible objective or policy. . . . There is nothing better than the uneasy solution offered by liberal society, which means legal equality plus private 'discrimination.'"[3]

The reference to discrimination reminds us that the line between public and private is not in all respects bright. Democracy in America did not cease to be liberal when the 1960s civil rights laws defined restaurants and hotels as "public" accommodations, nor when rental properties above a certain size were subjected to antidiscrimination norms. Something more basic would have been at stake if homeowners with a basement apartment to rent had been brought under this authority; tacitly respecting the intuitive distinction between public and private, fair housing laws did not go this far. Nor did liberalism totter when the law sought to prevent, or punish, physical abuse directed against one's children or spouse. Within certain limits, political authority may shift the location of the legal line between public and private without fundamentally transforming the character of the regime.

Why is there nothing better than the liberal solution? Strauss offers two answers, one negative, the other positive. Negatively: the experience of the twentieth century teaches us that the most likely outcome of abolishing the private sphere is not justice but rather tyranny that not only oppresses individuals but actually expands the sway of discrimination. Positively as a sphere of freedom, the private sphere protects the high as well as the low: "While we are not permitted to remain silent on the dangers to which democracy exposes itself as well as human excellence, we cannot forget the obvious fact that by giving freedom to all, democracy also gives freedom to those who care about human excellence. No one prevents us from cultivating our garden or from setting up outposts."[4]

The second objection to liberal democracy rests on an appeal to democracy itself. The argument is that the only legitimate political authority is democratic self-government and that the only limits on the scope of legitimate government are those that reflect the principles of democracy. There is accordingly no basis for invoking an independent conception of the private sphere, individual rights, or any other external limits, and no need to do so, because democratic norms suffice to secure everything that is morally attractive in liberal limits. (John Dewey, Robert Dahl, and Jürgen Habermas, among others, have offered theories along these lines.)

I have argued at length against this thesis elsewhere and will not repeat myself.[5] To mention but one of many counterarguments: it turns out to be impossible to justify (for example) all of the protections for individuals in the Bill of Rights (or even in the First Amendment) on the basis of democratic norms and procedures alone. The proponents of plenary democracy must therefore abandon either their adherence to many liberal rights, which they are loath to do, or their advocacy of total democracy.

The third objection to liberal governance invokes neither the negative consequences of limiting political authority nor the redemptive virtues of democracy, but rather the nature of politics itself. Carl Schmitt famously contends that "We have come to recognize that the political is the total, and as a result we know that any decision about whether something is *unpolitical* is always a *political* decision, irrespective of who decides and what reasons are advanced."[6] In the 1932 edition of *The Concept of the Political*, Schmitt insists that politics dominates all other considerations: "The ever-present possibility of a friend-and-enemy grouping suffices to forge a decisive entity which transcends the mere societal-associational groupings. . . . Only as long as the essence of the political is not comprehended or not taken into consideration is it possible to place a political association pluralistically on the same level with religious, cultural, economic, or other associations and permit it to compete with these."[7] And in the 1933 edition, he expands the text to make his opposition to liberal limitations on political authority clearer and more pointed than ever before: "The political unit is always, as long as it is present at all, the authoritative unit, total and sovereign. It is 'total' first because every matter can potentially be political and therefore can be affected by the political decision; and second because man is totally and existentially grasped in political participation."[8]

Schmitt's intervention forcefully raises the core issue: Is the state/society or public/private distinction a political artifact based on (shifting) considerations of convenience, public opinion, and prudence? Is it an evasion of reality that is bound to crumble under the pressure of truth-revealing extreme situations? Or does this distinction have a solid theoretical basis? If the latter, what is it, and what does it imply about the nature of limited politics and content of the private realm?

The Theoretical Basis of Limited Government: Five Possibilities

In this section, I lay out and briefly examine five significant kinds of theoretical arguments, which are not necessarily mutually exclusive, in favor of limited governmental authority.

Rights as Limits on Government

In the United States, especially, we must begin our canvass of alternative bases for limited government with individual rights, which define the legitimate aims of government ("To secure these rights . . .") and at least some of the limits on its "just powers."

The idea of rights raises a host of theoretical issues. Let me raise just two. First, we must ask whether it is possible to defend anything like our ordinary understanding of rights without relying on the premise that human beings are not by nature political. To put it the other way around: does the Aristotelian proposition compel the conclusion that all rights are provisional and must yield to obligations to the political community (and its duly constituted authority) whenever conflicts arisen between them?

For example: On what basis can a polity founded on, inter alia, a prepolitical right to life legitimately order its citizens to fight for the preservation of the community at the risk of their own lives? Strauss and Schmitt seem to agree that it cannot. Strauss maintains that "Hobbes . . . is the founder of liberalism. The right to the securing of life pure and simple—and this right sums up Hobbes's natural right—has fully the character of an inalienable human right, that is, of an individual's *claim* that takes precedence over the state and determines its purpose and its limits."[9] More broadly: "Hobbes . . . did not recognize any primary obligation of man that takes precedence over every claim *qua* justified claim because he understood man as by nature free, that is, without obligation; for Hobbes, therefore, the fundamental political fact was natural right as the justified *claim* of the individual, and Hobbes conceived of obligation as a *subsequent* restriction upon that claim."[10] Schmitt draws what seems to be the inescapable conclusion: "In case of need, the political entity must demand the sacrifice of life. Such a demand is in no way justifiable by the individualism of liberal thought. No consistent individualism can entrust to someone other than to the individual himself the right to dispose of the physical life of the individual."[11]

We might explore a way of meeting this difficulty via an argument that seeks to coordinate individual rights with an understanding of human beings as naturally political, an argument moreover that is consistent with Aristotle's observation that while "there is in everyone by nature an impulse toward this sort of [political] partnership, yet the one who first constituted [a city] is responsible for the greatest of goods."[12] Suppose, as seems plausible, that rights help define the aims of government and that rights cannot be secured and exercised without government. Suppose further that government cannot be "constituted" (or as the Declaration puts it, instituted) unless all individuals party to the act of constitution are willing to surrender a portion of their rights. It would then be a dictate of natural reason to consent to such a surrender, an act that helps define the "just powers" with which the government is endowed.

However this may be, there is a further difficulty: it is not obvious how to move from the abstract concept of individual rights to a concrete specification of the rights we have. Consider again the familiar words of the Declaration: "We hold these truths to be self evident, that all men are created equal, that they are endowed by their Creator with certain unalienable Rights, that *among these* are Life, Liberty, and the pursuit of Happiness . . ." I have italicized the words relevant for the current discussion: if life, liberty, and the pursuit of happiness are only some of the rights with which we are endowed, how do we know (or discover) what the others are? A similar difficulty arises in the Constitution. The Ninth Amendment tells us that "The enumeration in the Constitution, of certain rights, shall not be construed to deny or disparage others retained by the people." These words are more than a general guide to constitutional interpretation, and more than a different way of phrasing the Tenth Amendment; they point directly toward substantive rights-based limits on governmental power, but they do not tell us what those limits are.[13]

Notwithstanding these and other difficulties, there is a core of the concept of individual rights that makes intuitive sense. While individuals may be understood as part of a larger social whole, they are not only that; they have a separate, independent existence that entitles each one to a measure of respect, as a being with distinctive developmental needs when young and, on reaching adulthood, as capable of articulating a view of justice and the common good. "Rights" are a way of expressing the fact that there is an element of reciprocity, not just one-way obligations individual citizens owe government, in the moral constitution of political communities.

The Distinction between Harm to Self and Harm to Others

It is generally agreed that a wide range of harms that individuals inflict on others may be brought under legal restraints. (The extent of that range is a matter of continuing dispute; witness the controversy over the criminalization of "hate speech.") More controversial is the extent to which government should regulate the harms individuals impose on themselves. John Stuart Mill argues that at least in the cases of adults in full possession of their faculties and equipped with the requisite knowledge of their surroundings, the state should not deploy its power to prevent them from harming themselves, when their actions involve what he calls the "merely constructive injury which the person causes society by conduct which neither violates any specific duty to the public, nor occasions perceptible hurt to any assignable individual except himself."[14]

Mill's proposal raises a number of problems that have been discussed extensively in the nearly 150 years since he first made it. The "no man is an island" objection suggests that in practice, few actions will meet Mill's criterion of de minimis harms to others. The "why liberty?" objection points out that while Mill makes a strong case for liberty as a human good, he is far from proving that it is anything approaching the highest good, trumping others in cases of conflict. In justifying the harm principle by adverting to the "greater good of human freedom," then, he avails himself of a foundational premise to which he is not entitled.

In the end, moreover, Mill does not remain true to his own principle. If human freedom is that greatest good, it would seem to follow that the greatest harm a human being can inflict on himself is to deprive himself of liberty. Mill rules this out, and is prepared to use the full force of the law to prevent it, without even trying to show that voluntary self-enslavement harms other individuals or society as a whole: "The principle of freedom cannot require that he should be free not to be free. It is not freedom to be allowed to alienate his freedom."[15]

The question is why not. Mill goes on to draw the logical consequence of his stance—namely, that the law should not permit individuals to enter into irreversible contractual relations, including marriage without the possibility of divorce.[16] On the face of it, one could just as easily maintain the reverse, that the legal nonenforceability of marriage for life diminishes the liberty of individuals who sincerely want to enter into such as relation but are prevented from doing so.

Having said this, there remains (as in the case of rights) an intuitively appealing core of the position Mill advances. It is difficult to maintain that individuals are in any meaningful sense "responsible" for their conduct unless they are allowed to exercise their capacity for responsibility in actions they originate without compulsion. A zone of responsibility is all but certain to generate a mix of acts proper and improper, beneficial and harmful. It is hard to justify, in the name of responsibility, permitting individuals to perform acts harmful to others. But to some extent, it is possible to justify otherwise questionable acts the principal effects of which fall on the agent. A homely example: Parents should not allow their children to hit other children, just in order to learn about the retaliation and blame that will follow. But they may (and within limits should) allow their children to engage in risky activities such as climbing small trees, knowing that children may fall and scrape their skin. (Our judgment would be different if there was a significant chance that one child might fall on, and seriously injure, another standing below.)

The Nature of Religion as a Source of Limits on Government

There are well-known prudential arguments, drawn from the history of religious wars, in favor of religious toleration. Different from these are arguments resting on the nature of religion itself. In his *Letter Concerning Toleration,* John Locke offers a classic version of this thesis: "True and saving religion consists in the inward persuasion of the Mind, without which nothing is acceptable to God. And such is the nature of the understanding, that it cannot be compelled to the belief of any thing by outward force." Francis Hutcheson, who exerted an intellectual influence on the Founding generation second only to Locke, makes a parallel if broader claim: "Our rights are either *alienable* or *unalienable.* . . . Thus our right to our goods and labours is naturally alienable. But where the translation cannot be made with any effect . . . the right is unalienable. . . . Thus no man can really change his sentiments, judgments, and inward affections, at the pleasure of another. . . . The right of private judgment is therefore unalienable."[17]

These arguments are true in certain respects. Belief is subject neither to the will nor (at least in the short run) to external compulsion, which is why forced conversions can only represent external and expedient compliance. But in other respects, they are not true.

In the first place, the claims of Locke and Hutcheson rest on a classic Protestant account of religion as inner faith, private judgment, and individual conscience. They are of limited application for religions, such as Judaism and Islam, that express themselves at least as much in ritual and law as in creedal terms. (As a sociological matter, non-Protestant religions in the United States typically tend over time to get restructured along Protestant lines, which may explain why Lockean toleration has worked better here than in other nations where faith is pervasive.)

Second, as Jonas Proast observed soon after the publication of Locke's *Letter,* in the long run coercion can create circumstances in which individuals (particularly the young) are more likely to acquire certain beliefs over time and are less likely to be disturbed in the possession of these beliefs, once acquired. As an astute contemporary scholar has observed, "Despite the enormous amount of ink that he devoted to his response [to Proast], Locke failed to provide any adequate answer to this point."[18]

For these reasons, among others, I am less inclined than I once was to accept on its face Locke's official argument for religious toleration. This does not mean that there aren't others that may work better. In that vein, toward the end of this essay, I shall return to the arguments of James Madison and Thomas Jefferson.

The Search for Truth as a Limit on Government

The nature of the search for truth imposes limits on the authority of political institutions (including democratic institutions) over scientific inquiry. It seems perfectly appropriate for democratic institutions to determine the distribution of resources devoted to various domains of inquiry. It is legitimate, moreover, for them to make those judgments based, in part, on their assessment of the kinds of inquiry that are most likely to benefit the citizenry or to sustain democratic institutions. Democracies can impose restraints on allowable research methods (on indubitably human subjects, for example, or on gray-area entities such as human embryos), even though these restraints may make it more difficult for research to succeed. In certain circumstances, it may be appropriate for democracies to restrict international scientific collaboration (for example, for reasons of national security) or to prohibit the publication and public discussion of specific research results.

Distinct from all these actions is government intervention to determine the *outcome* of inquiry. The quest for truth is an autonomous activity shaped by its own rules. One of the sorriest episodes in the sordid history of the Soviet Union was the use of state power to impose the pseudo-Lamarckian views of the quack agronomist Trofim Lysenko on the whole of Soviet biology. Plant scientists of unimpeachable international standing were forced to repudiate Mendelian genetics and to conduct their research based on a theory driven by ideology—the environmental rather than genetic determination of species change.

This affair is frequently presented as the epitome of totalitarianism, which in a way it was. But the real point is broader: Lysenko's biology would have been no better, and no more legitimate, if it had been imposed by a democratic vote after full public deliberation. The political sphere has no rightful authority over the processes internal to the various disciplines that guide their quest for truth.

I have used modern science as an example of truth-seeking activities, but of course there are others. While governments can run huge budget deficits and intentionally obscure the cost of their programs, they have no authority over the laws of arithmetic. And while governments often claim the authority to restrict the public expression of philosophic questioning, they have no authority over its content: if philosophical dialogue establishes that propositions A and B contradict one another, no government can intervene to alter that fact. Truth and the quest for it possess their own distinctive authority, separate from that of politics.

In this context, forms of contemporary relativism inspired by Nietzsche can be seen as threats to liberty. If knowledge claims are nothing more than covert assertions of power, then truth can no longer limit political authority. Indeed, politics enjoys a certain superiority, because it is the frank, open, courageous expression of the drive for domination that is the unspoken and dishonestly denied motive of those who claim "objectivity." One sees the practical effects of this outlook in the growing tendency to regard all journalists as the biased instruments of political partisans. The idea that some journalists are moved by a passion to find and expose the truth, and that all of us should be open to their findings even when inconvenient for our "side," is increasingly regarded as naive and quaint. Reducing truth to a malleable instrument of power removes an essential obstacle against tyranny.

Multiple Authorities as Limits on Political Authority

The previous remarks about the independent authority of truth suggest a more general observation: the experience of everyday life points us toward multiple, potentially conflicting, sources of authority—that is, multiple kinds of obligations and binding claims—of which politics is only one. I call this understanding of multiple authorities within a shared social space *political pluralism.*

It is of course possible that we should understand political authority as dominant in cases of conflict between authorities. But as we've seen, examples drawn from the life of the mind point toward the opposite conclusion. And other examples do as well.

Consider the family. Those who believe in the plenary authority of politics will urge the subordination of family relations to political considerations. In Susan Schechter's vision of a society restructured along radical feminist lines, "Family life would be open for community scrutiny because the family would be part of and accountable to the community. Community-based institutions could hear complaints and dispense justice, and community networks could hold individuals accountable for their behavior."[19]

John Rawls exemplifies the tension between, on the one hand, the liberal distinction between public and private matters, and on the other, the desire not to be seen as enabling inegalitarian and antidemocratic family relations. "It is clear," he declares, "that liberal principles of political justice do not require ecclesiastical governance to be democratic. Bishops and cardinals need not be elected; nor need the benefits attached to a church's hierarchy of offices satisfy a specific distributive principle, certainly not the difference principle. . . . [T]he principles of political justice do not apply to the internal life of a church, nor is it desirable, or consistent with liberty of conscience or freedom of association, that they should."[20] He treats the family differently, however: "Mill held that the family in his day was a school for male despotism: it inculcated habits of thought and ways of feeling and conduct incompatible with democracy. If so, the principles of justice enjoining a reasonable constitutional democratic society can plainly be invoked to reform the family."[21] This is puzzling, because many hierarchical religious associations have inculcated habits, feelings, and thoughts that are at least as inharmonious with democracy as anything the family can produce. Why not employ the law to "reform" them as well?

The realm to which Rawls's enforceable principles of political justice apply directly is what he calls the "basic structure of society." These principles constrain and indirectly shape the institutions and associations outside the basic structure but do not authorize legal intervention within them. The equivocal position he assigns to the family becomes manifest when in the course of a single page, he both affirms and denies that the family is part of the basic structure.[22] Clearly, the family is not immunized from the restraints that apply to all citizens: physical assault within the family is no less legally actionable than is the same conduct on the street among strangers. But that is a far cry from the sort of gender-based differential or hierarchy within the family to which the would-be reformers object.

The problem is only intensified when we focus on conflicting loyalties and obligations. Arlene Saxonhouse puts it well: "What emerges from a consideration of ancient Greek thought on public and private is a sense of the tragic interdependence of the realm of the city and the family. It is a tragic relationship because each realm demands full, and not partial, devotion: one cannot die for the city and yet live for the family. Each realm cannot get that complete devotion it demands without leading to the destruction of the other."[23] These tensions are hardly confined to a vanished past; they play out before our eyes on television every day, as parents with sons and daughters deployed overseas wrestle with competing civic and private affections.

We may conjecture that if the highest kind of friendship is between those who resemble one another in virtue and goodness, and if the friend is truly another self, then bonds between friends also entail genuine and weighty obligations that can conflict with those arising from political authority, as well as from the biological family. The biblical relationship between David and Jonathan vividly illustrates these possibilities.

I now return, as promised, to the question of religion, understood as a source of obligation that may stand opposed to political authority. To underscore the importance of this possibility, I quote Madison and Jefferson's "Memorial and Remonstrance" at some length:

> It is the duty of every man to render to the Creator such homage and such only as he believes to be acceptable to him. This duty is precedent, both in order of time and degree of obligation, to the claims of Civil Society. Before any man can be considered as a member of Civil Society, he must be considered as a subject of the Governour of the Universe: And if a member of Civil Society, who enters into any subordinate Association, must always do it with a reservation of his duty to the General Authority; much more must every man who becomes a member of any particular Civil Society, do it with a saving of his allegiance to the Universal Sovereign. We maintain therefore that in matters of Religion, no mans right is abridged by the institution of Civil Society and that Religion is wholly exempt from its cognizance.

Here the argument is not, as in Locke's *Letter*, the irrational futility of coercion in religious matters. Rather, religion represents a form of authority that precedes political arrangements, generates binding obligations, and limits the rightful authority of the state. Duty to God is one thing, duty to the state another. Madison and Jefferson did not claim that all religious practices are exempt from political control; they accepted the existence of the realm of what Locke called civil concernments within which political authority trumps competing obligations. Animal sacrifice was one thing, human sacrifice quite another. Still, they contemplated a division of authority between politics and religion, and a substantial sphere within which religious obligations limited the rightful reach of political authority.

This line of argument is bound to leave many readers unsatisfied. No, religious communities may not engage in human sacrifice, and if they try, political authorities have the right and duty to stop them. Yes, religious communities may assign positions of religious authority on grounds that would not be permitted in the public domain, and it would be wrong for political authorities to prevent them. But isn't there a broad middle ground of issues between these extremes, which a pluralist understanding of society doesn't help us resolve?

This is a fair objection, as far as it goes, but it doesn't go as far as those who urge it think it does. It reflects, I would suggest, more of a disagreement about the possibilities of theory than a critique of pluralism in particular. In my view, theory mostly provides a template of considerations that the sound exercise of practical reason must take into account. It will yield very few bright lines that neatly resolve entire categories of controversies. Rather, it structures the productive conduct of the form of practical reasoning known as casuistry. It yields results that look much more like common law than the clear rules of law that many students of jurisprudence crave. Broader patterns are inductive and emergent, not laid down in advance.

This is not to say that a pluralist perspective precludes some important conclusions about the role of political authority vis-à-vis other authority claims. In the first place, the social space within which differing visions of the good are pursued must be organized and sustained through the exercise of public power; to solve inevitable problems of coordination among divergent individuals and groups, the rules constituting this space will inevitably limit in some respects their ability to act as they see fit. Second, there are some core evils of the human condition that states have the right (indeed the duty) to prevent; to do this, they may rightly restrict the actions of individuals and groups. Third, the state cannot sustain a free social space if its very existence is jeopardized by internal or external threats, and within broad limits it may do what is necessary to defend itself against destruction, even if self-defense restricts valuable liberties of individuals and groups. A free society is not a suicide pact.

Conclusion

This preliminary mapping of the terrain points toward the following conclusion: while there is some important truth in each of the theoretical sources of limited government that I have canvassed, the existence of multiple and competing authorities making claims on our allegiance represents the deepest basis on which liberal governance in some form may be defended. It cannot be denied that the fact of such authorities generates large, unending difficulties. Life would be simpler in the political community of civic republican dreams, where religion is wholly "civil," where citizens fly to the assemblies, where parents care only whether their slain warrior sons fight bravely and whether their city prevails over its foes. But this is not the world in which we live. An honest examination of our experiences suggests that our obligations are plural and heterogeneous, that they often conflict, and that our civic obligations should not always prevail over the rest.

Recall Carl Schmitt's assertion that politics is total because human beings are fully grasped in their capacity as political agents, particularly in moments of crisis and existential danger. The burden of my argument is that Schmitt is wrong, that many important elements of human life evade the grasp of politics, at least in part. To say this is not to trivialize politics. Taking politics seriously, as we must, does not mean granting the domain of politics total authority over our lives. This proposition points toward the deepest basis on which liberal governance may be defended.

My thesis is exposed to a practical objection: in the contemporary United States, one may well argue, the denigration of politics and the retreat toward private life are far more pervasive and troubling than is the opposing threat of totalizing politics. What is most needful in our current circumstances, then, is a robust vindication of the public realm over against the pull toward privacy.

On one level, it is hard not to agree with this objection. American citizens today are less inclined to inform themselves about and participate in public life than they were even three or four decades ago. The increasing polarization of partisan conflict and political discourse has left the broad center of the electorate feeling unrepresented and disaffected, and Americans are less likely to respect the competence or trust the motives of elected officials than they once were.[24] If government cannot manage to carry out even basic functions, such as responding to natural catastrophes, many reason, what basis is there to believe that it can improve our society? Surely it is more prudent to rely on the family for care, on civil society for mutual assistance, on religion for community and social reform. Not surprisingly, many American do just that.

And yet, there is a perennial temptation, not always avoided, to lurch to the other extreme. Many have come to believe that for every private harm there must be a public response and that the inevitable vicissitudes of daily life somehow imply a public responsibility to remedy them. Many resort to courts and legislatures to address problems within the authority of families and faith communities. And when our safety is in jeopardy, many are all too willing to expand public power at the expense of private liberty—often the liberty of those seen as "others" (recall the shameful incarceration of Japanese-Americans during World War II), but sometimes our own liberty as well.

By embracing private as well as public liberty, liberal democracy rejects in principle the claim that we may pursue public aims, however worthy, by "all means necessary." Not even the great ends of justice and security straightforwardly legitimize everything that may be done in their name. As an end in itself, private liberty limits public authority.

That these limits generate not just temptations, but genuine difficulties, cannot be denied. Circumstances may arise in which it is impossible to honor fully the claims of private liberty, either because one private liberty proves incompatible with another or because the defense of the system of liberty as a whole requires the abrogation of particular liberties. These facts remind us of what should be an obvious truth, that no political system or theory can be fully adequate to the complexity of our existence. And they point as well toward a deeper truth: in the end, the protection of liberty depends on good fortune that no constitution can ensure—namely, the presence of leaders at crucial moments who are motivated by concern for the preservation of liberal democracy rather than the *libido dominandi*.

NOTES

1. Leo Strauss, *Liberalism Ancient and Modern* (New York: Basic Books, 1968), 230.

2. *Kelo v. New London*, 125 S. Ct. 2655 (2005).

3. Strauss, "Why We Remain Jews," in *Jewish Philosophy and the Crisis of Modernity*, ed. Kenneth Hart Green (Albany: SUNY Press, 1997), 314–17. While one might question relying on the transcript of a public lecture delivered from notes rather than a text, the quoted thoughts track, while fleshing out, arguments made in carefully written articles, including Strauss's remarkable 1965 preface to his *Spinoza's Critique of Religion*, first published four decades earlier.

4. Strauss, *Liberalism Ancient and Modern*, 24.

5. See *The Practice of Liberal Pluralism* (New York: Cambridge University Press, 2004).

6. Carl Schmitt, *Political Theology: Four Chapters on the Concept of Sovereignty*, trans. George Schwab (Cambridge: MIT Press, 1985), 2.

7. Schmitt, *The Concept of the Political*, trans. George Schwab (Chicago: University of Chicago Press, 1996), 45.

8. Quoted and discussed in Heinrich Meier, *Carl Schmitt and Leo Strauss*, trans. J. Harvey Lomax (Chicago: University of Chicago Press, 1995), 16.

9. Strauss, "Notes on Carl Schmitt, *The Concept of the Political*," in Schmitt, *Concept of the Political*, 91.

10. Strauss, "Notes on Carl Schmitt," 99.

11. Schmitt, *Concept of the Political*, 71.

12. Aristotle, *The Politics*, trans. Carnes Lord (Chicago: University of Chicago Press, 1984), 37 (book 1, chap. 2).

13. See especially Randy E. Barnett, ed., *The Rights Retained by the People: The History and Meaning of the Ninth Amendment* (Fairfax, Va.: George Mason University Press, 1989). Barnett suggests (pp. 34–44) that some combination of history, theory, and what he calls a "general . . . presumption in favor of individual liberty" offers the best way of filling in the broad outlines of the Ninth Amendment; others disagree.

14. John Stuart Mill, *On Liberty*, ed. Currin V. Shields (Indianapolis: Bobbs-Merrill, 1956), 100.

15. Mill, *On Liberty*, 125.

16. Mill, *On Liberty*, 126–27.

17. Quoted in Daniela Gobetti, "Humankind as a System: Public and Private Agency at the Origins of Modern Liberalism," in *Public and Private in Thought and Practice: Perspectives on a Grand Dichotomy*, ed. Jeff Weintraub and Krishnan Kumar (Chicago: University of Chicago Press, 1997), 129.

18. Jeremy Waldron, "Locke: Toleration and the Rationality of Persecution," in *Justifying Toleration: Conceptual and Historical Perspectives*, ed. Susan Mendus (Cambridge: Cambridge University Press, 1988), 84.

19. Quoted and discussed in Jean Bethke Elshtain, "The Displacement of Politics," in Weintraub and Kumar, *Public and Private*, 174.

20. John Rawls, "Public Reason Revisited," *University of Chicago Law Review* 64 (Summer 1997): 789.

21. Rawls, "Public Reason Revisited," 790–91.

22. See Rawls, *Justice as Fairness: A Restatement* (Cambridge: Belknap Press of Harvard University Press, 2001), 10.

23. Arlene Saxonhouse, "Classical Greek Conceptions of Public and Private," in *Public and Private in Social Life*, ed. S. I. Benn and G. F. Gaus (London: Croom Helm, 1983), 366.

24. For much more on these trends and their consequences, see William A. Galston and Elaine C. Kamarck, "The Politics of Polarization," Third Way, Washington, D.C., October 2005.

A Clear and Present Danger:
The Doctrine of Political Nonfoundationalism

James W. Ceaser

The greatest threat to America today comes from a theoretical doctrine that has been offered in all sincerity as the friend, even the savior, of liberal democracy. For want of a universally accepted name, this doctrine will be designated here by the label of *political nonfoundationalism*. Political non-foundationalism holds that liberal democracy is best maintained by re-nouncing public reliance on a first principle (or "foundation") that claims to embody an objective truth—something, for example, along the lines of the "laws of nature" that are invoked in the Declaration of Independence. Political life should either be neutral toward such principles or exclude them altogether. The implementation of nonfoundationalism would take place not by imposing new constitutional or legal rules, except perhaps in the case of religion, but by encouraging a new way of thinking. This new way of thinking, called "reasonableness" by one philosopher and "irony" by another, is already said to be trickling down from the intelligentsia to the people.[1] A public shaped by the doctrine of nonfoundationalism would re-gard the introduction of first principles into politics as retrograde (because all foundations are fictions), or divisive (because not all persons share the same first principles), or undemocratic (because a truth is held to be self-subsisting and thus beyond our own making).

The new doctrine draws its support from some of the most celebrated thinkers of our era, among them Richard Rorty, Jacques Derrida, John Rawls, Jürgen Habermas, and Gianni Vattimo. Each of these philosophers has his own school of thought, known respectively as "anti-essentialism" (or "neopragmatism"), "political deconstructionism," "the doctrine of pub-lic reason," "deliberative democracy," and "weak thinking" *(il pensiero de-bole)*. By no means are these positions all in perfect agreement. Some of these philosophers defend a thoroughgoing theoretical skepticism, while others insist that certain positions can be objectively established.[2] Yet regardless of their differences on these theoretical issues, nonfoundationalists join together in seeking to erect a high wall of separation between foundations and politics.

To put a clearer face on this doctrine, political nonfoundationalism in America would mean an end to public discourse about the "transcendent law of nature and nature's god" that has been invoked since the Founding.[3] "Metaphysical ideas" or "comprehensive doctrines" of this sort should have no place in the public discourse of an advanced liberal democracy. They are in a word, and the word is Richard Rorty's, "useless."[4] "A liberal society," he writes, "is badly served by an attempt to supply it with philosophical foundations. For the attempt to supply such foundations presupposes a natural order of topics which is prior to, and overrides the results of, encounters between old and new vocabularies."[5] A nation without foundations can move more easily from one language game to the next, free of the vexing constraints imposed by claims of truth. A nonfoundationalist public philosophy, Rorty continues, is a boon to liberal democracy; it "chimes . . . with the spirit of tolerance that has made constitutional democracy possible."[6] John Rawls, following his famous turn in the 1980s, argued much the same thing: "A constitutional regime does not require an agreement on a comprehensive doctrine: the basis of social unity lies elsewhere."[7]

The doctrine of nonfoundationalism would likewise exclude public acknowledgment of a religious basis of America's political system and civilization. Shortly before his death, Jacques Derrida contrasted contemporary "European" public philosophy, characterized by its exclusion of religion from sanctioned public discourse, with the backward views found in America, where "despite the separation in principle between church and state, [there is] a fundamental biblical (and primarily Christian) reference in its official public discourse and the discourse of its political leaders."[8] Derrida lamented the fact that American currency still displays the motto "In God We Trust" and that presidents regularly invoke the Almighty in their public speeches. Just as Rorty has urged the abandonment of metaphysical foundations, Derrida called on American political elites to dispense with these anachronistic references to religion and to follow the lead of advanced European nations in embracing a nonfoundationalist secularism.

No observer can fail to remark upon the highly political use of the doctrine of nonfoundationalism in recent times. Almost alone among the

Western liberal democracies, America exhibits strong foundationalist elements in its political discourse. For this stance, it has been roundly criticized by nonfoundationalists, especially in those instances when presidents have turned to foundational concepts in explaining and justifying American positions in foreign policy. Jürgen Habermas, probably Europe's most important contemporary philosopher, has argued that the kind of "universalism" invoked by Americans is of no help in spreading liberal democracy. The alternative, embodied in contemporary European nonfoundationalist philosophy, is predicated "on an equality that demands . . . one step outside of one's own viewpoint in order to put it into relationship with the viewpoints adopted by another, which are to be regarded as equal."[9] Pierre Rosanvallon, one of France's most prominent social scientists, has taken Habermas's thinking a step further, distinguishing between America's "dogmatic [or foundational] universalism," which is "characterized by an intolerable arrogance that is only made more so by its spontaneous naïveté," and Europe's "pragmatic" or "experimental universalism," which makes no foundational claims.[10] Nonfoundationalism, by his account, not only better supports liberal democracy in advanced nations, but it is also superior in promoting liberal democracy in developing nations. In this widely shared line of argument, nonfoundationalism is considered to be the basis of a new political science that can guide practical politics and be the saving doctrine of liberal democracy. No wonder, then, that most nonfoundationalists regard the debate about "foundationalism" as the central question of political theory of our day.

The widespread advocacy of political nonfoundationalism in America, where it still is a minority position, represents a dramatic departure from past ways of thinking. The change can be appreciated by juxtaposing two statements. The first comes from a speech by Abraham Lincoln delivered in New Haven in 1860, in which he reflected on how a democratic system must operate: "Whenever this question [i.e., the question of slavery] shall be settled, it must be settled on some philosophical basis. No polity that does not rest upon some philosophical public opinion can be permanently maintained."[11] Contrast this position with the nonfoundationalist statement of Richard Rorty: "The idea that liberal societies are bound together by philosophical beliefs seems to me to be ludicrous"; "philosophy is not that important for politics."[12] Of course, if philosophy were as inconsequential as Rorty asserts, he would have had no reason to waste so much of his philosophical career inveighing against it. His claim is a deliberate rhetorical provocation meant to support his central point: A polity that rests upon a philosophical foundation cannot long endure.

The doctrine of political nonfoundationalism in its full-blown form is a product of the recent past. This assertion may sound strange in light of the fact that so many nonfoundationalists are skeptics, a type of thinker as old as philosophy itself. But, to paraphrase Edmund Burke, boldness formerly was not the character of skeptical thinkers. Whatever their private doubts about truth, skeptics in the past ordinarily insisted that a political community needed a firm foundation. If no truths existed, it was necessary to act as if they did. Contemporary political nonfoundationalists, by contrast, hold that advanced societies could easily do away with any kind of foundation and would be much better off if they did so. Political nonfoundationalism is accordingly not the same thing as skepticism, although it has proven highly attractive to contemporary skeptics by allowing them to say in public what their predecessors once only dared to utter in private.

It might seem like an overly academic approach to characterize a theoretical view as the greatest danger to America when more tangible threats, like the menace of terrorism, are looming around us. But if Auguste Comte was correct when he observed that "ideas govern the world, or throw it into chaos," then it is proper to begin with intellectual doctrines.[13] The effect of ideas, though often less visible than those resulting from a practical disaster, can be more enduring. This is the case even in this instance, when the stated aim of nonfoundationalists is not a revolutionary change in the formal character of liberal democracy, but the seemingly conservative objective of maintaining and improving it. But this moderate posture hides a more radical project. The American polity today is not entirely defined by its formal political model (liberal democracy), but is also made up of its animating spirit, which includes devotion to a version of natural right and to biblical faith. An American populace that adopted the doctrine of political nonfoundationalism would therefore be a very different kind of people than the one that exists today. Under the benign cover of saving liberal democracy, this change is exactly what most nonfoundationalists are seeking.

The Character of Foundational Concepts in America

To understand what is at stake in the current theoretical debate, nonfoundationalism must be compared with what it aims to replace. Nonfoundationalists have deliberately obscured this understanding by defining terms to favor their position. As they frame this issue, their doctrine is a substitute for a parallel doctrine they call "foundationalism." But "foundationalism," to the extent any such notion previously existed, was never considered a doctrine; it referred only to a commonplace observation, of the sort made by Lincoln, that every polity needs a fixed first principle. What mattered was *which* foundation was adopted. Foundations could be as different (to keep with the situation Lincoln confronted) as the claim of the vice president of the Confederacy, Alexander Stephens, that "the negro is not the equal of the white man [and] that slavery—subordination to the superior race—is his natural and normal condition," and Lincoln's proposition that "no man is good enough to govern another man without the other's consent."[14] Viewed in this light, the important choice that confronts America today is not between nonfoundationalism and this recently coined abstraction of "foundationalism," but rather between nonfoundationalism and some particular foundation (or combination of foundations).

Beginning from this last perspective, the proper mode of theoretical inquiry is to commence by considering the concept of a foundation and by examining its different types. A foundation is a first principle that explains or justifies a general political orientation; it is offered as an authoritative standard, initially perhaps for a movement or party, but ultimately for the nation as a whole. In John Stuart Mill's words, it is "a recognised principle . . . which no one could either fear or hope to see shaken."[15] A political foundation is not in the first instance an academic tool of analysis invented by scholars to study politics from the outside, but something that arises within political life itself. Foundations have tended to be most apparent to political actors in America at critical moments. The concept—even the term itself—was present in America at the outset, when it arose in a seminal debate of the Continental Congress in 1774 on the justification for the colonial policy toward Britain. As recorded by John Adams, the great question confronting Congress was the "*foundation* of right" that should be adopted: "We very deliberately considered and debated . . . whether we should recur to the law of nature" along with the historical foundations of the tradition, such as the "common law" and "the charters" or "the rights of British subjects."[16] Participants considered not only which foundational concept was truest in theoretical terms, but also which one might best meet the political end of effectively mobilizing people and binding them together. Political foundations thus have a peculiar property when compared to their analogous concepts in philosophy; while they are generally proclaimed as "pure" theoretical propositions, political actors also judge them by their capacity to fulfill certain political requirements.

An example is worth a thousand arguments, so a listing of a few statements may help to illustrate better what a foundation is:

> Progress! Did you ever reflect that that word is almost a new one? No word comes more often or more naturally to the lips of modern man, as if the things it stands for were almost synonymous with life itself. . . . We think of the future, not the past, as the more glorious time in comparison with which the present is nothing. Progress, development—those are modern words. The modern idea is to leave the past and press onward to something new. (Woodrow Wilson, 1912)[17]

> We had no occasion to search into musty records, to hunt up royal parchments, or to investigate the laws and institutions of a semi-barbarous ancestry. We appealed to those of nature, and found them engraved in our hearts. (Thomas Jefferson, 1824)[18]

> It concerneth New England always to remember that they are originally a plantation religious, not a plantation of trade. The profession of the purity of doctrine, worship and discipline is written upon her forehead. . . . [W]orldly gain was not the end and design of the people of New England but religion. (John Higginson, 1663)[19]

These examples of foundations can be grouped into three general types according to whether the claim they raise is based on History, nature, or faith. Each of these terms needs to be further specified, with illustrations provided of some of the variants that have appeared in American politics.

A foundation in History offers ultimate justification by reference to what takes place in the flow of time. Something is said to be right or good either because it conforms to the past and our tradition, which is deemed almost sacred or unassailable, or because it accords with the direction in which the temporal process as a whole is said to be going, which can be downward (decline) or, as has more usually been the case, upward (progress). The first view, which emphasizes the particular traditions of different communities, is often called "Customary History"; the second, which stresses general and universal laws of historical movement, is known as "Philosophy of History." The use of History in this grandiose sense to supply a standard of right should be distinguished from "ordinary" history (with a small *h*) of the sort we usually encounter when we think of history—what Winston Churchill once defined, in one of his more cheerful moods, as "mainly the record of the crimes, follies and miseries of mankind."[20] History in this sense recounts and analyzes the past, but it makes no pretense to supplying the grounds for making ultimate judgments.

In America, a form of Customary History played the central role in the early stages leading up to the break with Britain, until it was largely replaced on the eve of the Revolution by a foundation of nature. The use of History derived the idea of right from the ancient sources of the tradition—from the great British charters such as the Magna Carta, or, still further back, from the gothic constitution originating from the "native wilds and woods in the north of Europe."[21] History was reintroduced as a major foundation in the 1830s. It appeared in two forms. Customary History was embraced by the Whig Party, while Philosophy of History was adopted by many Democrats. The Whigs, especially those in New England, sought to build an American tradition that relied heavily on the Puritan Fathers, whose merits were extolled in an attempt to create a doctrine of "two foundings," one at Plymouth and the other in Philadelphia. This appeal to Customary History was influenced by the conservative reaction in Europe to the French Revolution, where thinkers beginning with Edmund Burke worried about the consequences of appeals to nature. Unlike these European conservatives, American Whigs did not seek to replace natural right, which after all was central to America's tradition, but instead to add History to nature. This synthesis aimed to curb what they thought were the excesses of Jacksonian democracy and to promote older virtues that they feared were ignored under strands of "Lockean" thinking.

The Democrats turned to Philosophy of History to supplement the standard of nature. They connected universal progress to American democracy and to its expansion (Manifest Destiny). One of the best expressions of this view is found in the writings of the historian George Bancroft, who was also a prominent Democratic advisor and speechwriter. A student of Hegel who sought to democratize the Hegelian system, Bancroft famously wrote: "the voice of the people is the voice of pure Reason." He continued: "Everything is in motion for the better. The last system of philosophy is always the best. . . . The last political state of the world likewise is ever more excellent than the old."[22] Each political party maintained an uneasy mix of the two foundations of History and nature until the 1850s, when History acquired the upper hand in both parties. What remained of the Whig Party appealed to tradition, while northern Democrats, following Stephen Douglas, grounded the party in their idea of progress. A defense of natural right was then taken up by a new party, the Republicans, and given classic voice by its leader Abraham Lincoln.

There is no mystery about the basic foundational principle that dominated the Progressive Era. Progressivism, as its etymological root ("progress") indicates, subscribed to Philosophy of History. Progressives understood progress to be not merely a hope or sustaining faith, but an objective fact discernible through the study of history. They drew eclectically on different statements of this idea, taking pieces from German idealistic philosophy (mostly that of Hegel), from adaptations of Charles Darwin's evolutionary theory, and, most importantly, from the positivist approach of Comte and Condorcet. It was Condorcet, the good friend of Jefferson, who provided the classic definition of Philosophy of History as "a science that can foresee the progress of humankind, direct it, and accelerate it."[23] According to this understanding, which was widely shared among the Progressives, although the direction of History was fixed, those conscious of its laws needed to help it along and superintend its movement. This task now fell to the pragmatic philosophers and the policy scientists. A new era of governance that relied on the benign guidance of these experts, operating beyond all partisanship, was in the offing.

A foundation in nature provides justification by reference to something in the structure of reality as it can be accessed by reason. Nature designates a rational, meaning a scientific or philosophical, approach that humans can grasp without the direct need of Divine revelation. Different understandings of science as applied to politics may therefore produce alternative conceptions of nature. Think, for example, of the contrast between accounts that come from current theories of sociobiology, with its laws of movement and adaptation based on the machinations of the little selfish gene, and the account of the "laws of nature" invoked above by the Founders, which supplied a permanent standard of right.

The American republic was the first to bring the concept of nature down from the realm of theory and introduce it into the political world as the functioning foundation of a large nation. The turn from History to nature marked a revolution in the intellectual world comparable in importance to the political revolution that commenced at Lexington and Concord. Not myth, mystery, or History, but philosophy or science—the two terms were then synonyms—could serve, perhaps in a simplified version, as a public foundational concept. There could be "public philosophy." The "laws of nature" were taken by the Founders to be derivations from rational inquiry. For some of them, this investigation relied on forms of Christian rationalism ("natural law"), while for others it derived from a new science that combined inquiry into human nature ("psychology") with rational political analysis. The science that was derived from this combination became the basis for articulating the idea of natural rights or the rights of man.

Because the Founders' general version of natural right was solemnly promulgated in official public documents, it earned a "privileged" position in America and was often identified as *the* view of nature. Those holding contrary views of nature therefore had to consider whether to present their position as an alternative account of nature, or to attack the standard of nature outright. Both strategies have been followed. An early challenge to the Founders' view of nature drew on the science of ethnology (or "natural history") in support of a position of racial hierarchy. Proponents of this science promoted their position as the truly natural one, that is, based on science, while dismissing the Founders' view as nonempirical. Following the Civil War, the favored science became evolutionary biology ("Darwinism"). Darwinists likewise offered a version of a natural standard of right (or of necessity) that differed from that of the Founders. It stressed the notion of struggle derived from observation of the lower species. In the words of the sociologist William Graham Sumner, "The social order is fixed by laws of nature precisely analogous to those of the physical order . . . the law of the survival of the fittest was not made by man and cannot be abrogated by man."[24]

Progressive theorists launched the most sustained attack on the foundation of natural right and in some cases embraced the tactic of denying the very idea of a natural standard. According to John Dewey, natural right was a concept "located in the clouds . . . whose falsity may easily be demonstrated both philosophically and historically."[25] Criticism of the idea of permanency in nature, especially in human nature, was needed to sustain the most robust notion of progress, for the idea of an unchangeable human nature set limits to the possibilities of development. Dewey took the further step, so important for future philosophical development, of claiming that *any* philosophical proposition that implies a theoretical hierarchy or an idea of right is supportive of authoritarian political rule. A view that is "committed to a notion that inherently some realities are superior to others, are better than others . . . inevitably works on behalf of a regime of authority, for it is only right that the superior should lord it over the inferior."[26] True democracy is foundationless. Implicit in this contention is a "metaphysical" position of its own. Only if nature is understood as matter in motion possessing no natural hierarchy is democracy safe.

A final source of foundation derives from faith. Thus for the earliest Puritan communities, the "plantation[s] religious" were established "for the Glory of God and Advancement of the Christian Faith." Foundations of faith in the West, which derive from the Bible and Christian sources, appear in the form of deductions that fix a general and permanent law, which are analogous to statements of nature, or in the form of interpretations of the course of Providence, which are analogous to statements about History. By the time of the American Founding, the faithful took the decisive step of abandoning claims to make a religious foundation serve as the sole or primary official source for political life, if only because revelation is something to which all do not have access. Foundations deriving from faith became part of a "second constitution" that operated in the minds and hearts of many alongside the official or legal constitution. Religious foundations were invoked to support (or sometimes almost to merge with) the other kinds of foundations, beginning with the phrase in the Declaration of "the laws of nature and nature's God." While the faithful have not insisted on the exclusivity of religious foundations, they have often considered them as indispensable, providing a source of guidance and support for other foundations. Religious foundations have received public recognition and acknowledgment in the platforms of parties, the campaign speeches of candidates, and in the addresses of American presidents and their official pronouncements.

Foundations in the Modern Era

The authority of America's major foundational ideas came under challenge beginning in the early twentieth century. In a first phase, just noted, progressive intellectuals guided by a positivist spirit rejected the concept of natural right as pure "metaphysics" (in the pejorative sense). They continued, however, to embrace as scientific history the idea of progress, which was understood to include economic development, scientific advancement, greater equality, and the spread of liberal democracy. In a second phase, which began in the 1930s, the idea of progress itself came under assault. Confidence in this idea was shaken by the emergence of Fascism and Communism, which directly challenged liberal democracy, and by the arrival in America of the powerful theoretical nexus of ideas often labeled "historicism." Historicism held that there was no permanent basis or standard for making judgments; instead, all values derived from the shifting and contingent views of the framework of the era in which one lived. The idea of progress, only recently considered to be an objective truth, was now said to be merely an opinion of the age. The historian Charles Beard, who began the century as a progressive, shifted ground in his Presidential Address to the American Historical Association in 1933, entitled, significantly, "Written History as an Act of Faith." Beard now declared the notion of a "science of history embracing the fullness of history" to be an "illusion." Each era— each historian within each era—had to choose a frame of reference, which ultimately was a "subjective decision."[27] Like many other American intellectuals, Beard opted for progress, but on the basis of nothing more than "an act of faith."

In a well-known account of the development of Western thought in the twentieth century, the French philosopher François Lyotard in 1979 traced the emergence of what he called "the postmodern condition." Postmodernity is an intellectual situation in which philosophy had rendered untenable belief in any grand "metanarrative" or permanent truth.[28] Western thought had entered a postfoundational age. While Lyotard's analysis bore certain similarities to a set of earlier assessments made in the United States in the 1950s and 1960s by Leo Strauss and Walter Lippmann (among others), these thinkers did not hesitate to label the condition a "crisis" of Western thought. This crisis was likely to have dire consequences for liberal democracy in general and for American liberal democracy in particular. In Strauss's words, "a society which was accustomed to understand itself in terms of a universal purpose cannot lose faith in that purpose without becoming completely bewildered."[29] In the immediate context of their day, both men worried whether America could sustain its efforts in the struggle against an ideology (Communism) that was unscrupulous in its means and that, for the moment, professed greater surety about its future.

Two responses to this condition have been evident in American politics: a revival of natural right and the advent of the doctrine of political non-foundationalism. The first can be traced back in large part to the writings of Strauss and Lippmann.[30] Despite their analysis of the powerful trends in modern thought that produced the crisis, neither thinker judged it to be a permanent condition or an unalterable fate. Time and philosophy did not stop in the middle of the twentieth century. Strauss made an appeal to re-open the question of natural right, and he suggested that the very crisis into which the West had fallen had prompted such an inquiry. Lippmann went further and, perhaps prematurely, began to sketch his idea of "the public philosophy." Since the 1970s, relatively small but important parts of the American intellectual community have sought to recover the underpin-nings of natural right thinking from the classical philosophers, the Scholas-tic natural law theorists, and the American Founders. This investigation has achieved the status of a full-scale theoretical project that has lent support to a reintroduction of the idea of natural right in American political life. The intellectual situation in America today accordingly bears only partial re-semblance to the one that Strauss or Lippmann described a half-century ago.

The second response has been the doctrine of political nonfoundation-alism, many of whose proponents stress its direct connection to the condi-tion of postmodernity. After all, if there are no theoretical foundations available to us, then political nonfoundationalism would seem to be the best fit with the times in which we live. But it would convey a false impres-sion to suggest that nonfoundationalists greeted postmodernity in a spirit of glum resignation, as a condition that contemporary man and woman had reluctantly to bear. Just the contrary, in fact, has been the case. Non-foundationalists have regarded postmodernity as a great liberating mo-ment, a gift of fate that they celebrated in a mood reminiscent of one fa-mously described by William Wordsworth: "Bliss was it in that dawn to be alive / But to be young was very heaven!" Postmodernity has placed the ad-vanced portion of humanity in a much better position both politically and morally—politically because nonfoundationalism provides the first theo-retical basis for the establishment of full and genuine democracy, and morally because people now face the world as it really is, without the illu-sions once supplied by philosophical and religious foundations. Despite their formal contention that all "vocabularies" are relative to the age in which one happens to live, postmodernists clearly believe that we live in a "privileged" time when our vocabulary provides access to what the world really is.

The striking fact is, then, that nonfoundationalists are heavily invested in the condition of postmodernity, so much so that they cannot seem to contemplate ever letting it go. It is Richard Rorty's "hunch" that "Western social and political thought may have had the last conceptual revolution it needs."[31] Only this attitude can explain the nonfoundationalists' unwillingness to entertain the possibility of a new period of thought, that is, a post-postmodern era. They regard what has been happening recently in America as a weird aberration—a temporary return to "fundamentalism"—that cannot represent a real theoretical development. Still, beneath the surface, their growing uneasiness about where history is going is all too evident, as seen by the rising chorus of harsh attacks on "foundationalism." If the horse were really dying, what need would there be to keep flogging it so unmercifully?

There has been a parallel development in America to the revival of natural right. It is a renewal of religious faith. This change has, if anything, been even more unexpected than the shift that has taken place in philosophy. At roughly the same time as the emergence of the idea of historicism in the West, when philosophical foundations were said to be moribund, religion was also declared to be entering into its last stage. Max Weber's famous pronouncement of a growing "disenchantment of the world" in his *Protestant Ethic and the Spirit of Capitalism* (1904) helped give birth to the thesis of secularization, which held that religion in the West was fated to lose its influence over the sphere of public life and to begin to die out altogether. For years all evidence confirmed the veracity of this thesis, and the expected trends have continued in most Western democracies. But in the United States, there has been a reaction in the form of a religious movement in politics, which formed to contest the political arm of the secularist cause. It has sought to win a place for religious faith inside public life and has promoted a religious foundation as a supporting element to the other foundations. America once again stands out as the exceptional case among the Western democracies.

Political Nonfoundationalism and Modern American Politics

If examined strictly on the basis of its formal properties, there is no reason why nonfoundationalism should be on one side of the political spectrum in America today. Yet as matters now stand, most nonfoundationalists are found on the left. A partial explanation is that most of those who stress foundations today are clustered on the right, which has induced nonfoundationalists to join the other side. The reverse may be equally as true. Either way, it appears today that the theoretical dispute about foundations, independent of all other causes, has contributed to the political division among elites in America.

It is too simplistic, however, to think that the theoretical debate perfectly tracks the political division or that it is the only cause. While the Right is home to most of those who espouse foundations, it contains elements that lean toward a kind of nonfoundationalism, although usually not in name. Of all of the foundational concepts mentioned earlier, Customary History, which has a significant constituency among conservatives today in the form of traditionalism, is clearly the "weakest" kind of foundation. Customary History celebrates the particular, that is, our tradition and our History, against the universal. This position is only one small step from the conclusion that if we have "our" tradition that is right for us, everyone else has "their" tradition that is right for them. There is no standard higher than traditions or cultures. For this reason, Customary History in its advanced stages in the nineteenth century contributed to the rise of historicism and thus indirectly to postmodernism. Customary History was also adopted in the aftermath of the French Revolution by those critical of the use of rational and universal prescriptions; it became the leading source, from the Conservative side, of the attack against natural rights and natural law. Finally, a part of the Right in America today takes its bearings from neoclassical economics, which, as Francis Fukuyama has argued, "is basically a kind of anti-foundationalism. The whole tradition that begins with Alfred Marshall's marginalism takes individual preferences as essentially sovereign; the job of the government is not to shape individual preferences, it's simply to aggregate them."[32]

The situation on the left is interesting in a different way. Given that so many on the left today embrace nonfoundationalism, it has become almost the public face of the left, at least among intellectuals. At the same time, as all acknowledge, there is no dearth of expression of broad values and ideals on the left, like social justice and humanitarianism. The result is that the left today is characterized by the curious combination of a scrupulous denial of foundations together with a persistent affirmation of values, a position that might best be described as "idealistic nonfoundationalism." Whether the leftist program is salable to a broad public on this basis has concerned some nonfoundationalists. To help rally the faithful to the political cause, Richard Rorty has recommended the mild opium of "spinning . . . narratives of social hope" that will "tell a story about how things get better."[33] This task, to be performed by novelists, journalists, and artists, will supply the needed solidarity for a liberal democratic people. It is to be supplemented by a sentimental education that cultivates compassion or the "recognition of a common susceptibility to humiliation [as] the only social bond that is needed."[34]

Nonfoundationalism: An Assessment

Political nonfoundationalism has been widely accepted by the intellectual class in America, which now considers it to be virtually a self-evident truth. It appeals to this class's belief in the dogma of theoretical relativism while offering simultaneous assurances that nothing in this position endangers the promotion of the same class's cherished progressive values. Although the support for this doctrine by intellectuals is impressive, the intelligentsia has been known on occasion to err before, as when it prostrated itself for so long before the idol of Marxist ideology. The only honest way to proceed is to consider the doctrine of political nonfoundationalism on its own merits, testing the strength of the arguments and weighing its likely consequences. By these criteria, there are a number of reasons to doubt the wisdom of embracing this new product of modern philosophy.

First, the doctrine rests on a simplistic binary schema that falsely collapses all thought into the categories of foundationalism and nonfoundationalism. All ideas labeled "foundationalist," which include almost all first principles ever conceived before the birth of John Dewey or John Rawls, are treated as part of a supposed class of things that is said to share certain important properties. This step allows nonfoundationalists to impute qualities of the most dangerous or odious of foundations to the most reasonable of them. Thus, the concept of natural right and the Marxist idea of History, though obviously not the same thing, are both grouped together as instances of "foundationalism"; they therefore participate in the same sin of intellectual rigidity, preempting "encounters between old and new vocabularies" and working "on behalf of a regime of authority." By this technique, a purely academic distinction between foundationalism and nonfoundationalism is used to obscure the real political distinction between free societies and regimes of authority.

And what of the category of nonfoundationalism? Proponents of this position almost never speak of the variety of its possible political manifestations, but identify it with the single form of a liberal democratic doctrine while arguing that "foundationalism" has supported authoritarian systems. But what is good for the goose should be good for the gander. Nonfoundationalist theory has served as a nursery for authoritarian systems. The list of philosophers who have embraced theoretical nonfoundationalism includes such figures as Martin Heidegger, Ernst Jünger, and Michel Foucault, all of whom favored nonliberal positions, whether of the Right or the Left. While the premises of nonfoundationalism may "chime with the spirit of tolerance" for thinkers today, they have tolled for tyranny for many in the past.

None of this is to question the intentions of contemporary proponents of nonfoundationalism, who are generally tolerant of others' views, with the exception of those that support foundations. The real issue today, however, is not the sincerity of nonfoundationalist thinkers, but whether their doctrine is sustainable and supportive of liberal democracy. Nonfoundationalism creates a vacuum in the public realm in regard to the truth of first principles. It claims, with no experience to prove it, that a polity of this kind will be stable. But is not this circumstance of an empty public square the most fertile soil in which holistic political religions and ideologies are most likely to grow and take hold? Did not the destruction of real religion among the elites in France in the eighteenth century prepare the way for the creation of the political religion of the Revolution, in much the same fashion as the nihilism of the early part of the twentieth century opened the doors to Fascism and Communism?

Second, political nonfoundationalism trades on false hopes to win adherents. The binary distinction demarcates not only two categories of thought, but also, seductively, two epochs of history. For centuries the nations of the West suffered under a politics that saw continuous conflicts among different foundations. Now, with the emergence of nonfoundationalism, Western man is ready to enter a new era, likely to be the final one, in which a new kind of logic will prevail. Political life will be delivered from its past woes. The essentialist will lie down with the historicist; neither will there be strife anymore. Despite the nonfoundationalist's denials of History, this extravagant "narrative of hope" would seem to have little to separate it from what used to be called Philosophy of History.

Third, the doctrine of political nonfoundationalism has been constructed from abstract philosophical propositions, not from actual inquiry into political life. The source of theorizing about "essentialism" and "foundationalism" originally had nothing to do with politics, but derived from pure philosophy and the interpretation of literary texts. The transfer of these categories to politics came as an afterthought. Instances can certainly be cited in which the application of a concept from another field to politics has produced an intellectual payoff—the biological notion of organic development might be one such example—but this result has always required that the concept in question prove its utility as a tool of real political analysis. This test has not been met in this case—far from it. Pages, nay volumes, have been written, filled with airy generalizations about the dangers of foundationalism. But which thinkers have taken the trouble to investigate the record of foundations in order to assess how they have performed in American history? Certainly not John Rawls, who is systematic to the point of painfulness about everything except the exploration of the actual performance of foundations. A quick look, for example, at the index of his *Political Liberalism* shows that he has discussed "Adams" once, but it is a contemporary academic, Robert Adams, not John. Thomas Jefferson appears twice, once in a footnote. Lincoln makes only a brief cameo appearance. Nor has Richard Rorty been especially well known for the depth of his historical inquiries. His brief accounts exhibit all of the charming casualness of invented narratives. And why not, for, as he notes, "there is no nonmythological . . . way of telling a country's story. . . . Nobody knows what it would be like to try to be objective when attempting to decide what one's country really is, what its history really means."[35]

If the concern of nonfoundationalists is with the performance of political foundations, they should have found it instructive to examine the role played in America by the foundation of the "law of nature" supported by an invocation of faith. No doubt such an examination would have pointed to certain difficulties, enough so that many over the course of American history have been moved to attempt to supplement or alter it. But would this investigation demonstrate, as nonfoundationalists would lead one to think, that Nature and Nature's God on balance thwarted liberal democratic development? Was this foundation an impediment to the Revolution in the 1770s, to the fight against slavery in the 1860s, to the struggle for civil rights in the 1960s, or to the efforts in Eastern Europe to overthrow Communist tyranny in the 1980s? Where, exactly, is the evidence of the millions who have suffered under its iron boot? It is a well-regarded counsel of prudence that a system should not be overthrown for "light and transient causes," or until there is an alternative that offers the prospect of a better result. Have nonfoundationalists followed this counsel, or for that matter even considered it?

If a real examination of the record has been lacking, one must never-theless concede the existence of a highly imaginative "discourse" adamant in its opposition to natural right. In one typical and prominent version, it is argued that all essentialist thought, including the natural rights thinking of the American founders, creates a "logic of identity" that "denies or represses difference."[36] Foundationalism has thus been linked over the past quarter century with opposition to progressive positions on issues of race and gen-der. Foundational thinking in America, as Shelby Steele has explained, has come to be "stigmatized" for its involvement in the sins of the past: "Amer-ica was a foundational nation, but we were hypocritical . . . Many people ar-gued that foundational principles were really a pretext for evil, out of which came this darker evil—the West—that dominated the world and oppressed people." To the rescue comes the saving doctrine of nonfoundationalism, whose proponents have no difficulty claiming the moral high ground. In Steele's words: "They're saying, we're not partaking of that hypocrisy and we've got new things like diversity and tolerance that don't have any foun-dational basis and aren't grounded in principle. They're just grounded in wonderfulness."[37]

Fourth, the doctrine of political nonfoundationalism is a cover for a (sub)regime change that seeks to alter the character of the American people. When speaking in a pragmatic vein, proponents of nonfoundation-alism often claim to rest their case on the political ground that their doc-trine is best for promoting liberal democracy. Nonfoundationalists, by this argument, have nothing against religion or natural right per se; it is just that these foundations turn out to be unhealthy for liberal democracy. But even the most superficial acquaintance with the thought of some of the leading nonfoundationalists reveals the disingenuousness of this argument. It comes far closer to the mark to say that nonfoundationalists believe in the "moral" superiority of nonfoundationalism and that their political argu-ment is advanced for the sake of promoting their moral positions. They lav-ish praise on the "ironic" or "reasonable" personality, while dismissing the rigid or dogmatic one; and they generally make no secret of their support for secularism over the promotion of religion.

Even if it were the case, however, that the doctrine of nonfoundational-ism promoted greater safety for liberal democracy, there might be sound reason to reject it. The reason why many in America have favored a liberal democratic system is not merely to cultivate "pure" liberal democracy. Lib-eral democracy as a political form is not the full American regime. Liberalism supplies the "floor" of the system, meaning its fundamental political premises and the rules that must not be violated. What a people chooses to construct above that floor, so long as it is not inconsistent with the principles of liberalism, can rightly be considered an integral part of the full polity. Americans have sought to maintain the recognition of faith, supported in forms of public discourse and by incidental forms of public acknowledgments, as a central element of the political order. Nonfoundationalism, which demands public neutrality between faith and nonbelief, aims at a profound alteration of the character of the polity.

Finally, the doctrine of political nonfoundationalism would promote listlessness in the American public. Without a foundational principle—without the moral energy that derives from efforts to establish foundational principles—a community ceases to exist in a deep or meaningful sense; and without this energy, a nation will be unable to extract from its members the added measure of devotion and resolve needed to guarantee its survival and to enable it to undertake important projects. People may sacrifice for a truth, but in what measure will they do so for a "narrative"? Embracing a public philosophy of nonfoundationalism would therefore lead to the evacuation of the spirit that is essential to a vigorous nation. Nonfoundationalists will doubtless reply that many nations today are happily dispensing with foundations while blazing new paths to a higher form of liberal democracy. Perhaps it is too soon for social science to resolve this question definitively. But even if the cheerful assessment of nonfoundationalists about its success in other nations should prove correct, this would hardly be dispositive for the United States. Each nation is particular, and fate has assigned different roles to different nations. Western civilization today confronts two great challenges: saving itself from a new barbarism that aims to destroy it and sustaining the religious faith that helped to give it birth. As the world's leading power, the United States has responsibilities in meeting these challenges that are of a different order of magnitude than those of countries like Luxembourg or Canada or France.

If the seductive doctrine of nonfoundationalism can be resisted in America, there will be very little positive to show for it, other perhaps than the reinvigoration that comes from having knowingly resisted an enormous danger. It is in such modest terms that victories in politics are often counted. Our reward will nevertheless be a real one: the chance to return to the perennial challenge of seeking foundational remedies to the problems most incident to foundational thinking.

1. John Rawls, *Political Liberalism* (New York: Columbia University Press, 1993), especially 48–54; Richard Rorty, *Contingency, Irony, and Solidarity* (Cambridge: Cambridge University Press, 1989).

2. For the differences between Rorty and Habermas, see Jürgen Habermas, Richard Rorty, and Leszek Kolakowski, *Debating the State of Philosophy* (Westport, Conn.: Praeger, 1996). Rawls and Habermas carried out an extensive debate in the *Journal of Philosophy* 92, no. 3 (1995). See Jürgen Habermas, "Reconciliation through the Public Use of Reason: Remarks on John Rawls's *Political Liberalism*," 109–31, and John Rawls, "Reply to Habermas," 132–80.

3. Alexander Hamilton, James Madison, and John Jay, *The Federalist Papers* (New York: New American Library Press, 1961), 279 (number 43).

4. Abraham Lincoln, Letter to Henry L. Pierce, April 6, 1859, in *Selected Speeches and Writings* (New York: Library of America, 1992), 215; Rorty, *Objectivity, Relativism, and Truth* (Cambridge: Cambridge University Press, 1991), 187.

5. Rorty, *Contingency, Irony, and Solidarity*, 51–52.

6. Rorty, *Essays on Heidegger and Others* (Cambridge: Cambridge University Press, 1991), 132–33.

7. Rawls, *Political Liberalism*, 63.

8. *Philosophy in a Time of Terror: Dialogues with Jürgen Habermas and Jacques Derrida*, ed. Giovanna Borradori (Chicago: University of Chicago Press, 2003), 117. Derrida puts "European" inside quotation marks to indicate that this position is not quite official. In actual fact, there is much more legal involvement between church and state in many European countries than there is in the United States.

9. Jürgen Habermas, "La statue et les révolutionnaires," *Le Monde*, May 3, 2003.

10. Pierre Rosanvallon, "Europe—les États-Unis, les deux universalismes," *Le Monde*, February 22, 2005.

11. Lincoln, Speech of March 6, 1860, at New Haven, in *Selected Speeches and Writings*, 257.

12. Rorty, *Contingency, Irony, and Solidarity*, 86; *Essays on Heidegger*, 135.

13. Auguste Comte, *Cours de Philosophie Positive* (Paris: Bachelier, 1830), 1:40–41.

14. Stephens, "Cornerstone" speech, in Henry Cleveland, *Alexander H. Stephens in Public and Private* (Philadelphia: National Publishing, 1866), 721; Lincoln, Speech on the Kansas-Nebraska Act, October 16, 1854.

15. John Stuart Mill, "Coleridge," in *Collected Works*, ed. John Robson et al. (Toronto: University of Toronto Press, 1963–91), 10:133–34.

16. *The Works of John Adams* (Boston: Charles C. Little and James Brown, 1850), 2:371 (emphasis added).

17. Woodrow Wilson, *The New Freedom* (New York: Doubleday, Page, 1913), 42.

18. Letter to Major John Cartwright, June 5, 1824, in *The Portable Thomas Jefferson*, ed. Merrill D. Peterson (New York: Viking Penguin, 1975), 578.

19. "Election Sermon," cited in Alexis de Tocqueville, *Democracy in America*, trans. and ed. Harvey C. Mansfield and Delba Winthrop (Chicago: University of Chicago Press, 2000), 688–89.

20. Winston Churchill, *The Gathering Storm* (Boston: Houghton Mifflin, 1948), 345–46.

21. Thomas Jefferson, "A Summary View of the Rights of British America," in *The Portable Thomas Jefferson*, 4.

22. George Bancroft, "Oration of February 18, 1840" at Hartford, Connecticut (Hartford, 1840); "Speech to the New York Historical Society, 1858" (New York, 1858).

23. Jean Antoine Nicolas Condorcet, *Esquisse d'un Tableau Historique des Progrès de L'Esprit Humain* (Paris: Flammarion, 1998), 88 (my translation). Published in English as *Sketch for a Historical Picture of the Progress of the Human Mind* (London: Weidenfeld and Nicolson, 1955).

24. William Graham Sumner, "Socialism," in *On Liberty, Society, and Politics*, ed. Robert C. Bannister (Indianapolis: Liberty Fund, 1992), 172.

25. John Dewey, *Freedom and Culture* (New York: Prometheus, 1989), 120; *Reconstruction in Philosophy* (Boston: Beacon Press, 1957, orig. 1920), 44.

26. *The Political Writings of John Dewey*, ed. Debra Morris and Ian Shapiro (Indianapolis: Hackett Publishers, 1993), 45.

27. Charles Beard, "Written History as an Act of Faith," American Historical Association Presidential Address, 1933, *American Historical Review* 39, no. 2: 219–31, http://www.historians.org/info/AHA_History/cabeard.htm (accessed March 13, 2008).

28. See François Lyotard, *The Postmodern Condition* (Manchester: Manchester University Press, 1984).

29. Leo Strauss, "The Crisis of Our Time," in *The Predicament of Modern Politics*, ed. Harold J. Spaeth (Detroit: University of Detroit Press, 1964), 44.

30. See especially Leo Strauss, *Natural Right and History* (Chicago: University of Chicago Press, 1953), and Walter Lippmann, *Essays in the Public Philosophy* (Boston: Little, Brown, 1955).

31. Rorty, *Contingency, Irony, and Solidarity*, 63.

32. Bradley Center for Philanthropy and Civic Renewal, "What's the Big Idea?": Bradley Symposium, May 25, 2006, http://pcr.hudson.org/index.cfm?fuseaction=publication_details&id=4044 (accessed March 13, 2008), 26.

33. Rorty, *Objectivity, Relativism, and Truth* (New York: Cambridge University Press, 1991), 212, 211, 219.

34. Rorty, *Contingency, Irony, and Solidarity*, 86, 91.

35. Rorty, *Achieving Our Country* (Cambridge: Harvard University Press, 1998), 11.

36. Iris Marion Young, *Justice and the Politics of Difference* (Princeton: Princeton University Press, 1990), 98–99.

37. "What's the Big Idea?" 28–29.

The Dangers of Conservative Populism

Alan Wolfe

I

Conservatism is at its best when liberalism is at its worst. Fortunately for American conservatives, liberals chose to be at their worst for a considerable portion of the post–World War II period. After uniting most of the country around a national security consensus in the early years of the Cold War, and then carrying forward an ambitious sense of national purpose, including a bipartisan commitment to civil rights, during the Kennedy-Johnson years, liberalism began to put its worst foot forward in the 1970s. Supreme Court decisions that seemed to flout democratic sentiment, an increasingly arrogant leadership class more familiar with what elite opinion considered correct than what ordinary Americans believed right, and an unwillingness to assign a high enough priority to national security—these were the features that, in discrediting liberalism, enabled conservatism to grow.

And conservatism grew indeed. Once a somewhat marginal movement confined to a reluctant South and agrarian Midwest, conservatism recovered from the 1964 Goldwater debacle to become the most vibrant political and intellectual force in the United States. To the great frustration of liberals such as myself, who once believed that the brightest and most talented people would always be attracted to the Left, younger politically engaged intellectuals began to flock to the Right, while the academic world, which retained its 1960s sensibilities long after the 1960s exhausted themselves, became buried in jargonistic abstraction and naked careerism. A conservative willingness to innovate with ideas such as school vouchers won support from inner-city minority parents. Conservative criticisms of affirmative action resonated with all those who remained attracted to ideas about rewarding individuals for their merit. Commitments to federalism and localism resonated, not only with those holding right-wing views, but with the temperaments of left-wing activists of the 1960s and 1970s who worried about concentrations of political power at the national level. The firm conviction that communism was incompatible with liberal democratic values, once associated with Democrats such as Harry Truman, became the province of Republicans such as Ronald Reagan, while the isolationism that had once been the singular weakness of the Right found itself inherited by the Left. Conservative ideas took hold throughout the last decades of the twentieth century not only because they were well funded—actually, liberal foundations during this period outspent conservative ones—but because they seemed innovative, even progressive, at a time of liberal exhaustion.

As perhaps befits a worldview that insists on responsibility and reward, conservatives had no sooner begun to fashion a compelling critique of liberalism than voters turned to them for a cure for their society's problems. Democrats, once the default political party of the postwar period, had never retained a firm grip on the presidency throughout those years, but by century's end, even their once seemingly impregnable control over Congress had been lost. A situation unimaginable in 1964—Republican control of all branches of the national government—became a brute fact of political life forty years later. (Although the midterm elections of 2006 allowed the Democrats back into majority status in both houses of Congress, this Republican ascent remains remarkable.) Rare is a political and intellectual movement that can move from opposition to power in so short a period of time. Fed up with liberal overreach, Americans gave conservatives an unusually free hand to do whatever they wanted. Indeed, after President Bush's reelection in 2004, no significant force in American politics—not the Democrats, not so-called moderate Republicans, not governors, and not any major court in the United States, especially the Supreme Court—seemed to be in a position of preventing Mr. Bush from implementing the conservative mandate he believed the voters had given him in that election.

Alas, however, if conservatism flourishes when liberalism is at its worst, conservatism fails most when liberalism is at its weakest. The 2004 election may have been a triumph for the Republican Party, but it also marked the defeat of the conservative intellectual revolution. This is not because, as some conservatives maintain, the interests of the Republican Party and those of the conservative movement diverged.[1] On the contrary, Mr. Bush was as indebted to conservatism as Lyndon Johnson was to liberalism; political ideologies exist to be realized through politics, and Republicans and conservatives needed each other desperately, the one to have ideas to put before the voters, the other to have a chance at turning those ideas into policies. As the Republican Party became increasingly embroiled in cases of corruption and revelations of incompetence, conservative intellectuals began to separate themselves from George W. Bush and former House majority leader Tom DeLay by claiming that such inside-the-Beltway machinations and big-government proclivities do not represent the best and brightest that the Right has to offer. This, however, is like saying that market failures have nothing to do with the theory of free markets or that socialism in practice has no relationship to Marxist or Leninist theory. No relationship between an ideology and a regime is ever perfect, but an effort to apply a theory cannot be held blameless when the theory fails.

Conservatism failed under Republican auspices in the early years of the twentieth century because the price it had to pay to gain access to political power was too high. That price can be summarized in one word: populism. America has long had a democratic political culture, and in the years since the 1960s, its participatory character has been further enhanced. The increasing democratization of American politics is reflected in a number of important developments, including the fact that both political parties stopped relying on unelected power brokers to nominate candidates in favor of contested primaries, began to use extensive fund-raising techniques and expensive advertising to bring out voters, and learned the arts of tailoring messages to win widespread support. A conservatism that sets itself up in opposition to these democratizing forces can offer an ideologically coherent, and even at times moving and persuasive, criticism of modern political life, but to do so has to welcome its status as "superfluous," to use Albert Jay Nock's term, in the hurly-burly of elections and governance.[2] A conservatism that opts to see at least some of its ideas become the law of the land, by contrast, will have to accommodate itself to a political culture characterized by instant gratification, message simplification, emotional satisfaction, and poll-tested policies. Operating in a political culture that allows little room for principle, less for reflection, and even less than that for introspection, conservatives in power are prevented from doing what conservatives, when out of power, do best, which is standing up and saying, as Martin Luther so famously did, that here they stand and they can do no other. Conservatism in power is conservatism without conscience, and since conscience is what conservatives do best, conservatism in power is hardly conservatism at all.

There has never existed one form of conservatism in the realm of ideas; on the contrary, conservatism has taken an Oakeshottian form of resisting ambitious transformations of the world as well as a more Straussian-inspired form of rejecting much of the modern world in favor of a classical understanding of virtue and politics.[3] The most striking aspect of today's populistic conservatism is that it resembles neither Oakeshott nor Strauss. Compared to small-bore conservatism, it has been bold and ambitious, willing to use government to support major transformations in public policy. But unlike Straussian conservatism, it never stands up and says no to modernizing trends, symbolized, almost too perfectly, by Mr. Bush's failure to veto any of the legislation that has ever reached his desk, at least until an effort to increase federal support for stem cell research did in the summer of 2006. The conservatism we have stands neither for principle nor for purpose. It is not the economic corruption manifested by a Jack Abramoff or a Tom DeLay that is contemporary conservatism's undoing. It is a deeper form of political corruption, represented by all those conservative politicians in contemporary America who would rather use power to reward the funders and voters who support them than rely upon the bully pulpit of office to educate and uplift. As dangers to democracy go, conservatism in power threatens to surpass the liberalism it had been elected to replace.

II

No domestic issue in American politics illustrates the corruption of contemporary conservatism better than its failure to take seriously the consequences of expanding budget deficits. This is in itself an astonishing political development because no other issue was historically so important to conservatives as their dismay at the willingness of liberals to pay for unaffordable public programs today by charging the costs against blameless future generations. Once upon a time the most important, as well as the most reprehensible, liberal in the conservative mind was John Maynard Keynes. The whole idea of dismissing the long run because in it we will all be dead struck at the heart of the Burkean conviction that generations are responsible for each other's fate. Keynes, for any self-respecting conservative, was a Tom Paine in economist's garb. Follow his advice, and you would instantiate into public policy the dangerous idea that people can get whatever they want without being asked to pay the price for their self-indulgence. It was Keynes's perceived moral laxity that bothered conservatives as much as his technical economic ideas.

Although he still fails to receive credit among conservatives, Bill Clinton was the first Democrat president to realize the political, and even to some degree, the moral problems with excessive deficit spending. Helped by a booming economy, Clinton was able to transform the reputation of Democrats as wild spenders just as he was willing to confront his party's negative reputation on issues involving welfare. With considerable political and financial skill, Clinton and his treasury secretary Robert Rubin not only balanced the budget, they held the line against pressures within the party to spend increased public revenue on new political programs. Al Gore may have proved inept at running for the presidency based on Clinton's economic performance, but eight years of Democrat rule left the American fiscal house in the best order it had experienced in decades.

Future historians are likely to judge the rapidity with which a conservative president wasted the Clinton surplus as the single most irresponsible act of the Bush presidency. Once again, economic circumstances played a role here, for Mr. Bush presided over a period of stagnancy just as Mr. Clinton did over a period of growth. (Why the economy did better under Democrats than under Republicans is a question I leave to others.) But it is also the case that politically, Bush refused to apply the politics of budgetary control adopted by Clinton. Like liberals before them, conservatives after 2000 were determined to pass legislation that would secure their standing among voters, no matter what the costs to the overall health of the economy.

The most illustrative example of big-government conservatism is the most expensive and far-reaching: Medicare reform. As it fashioned its most ambitious first-term legislative priority, the Bush administration not only refused to consider mechanisms that could cut the cost of pharmaceuticals, it misrepresented the actual costs of the legislation and engaged in wild horse-trading to win sufficient votes from reluctant conservatives to assure passage, in the process not only rendering Americans a new entitlement, but one likely to cost the taxpayers huge sums of money for as long as the eye can see. With the passage of time, numerous conservatives in Congress have come to regret their support for such an expensive public policy, and, with considerable irony, senior citizens themselves seem more willing to punish Republicans for complicating their choices than reward them for assuming the costs of their medications, but none of this changes the fact that the Bush administration, once the law was signed, has never rethought its commitment to one of the most flawed pieces of domestic reform legislation ever passed by Congress. Indeed, in the wake of Hurricane Katrina, the president presented himself once again as a big spender (although, as that even receded into memory, the administration did not follow through on its promises).

It is one thing to engage in a spending frenzy that would make Democrats blush and another thing to cut taxes at the same time, but this, of course, is what Mr. Bush was determined to do. Since its appearance on Arthur Laffer's napkin, supply-side economics has been to conservatism what the apple was to Adam and Eve: a temptation too delicious to resist. Forget, for the moment, that Arthur Laffer is no John Maynard Keynes, at least not in his abilities as an economist. But Laffer did offer to the Right what Keynes offered to the Left, a way of passing on the costs of today's follies to future generations. From the standpoint of deficits that will have to be paid by someone at some time, cutting taxes is the functional equivalent of out-of-control government spending (except that one gets neither an expanded military, nor public works projects, nor protections against catastrophic illness as a result). Supply-side economics in that sense is moral indulgence of the most irresponsible sort. Accept it as a given, which just about every Republican legislator does these days, and one need not make hard policy choices nor exercise restraint in one's legislative ambitions. The magic of economic growth will take care of all problems, and if sufficient economic growth eventually does not appear, well didn't some economist tell us what will happen in the long run?

If it represents anything but prudence to spend money the government does not have and is forbidden to raise, shifting the costs of public policy to those who can least afford to pay those costs represents a form of radical social engineering once promoted by the Left. There is an idea, long associated with conservatism, to rely on free markets and to let the chips fall where they may. But this has not been the guiding principle of the conservatives who have dominated American politics in the early years of the twenty-first century. Like liberals before them, conservatives believe in using government to do what the market by itself cannot, except that while liberals turned to the state to create more equality than the market would provide, conservatives do so to prevent the market from giving those with few resources a fair chance to compete with those who have more. Efforts to use government to promote the redistribution of income are fundamentally the same, whether those efforts involve shifting the burden away from the bottom toward the top or the other way around.

In its policy of tax cutting as well as in its efforts to reward industries and companies that finance its campaigns, contemporary conservatives are not engaged in promoting laissez-faire in any sense that Adam Smith would recognize. Tax cuts are designed not to cut taxes for everyone equally but to cut them the most for those who need relief the least, while attempts to lift regulatory burdens on industries benefit those firms that already have considerable clout at the expense of more innovative firms whose potential growth lies in the future. In this sense, conservative economic policy resembles the granting of privileges to those already well off irrespective of whether their relative advantage was earned by them. Adam Smith would recognize immediately the contemporary conservative tilt in favor of business and would just as immediately condemn it for its inegalitarian, unfair, and economically inefficient side effects. Republican political economy is protective more than it is competitive. Its goal is to fuse economic and political power rather than to separate them. The consequence is to reinforce unfairness rather than to open the field to talents.

This conservative preference for fiscal and economic irresponsibility does not represent some flawed approach that could, with tinkering, be corrected. It is instead intimately linked to a conservative quest for power and a willingness to use whatever means necessary to remain there. Liberals supported domestic reforms, but they also recognized the need to increase taxes to pay for them. Old-fashioned conservatives may prefer to cut taxes, but then they do not turn around and support programs that drain the treasury. Only conservative populists expand government's revenue obligations while cutting its sources of revenue, a surefire step on the road to fiscal disaster. Medicare reform was the most important piece of domestic legislation in Mr. Bush's first term not only because it was the most expensive, but because it came to symbolize the important choice that contemporary conservatives made. They could stand for principle or they could accommodate to power. They chose the latter, opting to reap the benefits of having voters on your side (hence the new programs) as well as those associated with paying off the interests that support you (hence their exorbitant costs). The choice, as it happened, turned out to be an easy one, certainly for Mr. Bush and, with a few exceptions, his Republican allies in Congress. Spend now, pay later: conservatives had heard all that before, only in those days it was meant as criticism. Now it is offered as policy.

III

Foreign policy during the Bush years was transformed as radically as domestic policy. Once again, the comparison with the Clinton years is especially instructive. To the great frustration of foreign policy activists such as General Wesley Clark, Bill Clinton was reluctant to take steps to deploy U.S. forces abroad in any kind of humanitarian capacity.[4] Ever sensitive to domestic opinion—Clinton was an avid reader of polls—the president realized that Americans have never willingly supported the costs, both financial and human, of overseas adventures that appeared to have little bearing on U.S. national security. Clinton also understood that Republicans were strong in Congress and that nearly all of them, especially those who leaned to the right of the political spectrum, would reflect their party's historic ties to isolationism and oppose actions designed to curtail genocide or promote human rights. In the instructive typology offered by Walter Russell Mead, Americans tend more toward a Jeffersonian and Jacksonian suspicion of the world than a Hamiltonian or Wilsonian engagement with it.[5]

Despite the possibility of intense opposition, Clinton nonetheless did commit American troops to humanitarian missions, sometimes failing badly and other times with commendable success. This left Al Gore vulnerable on these issues in the 2000 election campaign, and candidate George W. Bush—also, despite his frequent denials, an avid reader of polls—was quick to take advantage, insisting during the presidential debates that the United States should adopt a "humble" approach to foreign policy. Classic realism rather than humanitarian-inspired Wilsonianism seemed to be in the offing, especially as realists such as James Baker played such a prominent role in the controversy over disputed ballots from the state of Florida.

For obvious reasons, the terrorist attack of September 11, 2001, rendered irrelevant any discussion of humble foreign policies for the United States; decisive action was required in the wake of that event, and President Bush, cheered on by both parties, rose to the challenge. Still, September 11 did not answer the question of whether the strong response America could make and should have made was best guided by realism or by idealism. At first, realism constituted the operating assumptions of American policy. Identifying Afghanistan as the state sponsor of bin Laden's terrorist acts, the administration, in classic realist fashion, patiently assembled the forces necessary to toppling a government that had sided so strongly against the United States and used its military might to install a regime friendly to its interests. There was nothing in the way the administration intervened in Afghanistan to suggest that it was about to overthrow the caution and conservatism that has traditionally marked foreign policy realism in favor of the utopianism and messianism that can be frequently found among Wilsonians.

Iraq changed all that. But, once again, not at first. The administration's claims that Iraq had strong links to al-Qaeda and was in possession of weapons of mass destruction suggested a continuation of the realism that marked the war against the Taliban; no society can allow itself to be threatened either by terrorism or by WMDs. As the debate over whether the United States ought to invade Iraq began to heat up, realists generally took the position that it was important to know whether indeed Iraq did constitute such a threat to the United States and that the United Nations inspection process offered the best way of finding out. In addition, realists argued that any intervention contemplated by the United States, if it proved necessary, ought, like the war in Afghanistan, to be multilateral in nature. The coalition assembled by Mr. Bush's father, which had been put together by realists such as James Baker and Brent Scowcroft, seemed the appropriate model to apply. Aware of the prestige of such figures, Mr. Bush allowed himself to be persuaded by his secretary of state, Colin Powell, to bring his case before the United Nations.

Only with the passage of time did it become clear how internally divided the Bush administration had become over the pursuit of realistic foreign policy objectives—and how little influence Secretary Powell and other realists had over the direction of American foreign policy. Vice President Dick Cheney and Secretary of Defense Donald Rumsfeld were the key players in shaping America's approach to Iraq, and while both of them had the reputation of realists during their earlier period of government service, each had become persuaded to pursue a far more ambitious agenda for American foreign policy. The United States, in their view, ought to be willing to act alone if it so chooses, assembling coalitions of the willing for specific missions rather than fashioning grand alliances along the lines of NATO. More importantly, Cheney and Rumsfeld, whether or not they themselves belonged to the ideologically motivated group known as neoconservatives, were perfectly willing to cast foreign policy objectives in broad, ideological terms. Communism had collapsed, but international terrorism, they believed, was all too often associated with tyrannical states, and, in their view, bringing democracy to the societies that once sponsored it would eliminate the terror threat and in that way serve America's national security interests. In such a way did a Wilsonian insistence on making the world safe for democracy shift from Democratic liberals to Republican conservatives.[6]

Wilsonianism would become even more important to the Bush administration when its original rationale for the war in Iraq could no longer be sustained. After no weapons of mass destruction were uncovered in Iraq, and when no links to the September 11 terrorists could ever be found, the president appealed for public support by emphasizing the vital role the United States played in liberating Iraq from a dictatorship and helping the Iraqi people establish democracy. Such speeches resonated well with liberals who had supported President Clinton's efforts to promote democracy; there was no doubt in their minds of Saddam Hussein's evil, and many of them, some with great enthusiasm, gave the Republican president their support. Republicans themselves, especially those who had opposed earlier humanitarian interventions, were less likely to be enthusiasts for the Iraqi war on humanitarian grounds, but they were strong supporters of the president and, with one or two exceptions, most of them kept their reservations to themselves. Nor did the American people, traditionally suspicious of such interventions, at first oppose the president. Americans may tend toward isolationism, but they also believe strongly in taking whatever steps are necessary to protect their nation's security, and so long as they believed that Iraq was a threat to the United States, they gave President Bush their backing.

In their struggle against realists, the neo-Wilsonians around Cheney and Rumsfeld had one distinct advantage. True, their actual policies were not especially effective; Rumsfeld's efforts to win a military victory in Iraq while minimizing the number of troops deployed there seems especially wrongheaded in retrospect. But their understanding of domestic politics was far more sophisticated than the one offered by realists. Americans cannot be persuaded to sacrifice the lives of their children on behalf of the balance of power, but they can be rallied to support wars abroad if they are convinced that doing so will protect them against threats to their security. By combining an emphasis on bringing democracy to Iraq with the constant message that the situation in Iraq was directly linked to September 11, the neo-Wilsonians within the Bush administration were able to give their foreign policy a decidedly populistic coloration. Vote for us because we are strong, they claimed, and, equally important, do not vote for our opponents because they are weak. It did not matter if the war in Iraq was actually being won. What did matter was that Americans rarely deny presidents second terms when the country is at war, and they did not do so once again in 2004. For all the talk of moral values, foreign policy considerations were the most significant factor in President Bush's reelection. People liked him because they believed his toughness would protect them.

The way Iraq was discussed in the 2004 election had little or nothing to do with what was actually happening in Iraq itself, where the presence of American troops seemed to fuel the insurgency. But an emerging gap between domestic preference and international realities nearly always takes place when populistic considerations at home shape policies designed for abroad. As liberals were prone to do during the war in Vietnam, conservatives did during the war in Iraq; they constantly insisted on the light at the end of the tunnel, spoke in almost utopian language about the goals to be achieved, downplayed the costs involved in doing so, and turned a blind eye to the paradoxes and unexpected consequences of the American presence in that country. If Medicare reform was the perverse form that conservatism took in domestic policy to reproduce the flaws of the Great Society under Lyndon Johnson, the Iraqi war was the perverse form adopted by those conservatives seemingly bent on making all the mistakes Johnson did when he blundered into his unwinnable war in Southeast Asia. It all sounded so good, and Americans wanted to believe it would work, but as few results on the ground were achieved, opposition to the war began to increase. Populism could get the president and his team reelected. Populism could not win a war so badly justified and planned.

It was, in retrospect, too bad that so few conservative and realistic voices were heard in the initial years of the war against Iraq. For the war in Iraq would prove itself a near perfect example of why spending lots of money and speaking with the best of intentions cannot change the world, especially a world so foreign to Americans as Iraq. The war in Iraq represented nation-building of the most ambitious sort, undertaken with little knowledge of the nation to be rebuilt. It involved government waste on a scale that would put Boston's Big Dig to shame, complete with no-bid contracts, little supervision, and extensive cronyism. The notion that democracy could be brought to a land that was marked by ethnic conflict, and that was not even a country at the start of the twentieth century, flew in the face of history, experience, and prudence. Had liberals developed a plan for fighting a war as badly thought out, incoherently administered, and wildly unrealistic as this one, conservatives would have had a field day in opposition.[7] Because the plan was developed and implemented by conservatives, and because liberals, knowing full well that they would be attacked as treasonous if they opposed the war, mostly kept their thoughts to themselves, no significant opposition to the war in Iraq developed, with tragic consequences in terms of lives lost and dollars spent.

The question facing the Bush administration now, or any administration that follows it, is what to do in Iraq as the instability in that country continues or intensifies. (There is, of course, the possibility that a functioning democracy could emerge there, but this seems highly unlikely given Iraq's history and deep ethnic and religious divisions.) Here again the example of Vietnam may prove instructive. A war fought primarily by liberal presidents, Vietnam fueled a liberal opposition; the antiwar movement came from the Left and, because it turned violent, it ultimately worked to benefit the Right. Iraq, by contrast, is a conservative war and it has spawned no significant left-wing antiwar movement. Instead, opposition to the war in Iraq is most strongly manifest among groups usually identified with the Right: the military, which remains angry at Rumsfeld for his failures, isolationists and libertarians worried about the war's costs in money and lives, military families unable to understand the reasons why they sacrificed so much, and foreign policy realists of all political stripes aghast that their advice was ignored.

It remains to be seen whether conservatives will pay a political price for the failed war in Iraq the way liberals paid one for the failed war in Vietnam. But there is little doubt that as the public turns sour on the war, and as it becomes increasingly difficult to find new troops without a draft, the Bush administration will begin to withdraw Americans from Iraq; indeed, steps in this direction have already been taken. Once a democratically elected government is in place, the United States will almost certainly turn over more security tasks to Iraqis and increase the rate of troop withdrawal, even if pressures toward religious sectarianism increase and ethnic separatism intensifies. Any such instability in a country as strategically important as Iraq is likely to threaten America's own security, especially if Iran, whose nuclear ambitions constitute a real threat to American security, plays an enhanced role in the Shiite areas of Iraq. No realist could ever be pleased with such counterproductive results. But an administration that cares little about the long term in domestic policy can hardly be expected to make long-term security considerations part of its approach to foreign policy.

After liberalism overreached and began to lose its support among the American public, some liberals were extremely unwilling to admit mistakes, and even as Bill Clinton tried to move the Democrats more to the electable center, they held out for the purity of ideas fashioned in the heady days of the 1960s and 1970s. One can these days see a similar reluctance on the part of neoconservatives to acknowledge that the costs of trying to bring democracy to societies they view as threatening may be too high for Americans to pay. Iraq, after all, is not the only state in the world with a history of being run by bad people; there are the other two spokes of the axis of evil, Iran and North Korea, as well as numerous other societies that meddle in the affairs of other countries and treat their own citizens with marked brutality. The question of what the United States should do about such regimes is as serious and important as any question one can imagine. One cannot, and one certainly should not, turn away from such societies in the hope that the threats they pose will simply disappear. But nor can one solve the threat they pose by armed invasion. It may be the case that some combination of realism and Wilsonianism is the best formula for American foreign policy in future years. But the war in Iraq offers about as conclusive a proof as one can find that trying to impose democracy by outside force, especially in unilateral fashion without significant support from the international community, is neither wise nor possible. Conservatives, of all people, should have been the first to recognize this bitter truth.

IV

Populism, whether in left-wing or right-wing form, draws its energy from the democratizing energies unleashed under conditions of modern political life. But this does not mean that populism is by its very nature democratic. On the contrary, populistic movements are frequently accompanied by authoritarian tendencies that centralize political power in the state. If one believes, as conservatives such as Edmund Burke have believed, in the importance of institutions that stand as a buffer between the individual and the state, populism fails conservatism for two reasons: it gives too much power to the people *and* too much power to the state by bypassing the institutions and practices that flourish between them.

It should therefore not be surprising that while traditional conservatives bemoan the ever-increasing role of the state in modern political life, populistic conservatives encourage the centralization of state power. Politics is an unpredictable business, and it is impossible to know whether, thirty years from now, Americans will still be paying the costs of Mr. Bush's extraordinarily irresponsible ways of conducting both domestic and foreign policies. But given their relative youth, it is not out of question that thirty years from now, John Roberts and Samuel Alito will still be on the U.S. Supreme Court. And if both of them support the ideas of George W. Bush and Dick Cheney concerning the powers of the presidency, as their previous writings and decisions suggest, the centralization of power in Washington that Republican conservatives promoted in the early years of the twenty-first century is likely to be with us for some time to come.

A belief in the unchecked power of the president to act on behalf of the American people has been a constant theme reiterated by the Bush administration. No sooner did the attack of September 11 take place than John Yoo, deputy assistant attorney general in President Bush's Office of Legal Counsel, began to write memoranda arguing on behalf of extended presidential authority. In those memos, as well as in a book he wrote after leaving Washington to become a law professor in Berkeley, Yoo argued that the Constitution assigns to Congress a minimal role, and to the president a major if not exclusive role, in the conduct of war.[8] The text of that document does say that Congress has the power to "declare" war, but a proper understanding of the times in which the Constitution was written, according to Yoo, shows that this only means an acknowledgment by Congress that a war is already being fought. It is therefore perfectly within the spirit and letter of the Constitution for any contemporary president to choose whatever means he deems proper for purposes of fighting against America's enemies. In surely the most controversial of his arguments, Yoo claimed in one of his memoranda that if the president determines that torture is required for the United States to achieve its objections, he has the constitutional authority to allow torture to take place, even over the opposition of Congress.

Determined nonetheless to prevent other countries from torturing Americans, and then justifying their actions on the grounds that the United States does the same thing, Senator John McCain pushed hard for language attached to a defense appropriations bill to ban such actions. Equally determined to stop McCain's efforts, Vice President Cheney lobbied hard against it and, when that failed, lobbied for a CIA exception. McCain, however, carried the day, and the Bush administration was finally forced to accept the concerns of Congress. But not for long. Relying in part on advice offered in the past by Samuel Alito, the administration developed the practice of issuing signing statements putting into the record the president's interpretation of what was binding on him and what was not in laws passed by Congress and presented to him for his approval. In the signing language he used for the defense appropriation bill, the president once again indicated that he would not be bound by actions of Congress if he determined that such actions interfered with his powers as commander in chief.

An even greater controversy over presidential authority erupted after the *New York Times* revealed that the Bush administration had authorized wiretapping on American citizens without bringing the matter before special courts that Congress had created to protect Americans against abuses of the Fourth Amendment. Opposition to the president's authority, as with the case of torture, was bipartisan in nature and included Republican libertarians as well as Democrats. But the administration remained intransigent in its insistence on executive prerogatives, going so far as to launch an investigation, not into any individual liberties that may have been violated by the president's policy, but into the circumstances surrounding the leaking of that policy to the public. Clearly some key members of the administration, especially Vice President Cheney, believe that the president's powers have been too greatly curtailed in the years since Richard Nixon and Watergate, making it incumbent upon current occupants of that office to reassert such authority.

It is not just in the realm of foreign policy that the president should be able to assert his will over the other branches of government, many contemporary conservatives maintain. If the president is to govern effectively in domestic matters as well, he must, his defenders insist, be able to protect the prerogatives of his office, for example, by keeping secret such matters as the identity of those called to help formulate the administration's energy policy. When the administration (successfully) contested claims to make public the list of those who attended those meetings, it relied on the theory of the "unified executive," formulated by conservative legal scholars.[9] This theory holds that the presidency not only unifies all the powers of the executive branch, but that the president can be coequal to the other branches, including the Supreme Court, in interpreting the meaning of legislation. As applied to actual policy, the theory of the unified executive became the rallying point for legal scholars intent on making the case that presidents such as Ronald Reagan and George W. Bush could and should use all the powers of their office to promote a conservative agenda.

Whether the president should possess such broad powers is not the question to be posed here; a credible case could be made that he should. The more interesting point for present purposes is the way the debate over presidential power replays a situation in which conservatives find themselves justifying actions once advocated by liberals—and routinely condemned by conservatives. A half a century ago, liberals such as James Mac-Gregor Burns and Arthur Schlesinger, Jr., made the case for a strong executive. Enamored of the energy expended by Franklin Delano Roosevelt, and wary of the obstructionist proclivities of a more conservative Congress, they believed that the best way to protect and extend the New Deal—and, later on, to enter and succeed in the war against Germany and Japan—was to expand presidential authority.[10] It makes perfect sense, given this history, that when the Supreme Court stepped in to slap down the strong case being made on behalf of presidential power, it chastised a Democrat, Harry Truman, for his plan to take over U.S. steel companies.[11] For most of the postwar period, liberals became Hamiltonians while conservatives were Jeffersonians and Madisonians. The conservatism of a Richard Weaver or an M. E. Bradford, inspired by a preference for a southern way of life, would have been appalled by any aggrandizement of power at the national level. A conservatism rooted in the power of the president, however, would have especially aroused their ire; Lincoln, they believed, was the enemy at the gates, not the war president to be emulated.

Now, as the theory of the unified executive suggests, Republicans and conservatives find themselves more comfortable wearing Lincolnesque clothing. Doing so, however, drags them ever further away from the originalist doctrines conservatives once relied upon to denounce liberal activism. John Yoo makes strenuous arguments on behalf of the notion that the Constitution's framers understood the need for a strong executive, but to do so, he has little choice but to focus, not on the actual text of the document, but on the circumstances surrounding its writing. Others, including the legal theorists responsible for the theory of executive power, do not rely much at all on the original intent of the Framers; instead, they offer a comprehensive treatment of the way presidencies throughout American history acted on behalf of a unified executive in practice. These are all rich and fascinating arguments, but structurally, they are identical to arguments once made by liberals such as Bruce Ackerman, who insist that the Constitution is a living document that has been frequently amended through experience.[12] The theory of a unified executive may come to dominate Supreme Court jurisprudence with the arrival of justices sympathetic to the theory, but, in doing so, it will give strong support to the approach to constitutional interpretation developed by twentieth-century liberals.

This conclusion should not come as a surprise, because it only reinforces the fact that conservative legal theorists have been judicial activists for some time. The notion that the Supreme Court should be more protective than it has been toward property rights is little different in underlying logic from the efforts by liberal thinkers such as Ronald Dworkin to read the Constitution in a way protective of the rights of unpopular minorities; in both cases, a desired philosophic outcome is given preference over adherence to the text itself.[13] If judicial activism is defined as a willingness on the part of the Supreme Court to declare legislation unconstitutional—this is the definition frequently cited by Robert Bork is his defense of original intent—then conservatives on the court such as Scalia and Thomas are the true activists.[14] (The same could be said for Samuel Alito, who had no qualms declaring unconstitutional a ban on machine guns passed by Congress in his capacity as a circuit court judge.)[15] There is a certain honesty in all this; despite what advocates of original intent claim, interpretation is inevitable, and interpretation is frequently guided by preexisting political and ideological sympathies. But neither side in this debate can claim to adhere to fixed tradition. We are, in that sense, all liberals now, at least when it comes to relying on the judiciary to achieve political outcomes.

V

Liberalism in the postwar years may have had its flaws, but it had its strengths as well, and one of them—as it happened, one that would have a significant impact on the rise of neoconservatism—was its appreciation of irony. In the writings of Louis Hartz, Richard Hofstadter, and, most importantly, Lionel Trilling, liberals worried about the seeming success of liberalism.[16] All three writers understood that a liberalism that became too sure of itself ran the risk of losing its ability to question itself. A liberalism without skepticism would be a liberalism stripped of its capacity to treat politics with detachment, including the kind of detachment that liberals ought to bring to their own political outlook on the world.

One can express appreciation for contemporary conservatism's tactics, its ability to get its way in the world, and its capacity to turn liberalism into an object of scorn, but there is little appreciation of irony in the conservatism of a George W. Bush or Dick Cheney. This, more than its willingness to mimic liberalism's ambitious goals for political action and experience-driven means for reaching them, is the most striking way in which the conservatism of today resembles the liberalism of yesterday. As practiced by George W. Bush, conservatism never acknowledges error, rarely engages in introspection, and shows no signs of self-doubt. In contrast to the more whimsical conservatism of William F. Buckley, Jr., it has lost whatever sense of ironic detachment conservatism once displayed as it confronted the paradoxes and problems of modern political life. Populistic conservatism is serious business, deadly serious. Like the extreme Left, but quite unlike the ironic liberals who had turned their backs on Stalin and Trotsky, it is out to change the world, a task for which diversions into introspection and irony would be self-defeating.

None of this bothers conservative political activists such as Karl Rove and Grover Norquist, to pick two of the least ironic of contemporary conservatives; they would, I imagine, regard comparisons to someone like Lenin as a compliment. The goal of their conservatism is to win the next election—or even, which seems increasingly unlikely, to create a new era of Republican domination in American politics. But if the goal of a conservative movement is to leave a lasting imprint on American political thought, the unwillingness of conservatives to treat their own ideas with the same sense of detachment that liberals like Trilling advocated for the Left is a problem indeed. Modern democracy is not the best environment for conservatives to reduce the size of government, increase the power of business, or fight wars designed to increase America's power in the world. By adjusting its goals and its tactics to the realities of modern democracy, conservatism these days dominates the media, has transformed American politics, and will influence the judiciary for the foreseeable future. But it is unlikely to leave behind a sense of how the world ought to work that will guide future conservatives when liberals, as they inevitably will do, become popular once again.

NOTES

1. See, for example, Jeffrey Hart, "The Burke Habit," *Wall Street Journal,* December 27, 2005, at http://www.opinionjournal.com/ac/?id=110007730 (accessed March 13, 2008).

2. Albert Jay Nock, *Memoirs of a Superfluous Man* (New York: Harper, 1943).

3. I elaborate this argument in "The Revolution That Never Was," *New Republic*, June 7, 1999, 42–47.

4. Samantha Power, *"A Problem from Hell": America and the Age of Genocide* (New York: Basic Books, 2002).

5. Walter Russell Mead, *Special Providence: American Foreign Policy and How It Changed the World* (New York: Knopf, 2001).

6. The best account of these trends is James Mann, *The Rise of the Vulcans: The History of Bush's War Cabinet* (New York: Viking, 2004).

7. The best book on the war in Iraq is Thomas E. Ricks, *Fiasco: The American Military Adventure in Iraq* (New York: Penguin, 2006).

8. John Yoo, *The Powers of War and Peace: The Constitution and Foreign Affairs after 9/11* (Chicago: University of Chicago Press, 2005).

9. Christopher S. Yoo, Steven G. Calabresi, and Anthony Colangelo, "The Unitary Executive in the Modern Era, 1945–2001," *Iowa Law Review* 90, no. 2 (2005).

10. Presidential power is justified implicitly in Arthur Schlesinger, *A Thousand Days: John F. Kennedy in the White House* (Boston: Houghton Mifflin, 1965), and explicitly in James MacGregor Burns, *The Deadlock of Democracy: Four-Party Politics in America* (Englewood Cliffs, N.J.: Prentice Hall, 1963).

11. *Youngstown Sheet and Tube Co. v. Sawyer*, 343 U.S. 937 (1952).

12. Bruce Ackerman, *We, the People* (Cambridge: Belknap Press of Harvard University Press, 1991).

13. Michael Greve, *Real Federalism: Why It Matters, How It Could Happen* (Washington, D.C.: American Enterprise Institute Press, 1999).

14. Thomas M. Keck, *The Most Activist Supreme Court in History: The Road to Modern Judicial Conservatism* (Chicago: University of Chicago Press, 2004). See also Paul Gewirtz and Chad Golder, "So Who Are the Activists?" *New York Times*, July 6, 2005.

15. *U.S. v. Rybar*, 103 F.3d 273 (3rd Cir. 1996).

16. Louis Hartz, *The Liberal Tradition in America: An Interpretation of American Political Thought since the Revolution* (New York: Harcourt Brace, 1955); Richard Hofstadter, *The Age of Reform: From Bryan to FDR* (New York: Vintage, 1955); Lionel Trilling, *The Liberal Imagination: Essays on Literature and Society* (New York: Viking, 1950).

PART THREE

A Divided People?

The Future of the Liberal Family

Susan Shell

Recent evidence of a "baby bust" across most advanced liberal societies raises warning signs of a potential crisis. A new "specter" is haunting Europe (and not it alone): a precipitous decline in birthrates. Even as liberal societies succeed beyond all previous economic measure, many of them, it seems, are failing to sustain themselves at the most basic level: maintenance of a constant, liberally acculturated population from one generation to another. While this failure is more pronounced in some countries than in others, and while the phenomenon of declining population is by no means limited to societies that can plausibly be deemed liberal, a markedly declining birthrate among societies that are generally held up as models for political and moral emulation is cause for reflection and concern.[1]

To be sure, that material luxury should be accompanied by declining birthrates should not be altogether surprising. Moralists from the time of Caesar Augustus (who answered the alarm by instituting a "bachelor tax") have noted that the corruptions bred by wealth are reflected first and foremost in the family. Eighteenth-century thinkers such as Montesquieu gave new voice to the ancient worry that an urbanized aristocracy would not reproduce itself. Indeed, for Rousseau, the association between wealth, corruption, and declining birthrate seemed strong enough to make birthrate in itself a rough measure of civic health.[2]

But there is also good reason to believe that something new is going on. Today's wealthy liberal societies are different by many measures from urban aristocracies of the past—and not least, in the sheer numbers sharing in the wealth. One might be tempted to attribute today's low birthrates mainly to the "pill" and other such fruits of modern technology. But technology alone seems insufficient to explain the phenomenon in question. If we have new means of preventing pregnancy and otherwise dissociating sexual activity from procreation, we also are far better at combating the diseases to which roughly half of all children once succumbed. It is not only that we live longer; almost all children can now count on living to advanced adulthood. Parents no longer need fear the tragic losses that made earlier generations of parents hostages to fortune (as Bacon put it). And now that adults typically live into their eighties and nineties in relatively good health, parenthood is no longer a lifelong occupation. If children are no longer the economic blessing they once were, they are arguably also less burdensome both temporally and emotionally (if not financially).

It is true that here, as in much else, the United States is "exceptional," maintaining something close to a replacement-level birthrate among native-born Americans, and rates slightly higher among first-generation immigrants. But these relatively cheerful statistics are leavened by a relatively high rate of poverty, fatherlessness, and infant mortality among U.S. children in comparison with other liberal societies. We may be having more children than our European and Canadian counterparts, but it is not clear that we are investing more in raising them. The women who are best equipped, by middle-class standards, to bring up children in America (i.e., the relatively well educated and affluent) are less likely to do so than those whose life-chances are more marginal.[3]

Without doubt, some of the poor and less educated may be better parents than some of the rich and highly credentialed. Still, the large number of U.S. children raised without fathers and in poverty, and who also lack decent schools, a healthy diet, and adequate access to health care should give pause.[4] The physical stature of Europeans is growing while that of Americans (even after discounting for natural variations among ethnic groups) is shrinking. There may be more children in America, but it is not clear that they will grow up to be as civic minded or as physically and mentally productive as generations of the past.

Why then are most liberal societies failing to sustain themselves across generations (as seems currently to be the case)? And what, if anything, might or should be done about it? It is always difficult to assess complex phenomena like this one, especially at a time in which old patterns seem to be breaking down and new ones have not yet fully established themselves. We do not know what the present child-bearing generation will ultimately choose with respect to child-rearing. And public discourse often bears a tenuous relationship with actual conduct. If polling data is to be believed, most young people in America continue to aspire to conventional marriage with children. And yet . . . something seems to be amiss. Women—especially those who are relatively wealthy and well educated—are marrying later (and at lower rates) than ever before.[5] And young men seem increasingly eager to prolong the pleasures of adolescence into what was once considered early middle age. With both men and women having children later (if at all), a declining number of children is almost inevitable—along with a declining investment in child-rearing during adults' most energetic years.[6] At the same time, those who seem best able to provide children with the educational advantages and financial resources needed to succeed in an increasingly competitive and insecure economy seem less and less inclined to do so.

Not incidentally, the declining birthrate has gone hand in hand with new legal definitions of marriage and the family that assign childbearing and child-rearing an increasingly marginal status.[7] As Mary Ann Glendon, Daniel Cere, and others have argued, the old, conjugal understanding of marriage, oriented primarily toward generation, has given way, in many legal circles, to a new "relational" model that mainly emphasizes the needs and wishes of adults.[8] Families are, more and more, whatever adults choose to make them.

To be sure, the very posing of the question—whither the liberal family—will strike some as an illegitimate reprisal of "eugenicist" worries of the past, that is, as an alarming expression of the sort of racial and class-based anxiety once common among racial and economic elites on both sides of the Atlantic. To such an audience, "liberal" will sound like a code word for "white" (or rich).[9]

Interest in the liberal family, however, predates the eugenics movement (and related social and intellectual pathologies) by several centuries. Indeed, classic liberal theory is as deeply concerned with the family as it is with property and the social compact. We are prone to forget that the "family values" often trumpeted today presuppose the destruction of family values in their traditional form, which emphasized the authority of fathers, and often set family against family at the expense of common citizenship. Partly owing to the political and rhetorical success of earlier liberal thinkers, we are inclined to view the family as a pillar of society rather than as the shaker and destroyer it has sometimes been.

Alexis de Tocqueville, perhaps the greatest observer of American democracy in its formative period, did not doubt the crucial importance of a new kind of family to democracy's overall success. Never one to mince words, he goes so far as to declare that "in America, the family, taking this word in its Roman and aristocratic sense, does not exist."[10] In its place, he says, a new domestic arrangement has sprung up, in which the bonds of natural affection have largely replaced the chilly formalities of paternal rule. In the democratic family, "the father exercises little power other than what others are pleased to grant to the tenderness and the experience of an old man"—that, and the expectations that arise from his democratic freedom to dispose of his property as he sees fit. Siblings no longer defer to the eldest, gaining in friendship what they lose in dynastic loyalty. And women are raised to be mistresses of their own destiny—a freedom they combine, to Tocqueville's admiration, with a voluntary surrender to the chaste bonds of domesticity that is hardly known among their aristocratic sisters. This remarkable feminine "superiority"—to which he largely attributes America's "singular prosperity and growing force"[11]—is not, to be sure, without its drawbacks. In cultivating women's judgment at the expense of their imagination, America makes women "honest" and "cold" wives rather than "tender" and "amiable" companions.[12] In a society devoted to commercial enterprise and the art of getting on, even domestic retreat loses something of its European charm. The American woman has a feminine shape but a masculine mind and heart. In her free acceptance of social inferiority she becomes man's moral equal and perhaps even his superior. She sacrifices her freedom in part out of well-understood self-interest, given social conventions that present her with the stark choice of domesticity or the obliteration of her social existence. But the pride that elevates her choice beyond prudent selfishness is shadowed by sadness—as with those women of the frontier, raised in East Coast refinement, who steadfastly accompany their restless husbands westward. Their faces seemed drawn and pale, Tocqueville says, but their gaze was steady. They seemed both "sad and resolute."[13]

In sum, the family that Tocqueville encounters in America is a necessary leaven to the selfish individualism that prevails more generally. Natural affection and womanly noblesse oblige temper the cold calculation that would otherwise drive individuals and families apart; and they lend encouragement to the "small associations" that give scope to personal pride and without which democratic freedom cannot flourish.[14]

Tocqueville's powerful description of the American family would have been reasonably accurate through much of the nineteenth and early twentieth centuries. It would hardly be acceptable today, except, perhaps, with respect to certain isolated religious communities. The settlement that he describes between sentiment and calculation, self-interest and sacrifice, social inequality and moral superiority, seems to have broken down irrevocably. Still something of his depiction remains if only in our sense of what we have lost. We still aspire to form stable, child-rearing nuclear families, bound by some vaguely defined blend of affection, self-interest, and personal transcendence—an escape, on multiple levels, from the pettiness of a life wholly devoted to "getting and spending."

In investigating the weakening of the domestic ideal on behalf of which Tocqueville advocates, an examination of what earlier liberal thinkers had to say about the family proves most helpful. For that ideal (and the standards of normalcy that it continues to inspire) was partly the result of successive liberal efforts to refound the family from the ground up. To be sure, there are many other, nonintellectual factors that have shaped the contemporary American family, from geographic mobility to birth control. Still, to a degree not always sufficiently appreciated, the liberal democratic family as we know it was a deliberate social construct, designed to replace the illiberal family that still existed in Tocqueville's France as a living memory.

The importance of the family to classical liberal political thought often goes unnoticed—in part, because thinkers like Locke tried to make it so. By relegating the family to a "private" sphere in which public life takes no direct or immediate interest, liberalism sought to disrupt the fatal (natural) bond between obedience to fathers and obedience to rulers.

Early liberal thought not only aimed to decouple rulership from fatherhood—the main thrust of Locke's *First Treatise of Government*. Thinkers like Locke also entrusted to the family a variety of vital political functions traditionally claimed by Crown and Church. The family, from Locke forward, is a little laboratory of republican self-government, in which children absorb the core civic lessons they will need to perpetuate a society of free individuals. Democratic family life and liberal self-government are thus mutually implicated in complex ways to which Tocqueville (who still knew something of the alternative firsthand), among others, drew striking attention. It is perhaps not insignificant, in this regard, that George Washington, the "father" of our country, was also childless. Washington managed, somehow, to be the "father" of his country without making us all his "children" (in something like the royal manner). A Washington with his own children (with whom other citizens could identify) might have found it harder to avoid reawakening illiberal instincts of subservience that the founders, and not least Washington himself, were determined to put down.

Marriage, as conceived by Locke, is a voluntary contract between a man and a woman, not an affair of parents or extended families. It is an arrangement of "affection" as well as interest, the community of which flows from human foresight, combined with the natural duty and tenderness of parents toward their offspring. Locke appears to have no great illusions as to the attachment of parents, especially fathers, toward their children, absent a certain common affection, renewed and maintained by woman's dependence through repeated pregnancies.[15] Nor does he lay much stress on erotic attraction, which might well give rise to such "uncertain mixture" and "frequent solutions of society" as would "mightily disturb" provision for a couple's "common issue." Still, Locke would allow the dissolution of marriage once such provision is made, and even suggests, in private notes, some tolerance for "left-handed unions," whose terms depend entirely on the wishes of the two parties.[16]

Like property, marriage for Locke is an expression of natural rights more fundamental than anything we owe to civil society. The latter is thus limited—morally if not legally—in its authority over what goes on within the domestic circle: "conjugal society" is the first instance and example of a "private sphere," arising even before there is a public sphere. The conjugal relation, however, also differs from other natural exchanges of property. "Conjugal society" is "made by a voluntary compact between a man and woman," which consists "mainly in such a right in one another's bodies as is necessary to its chief end: procreation." Unlike other contractual exchanges in the state of nature, and like the civil compact itself, marriage has a predetermined purpose—preservation of the greatest number—that both defines it in advance and sets upon it certain necessary terms and limits.[17]

The relation between parents and their offspring starts with the rights of children, not with duties owed to parents; and these rights shape and limit what men and women are naturally entitled to agree to by way of rights to one another's bodies.[18] As with the rules concerning the acquisition of property more generally, the law of nature looks to human preservation.[19] Marriage thus draws with it "mutual support . . . and a communion of interest" necessary not only to unite the couple's care but also for the "nourishment and maintenance" of any common offspring.

But conjugal society differs from its civil counterpart in several crucial respects. First and most importantly: only civil society requires individuals to yield their natural right to "execute the law of nature" to the exclusive power of a magistrate. This not being necessary to secure the ends of marriage, fathers (and mothers) have no more power in the state of nature to punish those who break the law of nature (a power, with regard to children, that is much softened by both interest and affection) than human beings have generally. In sum, Aristotle's "Cycloptic" father, who rules tyrannically over wives and progeny (the two not necessarily distinguished), is replaced, in Locke's precivil "state of nature," by a head who is more CEO than brutal tyrant.

To be sure, fathers and husbands generally have, by virtue of those ends, a certain necessary prerogative. But Locke is careful to distinguish it from the traditional sway that it might seem to resemble superficially. Mutual consent as a requirement of marriage has deep roots in Christianity. Locke goes out of his way, however, to upset the underlying theological and political metaphor that usually accompanies that requirement (as in Filmer's *Patriarcha*): woman's willing submission to her husband is like that of the community of believers to Christ (and, by extension, that of subjects to their king); it is, that is to say, part of a chain of morally and religiously grounded authority and submission that stretches from God's vicar to the lowest of God's children.

The marital relation is, without doubt, special even by traditional Christian standards. The explicitly *consensual* character of the wife's submission (a consent largely lacking in the case of slaves and subjects) enables marriage to mirror with peculiar precision the relationship between Christ and the community of believers who have accepted him.[20] Locke, however, treats the "specialness" of marriage in a different way—that is, by carving out for it a special zone of protection against the state that is clearer even than that afforded other forms of private property. "All the ends of marriage being to be obtained under politic government, as well as in the state of nature, the civil magistrate doth not abridge the right or power of either naturally necessary to those ends, viz. procreation and mutual support and assistance whilst they are together, but only decides any controversy that may arise between man and wife about them."[21] Far from urging wives to submit out of Christian duty, Locke encourages them to consult their own advantage. Although "the rule," or last determination of the will, in matters of common concern falls "naturally" to the man's share as "the abler and the stronger" (as he generally is in transactions with the external world), the wife remains in "full and free possession of what is by contract her peculiar right, and gives the husband no more power over her life than she has over his." If husbands, for Locke, are "naturally" like CEOs, wives are naturally like members of the board who are empowered to select or fire him. Men and women, in short, enter into conjugal contract from a position of natural equality as concerns "dominion" if not ability and strength. And women are (quietly) advised to make additional provision, if they can, to keep some property under their own exclusive control. The essence of marriage, in other words, is not linked to "coverture," the traditional doctrine that cancels the wife's separate legal personality on the grounds that man and woman are "one flesh" of which he is the "head."[22] This may be a far cry from contemporary conceptions of legal equality, but it is a good deal closer than "common law" practice in Locke's time, when principles of primogeniture and coverture were still much in force.[23]

Without attempting a complete account of Locke's radical revision of traditional notions of marriage and the family, especially as it pertains to differences between parental and political power, one can say this much: the civil purpose of marriage, on Locke's account, lies primarily in the production of future members of society who are reasonable, industrious, and self-reliant. Parents, especially fathers, have a duty to educate their children accordingly, a duty whose fulfillment earns them a right to the "honor," though not obedience, of their adult offspring. (Mothers, it seems, earn that right from the sheer labor involved in giving birth to them.) The resulting understanding is a clearheaded, minimally "romantic," but also highly individualistic partnership, which puts major emphasis on the equality of the contracting parties (except where biology intervenes), and on the independence of adults, both male and female, from the authority of parents along with such traditional dispositions of family property as the rule of primogeniture. It also locates the principal source of stable, mutual affection between husband and wife in their common interest in providing for their children, an interest that has its own industry-inspiring and otherwise civilly benign effect. It also puts a premium on the ability of men to choose their own heirs, the better to control their adult children (over whom they have no claims to obedience other than those flowing from the honor and affection they have earned).

Locke does not go so far as to make generation a necessary aim of conjugal society in any particular case; but he does express doubts that without such a locus of mutual care most conjugal partnerships would readily endure, or inspire industriousness of the most reasonable and foresighted kind.[24] Marriage without prospect of children is a voluntary compact like any other.

The religious basis of marriage Locke hardly mentions (apart from a brief reference to a certain "rule of the Creator," whose stipulations concerning care of offspring apply equally if not more so to "the inferior creatures"). Evidently, the same principles sketched out in his "Letter on Toleration" would here apply. Religious ceremonies and rules concerning marriage are a matter for private life, and should be tolerated and encouraged so long as they foster, or at least do not undermine, the appropriate purposes of both marriage and civil government.[25] To underscore the fact that marriage is not essentially "sacramental" (or otherwise freighted with high religious meaning), Locke suggests that marriages might be dissolved, like "any other voluntary compacts," once "procreation and education are secured, and inheritance taken care of," there being "no necessity in the nature of the thing, nor to the ends of it, that it should always be for life"—at least where "positive law does not ordain such contracts to be perpetual." Further stipulations as to the character of marriage (such as its permanence) are matters to be decided civilly, on nonreligious grounds—for example, with a view to securing the power of both husband and wife insofar as it is "naturally necessary" to both "procreation" and "mutual assistance and support."

In sum, Lockean marriage, rightly understood, is a voluntary compact that is unique in kind. *Like* the civil compact, and *unlike* other voluntary contracts, it entails specific rights and duties necessary to the natural purpose of preservation. *Unlike* the civil compact, and *like* other voluntary contracts, marriage does not set up a head with the power of life and death over its members, a power that would be contrary to the law of nature.

At the same time, civil and conjugal society for Locke are mutually supporting counterparts. Without the civil equality of adult citizens on display, the natural equality of members of the family tends (as history shows) to fade from view. Habituated to obedience, adult children continue to defer to parents beyond the point that they are able to "shift for themselves" and parental duties cease along with their authority. Civil equality among all able adults sets up a clear goal toward which parents' efforts, and children's hopes, are naturally directed. This counters, in turn, the slavish and tyrannic habits that set in when families are left to their own devices, as with tribal societies of the past.[26] (Cyclopses, in other words, are also in their own way "natural.")

The family, for its part, is equally necessary to civil society, for which it is a school of both enterprise and common purpose. Children learn ways of industriousness, foresight, and personal independence and affection that offset the tendencies toward "quarrelsomeness" and "contentiousness" to which many human beings are naturally subject. If reason, or the "law of nature," governs those who "will but consult it,"[27] the Lockean family helps render that counsel habitual.

Many elements of the Lockean view of marriage have found an especially welcome reception in America. The relative equality and informality of the American family that so struck Tocqueville was partly the result, as Tocqueville notes, of a regime of abstract rights (similar to those espoused by Locke). And the United States, in contrast to Britain and other European nations, has historically treated marriage primarily as a contract rather than a sacrament (at least for civic purposes). Publicly recognized religious figures may officiate; but nothing legally distinguishes such religious ceremonies from wholly civic ones.

To be sure, all is not sweetness and light. The new freedom of individuals to bestow property as they wish, along with related breaks with legal and religious tradition, sets up new areas of familial conflict and hypocrisy that modern writers—from Jane Austen to Honoré de Balzac and beyond—have brilliantly exploited. (Indeed, the power thus to shape the future of one's heirs is not unlike the power of a novelist to plot the future of his characters.) A new "sentimental school" rose up in Britain partly as a reaction to the crasser implications of Locke's new domestic dispensation. But no one saw its limitations in starker terms than Jean-Jacques Rousseau, whose romantic reformulation constitutes a kind of second founding of the liberal family.

For Rousseau, the self-interested bond uniting members of the modern "Lockean" family destroys its essential character. Rousseau does not disagree with Locke as to the harmfulness of traditional notions of paternal power and wifely submissiveness. Nor does he dispute Locke's claim that the family's "natural" end mainly consists in preservation of offspring, just as its civil end consists in rearing law-abiding and productive citizens. But Locke's deliberately ambiguous blend of self-interest, duty, and affection works against those purposes by tending to turn natural partners into secret enemies. The Lockean family (like its civil counterpart) has too much to do with calculation, too little with love (a word Locke hardly mentions).

Rousseau's solution is an extraordinary feat of imaginative retrieval and redirection, as indicated by the title of his best-selling novel *The New Eloise,* and most thoroughly elaborated in *Emile,* his famous work on education. According to literary tradition, the lovers Eloise and Abelard were separated first by the violence of Eloise's relatives (who castrated Abelard), then by respective monastic seclusion. Here each achieved a kind of spiritual redemption—she through her letters to her beloved, he through his philosophic writings. Rousseau takes the longing and pathos that surrounds this medieval literary hero and heroine and redirects them toward ordinary men and women. If the altogether admirable and attractive Julie (Rousseau's "new Eloise") is unhappy, it is only because, deferring to her father's wishes, she did not marry the man she loved. All further complications derive from this fundamental error and crime against the heart.

But love, though it rests on natural sentiments, must be carefully cultivated, on Rousseau's account, if it is to serve as a support of family and civic life rather than subverting them. *Emile* is a guidebook to that new domestic garden. Here ordinary conjugal relations are invested with sentiments and longings formerly the preserve of religious life or the aristocratic subjects of medieval poetry. The key, for Rousseau, lies in natural differences between the sexes, rooted in biology and necessary to the reproduction of the species, differences that Locke only minimally acknowledged.[28] These differences give rise to distinct sentiments that are more crucial to the formation of the family than any compact based upon self-interested consent. At the same time, they do not make for a simple natural hierarchy of ruler and ruled, as in traditional, preliberal models of the family. Instead, they support relations of mutual dependence and equality that are expressed through different yet complementary sorts of mastery, men ruling directly through their strength, women indirectly through their modesty and prudence.

Rousseau's new "family romance" revolves around the mystery of woman's "refusal," which inspires in men both an intensification, and a sublimation, of a sexual interest that is otherwise episodic and without (for men at least) much psychological or moral consequence. Women, on this account, literally make the family, by arousing feelings of love in naturally asocial men. And the family, for its part, as a model of attachment without domination, provides the necessary foundation for a healthy politics more generally. Men who do not love their wives and mothers will lack the habits of mind and soul required to love their country.[29] In sum: self-interest does not suffice as a basis either for family life or for social life more generally, and must be supplemented by feeling and imagination, stimulated, in the first instance, by women's natural modesty.

The Rousseauian model of the family inspired a wave of moral and cultural reform, not least in post-Revolutionary America: the American family was characterized early on, as Tocqueville saw, not only by Lockean equality and informality but also by heightened bonds of familial affection that were at least partly inspired by new literary and artistic models that retain a significant hold on us.[30] Though today's youth may be less hopeful and less patient in their search than generations past, most young men and women still aspire to find a "soul mate." In sum: romantic love remains, to the contemporary liberal mind, a crucial element of individual happiness and a sustainer of social life, rather than (as Locke seems to have believed) an at best troublesome complication. Indeed, this implicitly Rousseauian understanding continues to inform the views of some contemporary social critics who presume that men are natural savages and loners who must be civilized by women and marriage.[31]

One can dispute an anthropology that makes men (but not their sisters) natural loners. Still, from a liberal perspective, this may be a useful fiction, at least up to a point. "Manly" virtue, in liberal societies, necessarily consists more in "self-reliance" than in martial valor or magnanimity. It may therefore be helpful to exaggerate the degree to which men's desire for independence naturally outweighs their desire to dominate. Sentiments of spousal, maternal, and filial attachment sustain relationships without setting up hierarchies between superiors and inferiors (as in preliberal understandings of the family). And they provide a haven of love and mutual regard that is more attractive by far than the society of schemers and secret enemies that the Lockean family can seem to resemble.

Still, in assigning to sentiment (and women) so great a role in the establishment and maintenance of social bonds that transcend selfish motives, the Rousseauian model may ask more than either sentiment (or women) can deliver—at least once background social and religious norms of sexual modesty and womanly self-sacrifice have been eroded. Certainly Rousseau never expected it to work except in small homogeneous communities, or for those otherwise protected from the corrupting influence of urban life and commerce.

The work of reconciling Rousseauian moral sentiment with Lockean self-concern falls to a third wave of liberal familial reform. Much of the strength of the American family, as Tocqueville portrays it, lay in its success in adapting the Rousseauian model to the needs and demands of an expanding commercial society. Liberal thinkers from the Framers' generation into the later nineteenth century adopted a sentimentally inspired hope that romantic love, appropriately domesticated, might give moral and spiritual depth to marriage without upsetting its enlightened core or interfering with its liberal civic goals. The resulting ideal attempted to combine the passion of erotic love with the dignity of self-imposed vows and the prudent self-control involved in getting on.[32]

This third wave was aided (somewhat improbably) by the moral and legal theories of Immanuel Kant. Though deeply influenced by Rousseau's understanding of the natural difference between the sexes, Kant's legal reasoning goes further even than Locke in reducing marriage to a contract between two formally identical and equal adults.

Kant's other important additions to Locke's conception of marriage are twofold: first, an insistence on the role of marriage, or legally recognized and enforced monogamy, in reconciling sexual intercourse with human dignity; second, a concern with the tendency of the enlightened to avoid fertility, at least in its legitimized monogamous form.

This latter worry on Kant's part (which, in current circumstances, seems especially prescient) leads him to recommend a "bachelor tax" (or other such device) for the support of poor and out-of-wedlock children.[33] Doubtful of the ability of the poor to raise up rational, self-sufficient citizens (Locke is content that fathers, whose condition requires it, put their young to work "as soon as they are able"), Kant also puts greater stress than earlier liberal thinkers on the duty of the public at large, especially on matters bearing on education, and a related role for public welfare as an extension of the state's normal police power. In short, Kant tweaks liberalism in the direction of a more active role for government in the maintenance and education of future citizens, and a more robust role for marriage in maintaining public decency and the moral dignity of (sexually active) adults.

But Kant's thought also reaches forward into the present in ways more subtle: Kant is famous for insisting that marriage, as a legal institution, has nothing directly to do with procreation, or any other natural end.[34] To be sure, Kant assumes that sexual activity is likely to result in children, who have a right to parental support and education (on the grounds that they have been brought into the world without their consent!). Still, Kant's formal concept of marriage is an important source of a new model of the family—one that is rapidly replacing romantic models of the past. This new ideal puts heightened emphasis on adult choice, not as a condition of romantic attachment (as with Rousseau) but as a vehicle of individual "free expression." Kant, a lifelong bachelor who famously defined marriage as a "contract for the perpetual use by each party of the other's sexual faculties," seems an unlikely source for this new "expressive" view of marriage. And in many ways, his theory of marriage falls short of, or otherwise contradicts, today's "progressive" thinking. And yet to the extent that choice today has assumed an almost "spiritual" dimension (as in current Supreme Court doctrine in regard to privacy), liberalism has Kant partly to thank for it. Without Kant's elevation of personal "autonomy" to the status of a fundamental moral principle, it seems doubtful that today's claims on behalf of untrammeled sexual choice would have the legal and moral traction that they now do. For Kant himself, as earlier mentioned, this legally protected right to choose is hedged by many ethical strictures, it being his deeply held view that sexual activity without a procreative purpose is, though legally permissible, intrinsically degrading.[35] Still, as such strictures have fallen by the wayside—due, in part, to liberalism itself—the remaining legal conception of marriage as a contract among adults for their own mutual satisfaction, and without any essential relation to procreation, is Kant's standing legacy on matters sexual and spousal. Kant's effort to invest marriage with transcendental meaning has thus had the perverse effect of undermining its larger civil purpose. This is especially so now that birth control and the new sexual mores that support it make childless marriage as respectable as it is easy.[36]

What can be learned from these consecutive philosophic formulations that both enabled and, in my view, ultimately disrupted the Tocquevillian domestic settlement? And what, if any, is their bearing on challenges facing us today?

For all their differences, each of the above approaches shares a common appreciation of the *peculiarity* of the liberal family in its relation to the larger powers and purposes of the state. Liberal societies depend on families to perform tasks "in private" that other regimes assume directly and in public. Liberal societies depend largely on the family to inculcate norms of self-reliance and equality. And they depend largely on the family to sustain religion and other sources of ethical restraint and aspiration. The private character of these efforts helps secure both the liberal freedoms that we treasure and the powerful but limited government needed to support them. But it also exposes these important functions to a crucial source of weakness that laws cannot easily remedy directly. As mores have changed, especially mores related to sex and generation, the unearned ethical capital inherited from preliberal times has been depleted. (Tocqueville partly attributed the domestic chastity he praised to the lingering legacy of Puritanism.) And as children become more and more financially burdensome to their parents, the problem only grows worse. Raising the next generation responsibly is a social good whose cost mostly falls on individual parents. Indeed, misplaced environmental worries can even make those who choose to have children seem "selfish." It is true that religion, especially in America, remains a potent cultural influence. But it is unclear whether religion in its current form suffices to ensure the investment in the next generation that is necessary to the maintenance of civic community, whether liberal or otherwise.

That each of these approaches sought to remedy perceived defects in the one preceding has further lessons for today—among them, the dubiousness of any simple return to earlier models. For better and for worse, the times in which Lockean or Rousseauian domestic ideals might be deemed sufficient are behind us. Individuals today enjoy a moral latitude that is interwoven with our bedrock conceptions of liberal justice. This latitude is, one might say, the price we pay for wishing to invest subjective satisfaction with a higher moral purpose without reverting to preliberal constraints on human freedom.

If something effective is to be done, it must acknowledge this new moral latitude, which expresses itself in everything from the disappearance of antiobscenity restrictions and the massive entry of women into the workplace to the movement for gay marriage.[37]

True, many Americans continue to be moved by religiously inspired models of marriage and the family. With the possible exception of the issue of gay marriage, however, such models seem unlikely to have much public effect, at least for the foreseeable future.[38]

I have neither the space nor competence to propose adequate solutions to the difficulties at hand. The following practical approaches, however, would seem to hold promise.

1. Reasserting the civic purpose and dignity of marriage. Marriage today is often treated as nothing more than a package of public benefits for the convenience of private individuals (as in the Uniform Marriage and Divorce Act of 1987). So construed, it is difficult to see why marriage, which expends public resources on some but not others, should exist at all. If getting married (and raising children) is nothing more than a personal "lifestyle" choice, the single have fair reason to complain when they are denied its fiscal benefits. Marriage needs to be seen for what, civically speaking, it is: an institution necessary to the long-term flourishing and perpetuation of a liberal society. Asserting that purpose, and the dignity that flows from it, should not be left to the efforts of private religious groups but set forth on public grounds in which all citizens of a liberal democracy can share. Pushing back against the civil disestablishment of marriage (e.g., by distinguishing between civil union, available to same-sex couples and other domestic partners, and marriage as such) can also help highlight the peculiar civic purposes of marriage in a liberal society.

2. *Reclaiming liberal fatherhood.* The very word *liberty,* from the Latin word for "brother," suggests the importance of a peculiar sort of fatherhood to the flourishing of liberal society. Liberal fathers are in a certain sense their children's civic siblings. They must perform the difficult task of guiding without ruling; they must teach their children to respect authority when it is reasonably and rightly exercised and to oppose it when it is abused. They must impose discipline on their children without cowing them or inhibiting their initiative. In short, they must help instill a sense of honor consistent with the spirit of equality. Of course, mothers too perform such tasks. But as Shakespeare's *Coriolanus* shows, motherly efforts to instill courage and similar qualities may have their own peculiar limits and distortions. At the very least, children who grow up without the consistent presence of a man they can admire and trust seem disadvantaged in a serious way. The extraordinarily high percentage of children growing up today without fathers (or other stable and protective male figures) is thus a kind of civic scandal—a scandal to which some combination of misplaced political correctness, anger at the poor, and sheer habituation has made us oddly and conspicuously indifferent.[39] This is not to say that mothers cannot raise children on their own (or with female partners) successfully; but to treat this as normative, or even "optimal" (as with some recent scholarship) is an affront to common sense.

Reclaiming a special *liberal* role for fathers differs from the position of some religious conservatives, who seek to restore what they regard as a more authentically biblical (and nonliberal) understanding of the family. George Lakoff is thus seriously off the mark when he contrasts "nurturing" and "strict father" models of the family—the former Democratic and progressive, the latter Republican and disciplinary—as if they were the only relevant options.[40] In truth, the liberal parent is neither. Neither a domestic regime of pure nurturance (which treats human beings like plants that grow properly so long as they are fed, watered, and sheltered) nor of harsh discipline (which treats them as evil creatures whose will must be broken for the Lord) is likely to promote qualities of liberal democratic citizenship at its best.

Lakoff thus presents us with a false choice: gender-neutral nurturance (his favored metaphor) or harsh and unbending paternal discipline (the "conservative" alternative). In my view what is instead needed—both by an electorally viable Democratic Party and by the country as a whole—is a public discourse (and accompanying policies) that makes greater room for men's special gifts in raising children to be liberal adults.[41] A first step is to acknowledge that men, too (despite George Gilder's sociobiological musings), take a natural interest, not always liberal, in their children.[42]

3. Adopting a more judicious, morally nuanced approach to criminal justice. The harsh sentences and extraordinarily high incarceration rates that have prevailed in this country over the last two decades may or may not have led to lower crime rates (the figures bear multiple interpretations).[43] Less controversial, but rarely publicly confronted, is the high level of collateral damage to the families and children of the incarcerated (and thus, indirectly, to society as a whole). As Bruce Western reports in *Punishment and Inequality in America,* as of 1999, one in ten African American children under the age of ten (or roughly two million) had a father serving time in prison or jail—a figure that today is certainly even higher. No doubt some inmates might have been abusive or otherwise inadequate parents, had they remained free. Still, it is hard to differ with Western's conclusion that, on balance, harsh sentencing, in some cases for relatively minor crimes, has exacted a heavy toll, economically, psychologically, and spiritually, on those children who can least afford it. Broken homes are, arguably, even more destructive to civic life than are broken windows. "Warehouse" prisons and morally disproportionate sentencing also sends a most destructive moral message to those affected, especially children: life is a jungle in which the toughest prosper, a message that is reinforced in the echo chamber of pop culture. It is not a question of "punishing perps" versus coddling them (as Ann Coulter and similarly minded conservatives would have it), but of punishing wisely and with a reasonable moral and civic purpose.

4. Rewarding parents. According to recent estimates, it now costs a middle-class family approximately $1 million (counting foregone income, but not college) to raise a child. At the same time, children provide few of the economic benefits they once did. Given these substantial economic disincentives, and a social need for greater investment in children, certain changes in medical and fiscal policy seem reasonable. These might include health insurance for children not otherwise insured, Social Security credits for parents who see children successfully through high school,[44] and, in general, greater public appreciation of the fact that raising children well benefits not only private individuals but also society at large.

As will immediately be seen, such recommendations are not "partisan" in any usual sense; they suggest a moderate course based on principles—not just compromises—with which many who identify themselves as Democrats or Republicans could agree. If this is so, such policies would have the added benefit of helping to overcome a too great polarization of American society at present into "right" and "left." They might thereby help us meet political challenges even more pressing than those that currently confront the liberal family.

NOTES

1. For some relevant statistics, see Phillip Longman, *The Empty Cradle: How Falling Birthrates Threaten World Prosperity (and What to Do about It)* (New York: Basic Books, 2004). The worries raised in the present essay are civic rather than economic (as in Longman's work).

2. See *Social Contract*, book 3, chapter 9 ("On the Signs of a Good Government"): "All other things being equal, the government under which—without external aid, without naturalization, without colonies—the citizens populate and multiply the most is infallibly the best."

3. According to a recent report by the National Marriage Project, 24 percent of women forty to forty-four years old with a bachelor's degree were childless, compared to only 15 percent of those without a high school degree.

4. The most recent studies suggest that despite strong economic growth in recent years the United States has not made much progress here. According to a recent (2006) report of the Annie E. Casey Foundation, measures of economic health and income for children and teens are in a state of relative stagnation. Children, in the words of Foundation president Doug Nelson, are "treading water" rather than moving forward. Among the findings are a continuing decline in teenage birthrates but no decline in the percentage of children living in single-parent families (currently around one-third). The

report also notes a slight climb in infant mortality (mainly due to low birth weight and other effects of inadequate prenatal care), despite dramatic medical advances in the treatment of congenital defects. The U.S. infant mortality rate is higher than that of most other industrial countries, and higher than all of the G7, despite a much larger outlay for health care in the aggregate. According to the Foundation's public database, approximately 12 percent of U.S. children (or around 8.5 million) lack medical insurance. As of the late 1990s, around a third of all U.S. children were born out of wedlock. Of these, around half had fathers with less than a high school education, and only one-fifth had fathers with education beyond high school. Recent findings referred to in the report suggest that children raised in two-parent families, especially when these do not involve stepparents, do substantially better on a variety of social indicators than their single- or stepparent counterparts.

5. Concern about the low fertility rate of better-educated and wealthier Americans is not altogether unprecedented. One hundred years ago critics complained that three out of four Bryn Mawr graduates remained childless. And President Elliot publicly worried that alumni were having too few sons to fill future Harvard classes. (See Longman, *The Empty Cradle.*)

6. According to a recent report by the nonpartisan National Marriage Project at Rutgers University (*The State of Our Unions*, 2006), "Women are now entering their active child-rearing years at older ages than in the past and ending child-rearing years at younger ages. In 1970, 73.6 percent of women, ages 25–29, had already entered their child-rearing years and were living with at least one minor child of their own. By 2000, the share had dropped to 48.7 percent. In 1970, 27.4 percent of women, ages 50–54, had at least one minor child of their own in the household. By 2000, the share of such women had fallen to 15.4 percent." The comparable figure for men declined from 57.3 percent and 39.5 percent (for those 25–29, and 50–54, respectively) in 1970 to 28.8 percent and 24.7 percent today. The bottom line: in contrast to times past, a majority of adults of normal childbearing and child-rearing age do not live in households with children. Among the report's more disturbing findings is lower marital satisfaction among those with children than among childless couples—a development that the report attributes, at least in part, to the growing cultural normativity of childlessness (and the greater opportunities that it affords for career success and luxury consumption) and an accompanying depreciation of the peculiar satisfactions of parenthood. As one might conclude from those findings, being a parent is no longer, as it once was, the normal indicator of adulthood.

7. The Uniform Marriage and Divorce Act of 1987 defines marriage as "a personal relationship between a man and a woman arising out of a civil contract to which the consent of the parties is essential." Marriage, so conceived, has nothing essentially to do with the having and raising of children.

8. See, for example, Daniel Cere and Michael Farrow, *Divorcing Marriage* (Montreal: McGill-Queens University Press, 2004); and Mary Ann Glendon, *The Transformation of Family Law: State, Law, and Family in the United States and Western Europe* (Chicago: University of Chicago Press, 1989).

9. For a helpful discussion see Longman, *The Empty Cradle*, 158–60. Books were

published in the early twentieth century with such telling titles as *Race Suicide, Birth Control* (by Michael P. Dowling, New York: American Press, 1916). Margaret Sanger replied that birth control, far from leading to "race suicide," would give the better sort a leg up against the racially unfit.

10. Alexis de Tocqueville, *Democracy in America*, translated, edited and with an introduction by Harvey C. Mansfield and Delba Winthrop (Chicago: University of Chicago Press, 2000), 558.

11. *Democracy in America*, 576.

12. *Democracy in America*, 565.

13. *Democracy in America*, 567.

14. *Democracy in America*, 577–78.

15. See *First Treatise*, § 57.

16. *Second Treatise*, §§ 80–81; see also the note to § 81 in the edition of the *Two Treatises* by Peter Laslett (Cambridge Texts in the History of Political Thought), which quotes from Locke's diary.

17. *Second Treatise of Government*, § 79. The "end" of political society is similarly ambiguous, referring both to the aim that the contracting parties can be assumed to have specifically in mind—i.e., preservation of their property (*Second Treatise*, § 85) and to the ultimate goal encompassed by the "law of nature"—i.e., the good of mankind generally understood as preservation of the greatest number (*Second Treatise*, § 229).

18. The conjugal compact is thus a kind of civil contract writ small: each setting forth a common goal that enlists individual desire for the common benefit. Accordingly, conjugal union "draws with it mutual support and assistance, and a communion of interest too, as necessary not only to unite [the couple's] care and affection, but also necessary to their common offspring, who have a right to be nourished and maintained . . . till they are able to provide for themselves." *Second Treatise*, § 78.

19. *First Treatise*, § 59. According to the Law of Nature, "every one as he is *bound to preserve himself* . . . when his own preservation comes not in competition, ought he, as much as he can, *to preserve the rest of mankind*" (*Second Treatise*, § 6). The main way, it seems, in which individuals are to carry out the latter duty is by refraining from doing injury to the property of others and by punishing those who commit such injury. Locke also justifies it—albeit, with less vigor—by appealing to an ensuing contribution to the "common stock" of mankind (*Second Treatise*, § 36). It is less than clear how the Law of Nature gives rise to the parental duties that set limits to marriage. (Locke's appeal to the natural "tenderness" of parents is followed by examples of human cannibalism and the like that belie the power of "nature" in any simple sense [see *First Treatise*, §§ 56–58].) One way to resolve the difficulty might be to understand parental care as a kind of "restitution" for direct if unintended hurt to another human being (whom one has caused to be brought into the world in a condition of incapacity). The positive duty to be "fruitful and multiply" is here replaced by a negative duty to "do no harm" (i.e., to raise the children one has begotten)—itself, perhaps, no small incentive to a reduced birthrate.

20. Cf. this prayer, still used in the Catholic wedding rite: "Father, to reveal the plan of your love, you made the union of husband and wife an image of the covenant be-

tween you and your people. In the fulfillment of this sacrament, the marriage of Christian man and woman is a sign of the marriage between Christ and the Church."

21. *Second Treatise,* § 83.

22. See, in this regard, William Blackstone's illuminating gloss on the principles of coverture in his *Commentaries on the Laws of England.* In explaining the traditional "excuse" of wives from criminal responsibility for action undertaken under the presumed direction of their husbands, Blackstone subordinates British custom to the "laws of nature" as understood by Locke:

> The principal case, where constraint of a superior is allowed as an excuse for criminal misconduct, is with regard to the matrimonial subjection of the wife to her husband; for neither a son or a servant are excused from the commission of any crime, whether capital or otherwise, by the command or coercion of the parent or master. ... And therefore, if a woman commit theft, burglary, or other civil offences against the laws of society, by the coercion of her husband; or even in his company, which the law construes as a coercion; she is not guilty of any crime, being considered as acting by compulsion, and not of her own will: which doctrine is at least a thousand years old in this kingdom. ... And it appears that among the northern nations of the Continent, this privilege extended to any woman transgressing in concert with a man, and to any servant that committed an offence with a freeman. ... But (besides that in our law, which is a stranger to slavery, no impunity is given to servants, who are as much free agents as their masters) even with regard to wives the rule admits of an exception in crimes that are *male en se,* and prohibited by the law of nature, as murder and the like, not only because these are of a deeper dye, *but also, since in a state of nature no one is in subjection to another, it would be unreasonable to screen an offender from the punishment due to natural crimes, by the refinements and subordinations of civil society.* (William Blackstone, *Commentaries on the Laws of England of Public Wrongs,* adapted by Robert Malcolm Kerr [Boston: Beacon Press, 1962], 26; emphasis added)
>
> Wives, in Blackstone's account, are no more exempted from criminal responsibility for a "natural offense" than are servants, given a legal regime in which (in keeping with the laws of nature) all "slavery" is alien. To extend to wives the "privilege" of criminal excuse would thus be to treat them as no better than slaves. What from an earlier point of view can be regarded as an act of deference to a wife's higher spiritual calling appears, from Blackstone's fundamentally liberal point of view, as a degradation contrary to the laws of nature.

23. Another crucial difference between paternal and political authority for Locke lies in his restriction to the latter of the power of life and death. Thus: "the power of a magistrate over a subject" is to be "distinguished from that of a father over his children, a master over his servant, a husband over his wife, and a lord over his slave," consisting as it does in "a right of making laws with penalties of death, and consequently all lesser penalties, for the regulating and preserving of property" for "the public good." *Second Treatise,* §§ 2–3.

24. See, for example, *Second Treatise,* § 80.

25. On complex changes in the concept of marriage in the Protestant Reformation (including, but not limited to, denial of its sacramental status) see John Witte Jr., *From Sacrament to Contract: Marriage, Religion, and Law in the Western Tradition* (Louisville: Westminster, 1997). Although Protestantism relegated marriage to the sphere of earthly rather than heavenly government, its main Lutheran, Calvinist, and Anglican branches continued to conceive of marriage on the analogy of Christ's relation to his church—hence, as essentially hierarchical both civilly and spiritually.

26. See *First Treatise*, § 57, discussed in Robert Faulkner, "Preface to Liberalism: Locke's *First Treatise* and the Bible," *Review of Politics*, Summer 2005, 451–72.

27. *Second Treatise*, § 6.

28. Rousseau's most extended treatment occurs in *Emile*, books 1 and 5. For a further elaboration of this point, see Susan Shell, "Nature and the Education of Sophie," in *The Cambridge Companion to Rousseau*, ed. Patrick Riley (Cambridge: Cambridge University Press, 1999).

29. See, for example, the "Dedication" to the *Discourse on the Origins of Inequality*.

30. On the influence of Rousseau on American domestic habits, see Paul M. Spurlin, *Rousseau in America: 1760–1809* (University: University of Alabama Press, 1969). According to Spurlin, the *New Eloise* was the most successful of Rousseau's works—a "runner up," in the 1790s, to such "best sellers" as Hannah Foster's *The Coquette, Gulliver's Travels,* and Shakespeare (p. 3).

31. See, for example, George Gilder, *Men and Marriage* (Gretna, La.: Pelican, 1986); for a more nuanced defense of this position, see James Q. Wilson, *The Marriage Problem: How Our Culture Has Weakened Families* (New York: HarperCollins, 2002).

32. As Nancy Cott and Kay Hymowitz have written, constitutional framer James Wilson called the "institution of the family" the "true origin of society." And John Adams sounded a similarly Rousseauian note in claiming that "the foundations of national morality must be laid in private families." In the affectionate and self-reliant nuclear family, later famously described by Tocqueville, children might learn to be free from what Jefferson called "authority in all its guises." See Kay Hymowitz, "Gay Marriage and American Marriage," *City Journal*, Summer 2004; Nancy F. Cott, *Public Vows: A History of Marriage and the Nation* (Cambridge: Harvard University Press, 2000).

33. *Metaphysics of Morals*, Ak. 6:326–27.

34. *Metaphysics of Morals*, Ak. 6:227–80.

35. Even in his own lifetime, Kant's views as to the intrinsically degrading character of sex struck thoughtful contemporaries such as J. G. Hamann and K. L. Reinhold as indefensibly prudish and, indeed, as a symptom of psychological weakness on Kant's part. For a fuller consideration see Shell, *The Embodiment of Reason: Kant on Spirit, Generation, and Community* (Chicago: University of Chicago Press, 1996), chapter 8. As Rousseau warned, and as recent American experience seems to bear out, traditional notions of sexual modesty and shame sit uneasily with "enlightened" notions of happiness. To what extent such notions arise from liberalism itself—as distinguished from popularizations of Nietzsche (and other postliberal thinkers)—is an important question that cannot here be adequately addressed.

36. One Kantian stricture that has lasted is the notion that in matters sexual, no one

should be treated as a "mere means"—a condition that today is generally thought to be satisfied so long as sexual acts are consensual. Kant's own very different view has the virtue of acknowledging the fundamental mystery that attaches to our condition as embodied rational beings—beings, that is to say, whose bodies can be construed as "property" only in a highly peculiar sense. See, for example, *Metaphysics of Morals,* Ak. 6:279n, and 6:359, where he calls carnal enjoyment outside of marriage *"cannibalistic* in principle" if not always in effect.

37. Whether some traditional constraints might not be restored on liberal grounds is a question that cannot here be adequately addressed.

38. Louisiana's recent experiment with "covenant marriage" is a case in point: according to the most recent figures, fewer than 1 percent of couples eligible have elected its more rigorous conditions, which include mandated counseling, and waiver of no-fault divorce. Perhaps the lesson here is that "optional" requirements are not true requirements.

39. Currently, around a third of all U.S. children live in single-parent homes (in the vast majority of cases, with their mothers). The current estimate for African American children raised without stable contact with their fathers approaches three-quarters. Comparisons with the relatively high number of European children now born out of wedlock are here seriously misleading. Unlike their American counterparts, most of these children are brought up in stable, two-parent homes (and by parents whose "unmarried" status is generally regarded by themselves and others as a mere formality).

40. See, for example, George Lakoff, *Moral Politics: How Liberals and Conservatives Think* (Chicago: University of Chicago Press, 2002), and, more recently, *Don't Think of an Elephant: Know Your Values and Frame the Debate: The Essential Guide for Progressives* (White River, Vt.: Chelsea Green, 2004). Lakoff seems to regard "conservatism" and "progressivism" as irreducible, emotively based mind-sets with their own unique cognitive features. There would seem to be no rational grounds, on his account, why anyone who isn't already a "progressive" should become one.

41. Unfortunately, many recent liberal theorists have touted a different line. See, for example, Susan Okin's claim that "a just future would be one without gender." *Justice, Gender, and the Family* (New York: Basic Books, 1989), 171.

42. "Family values" conservatives often make the mistake of treating fatherhood largely as a burden that men naturally seek to escape. As we have seen, this view is less traditional, in the old-fashioned sense, than it is Rousseauian.

43. Bruce Western estimates that these harsher policies are responsible for around one-tenth of the reduced crime rate, with the remaining nine-tenths attributable to other factors. See Western, *Punishment and Inequality in America* (New York: Russell Sage, 2006), 186–87.

44. For a description of one such policy, see Longman, *The Empty Cradle.*

Political Voice in an Age of Inequality

Kay Lehman Schlozman and Traci Burch

All men are created equal.
—THE DECLARATION OF INDEPENDENCE, 1776

All men are born free and equal.
—CONSTITUTION OF MASSACHUSETTS, 1780

I believe in the equality of man.
—THOMAS PAINE, *THE AGE OF REASON*, 1794

Amongst the novel objects that attracted my attention during my stay in the United States, nothing struck me more forcibly than the general equality of condition among the people. I readily discovered the prodigious influence which this primary fact exercises on the whole course of society; it gives a peculiar direction to public opinion, and a peculiar tenor to the laws; it imparts new maxims to the governing authorities, and peculiar habits to the governed.
—ALEXIS DE TOCQUEVILLE, *DEMOCRACY IN AMERICA*, 1835

All men and women are created equal.
—DECLARATION OF SENTIMENTS, SENECA FALLS, 1848

. . . a new nation, conceived in liberty, and dedicated to the proposition that all men are created equal.
—ABRAHAM LINCOLN, GETTYSBURG ADDRESS, 1863

In respect of civil rights, all citizens are equal before the law. The humblest is the peer of the most powerful.
—JOHN MARSHALL HARLAN, DISSENTING OPINION, *PLESSY V. FERGUSON*, 1896

Since the colonists chafed under the rule of the British king, a commitment to equality has formed a thread in American political discourse.[1] But perhaps uniquely among values on which democracies rest, equality is a vexed concept. The men who met at Philadelphia to write the Constitution that continues to govern us were not equally committed to equality. With Shays's Rebellion and the threat of civil disorder in the background, some were concerned to protect the new government from the "temporary errors and delusions" of the people. Even dedicated egalitarians have not necessarily agreed about what democratic equality requires—at a minimum, equality before the law and equality of rights, but what about equality of opportunity? Equality of result? If equality of result, then equality with respect to which of many valued outcomes: economic reward? political power? social respect? To what degree do individual inequalities of condition become more acceptable if they do not aggregate into inequalities between groups defined by, say, race, ethnicity, or gender?

In both political discourse and policy outcome, concern with equality has intensified and diminished throughout American history.[2] The Revolutionary era, the years leading up to the Civil War, the decades of the New Deal and the Great Society were periods of greater rhetorical and policy commitment to equality. In contrast, our own era is one that celebrates the language of markets and has witnessed changes in an inegalitarian direction in policy areas that range from taxes to welfare.

At the same time that Equality Talk has fallen into relative disrepute over the past generation, actual economic inequality has sharpened in the United States. While expert opinion converges in the conclusion that, by a variety of measures, economic inequality has become more pronounced since the late 1970s, there has been less attention—and less agreement—with regard to changing political inequalities among citizens. In this chapter, we consider the extent of inequalities among citizens in the expression of political voice, assess the degree to which those inequalities of political voice are changing in tandem with growing economic inequalities to become sharper, and consider the extent to which—if at all—substantial inequalities of political voice pose a grave threat to American democracy.

These are matters about which facile conclusions are sometimes drawn before the facts are known. Our modus operandi is somewhat different from the approach taken by the other authors in this volume. An important part of our intellectual project is to lay out the evidence from a number of sources, including an important new data set about organized interests in Washington. The realities are more complicated than is sometimes appreciated. Doing justice to this complexity demands tolerance for quantitative evidence and circumspection in interpreting it.

The Economic Context: Growing Inequality

A considerable body of evidence demonstrates that, by a variety of metrics, economic rewards have become more unequally distributed over the past generation.[3] Time-series data beginning in 1917 show that, between the two world wars, there was variation, but no long-term trend, in the share of income commanded by the top tenth. Then, during World War II, it decreased markedly, remaining relatively stable until the 1970s, when it began to climb.[4]

The figures presented in table 1 show what has happened since then. As measured in constant dollars, average after-tax household income for those at the bottom of the economic ladder—and for the middle-class households in the middle three-fifths—grew quite modestly over the period from 1979 to 2003. In contrast, household incomes for those in the top fifth increased substantially: the *growth* in household income in the highest fifth was larger than the average 2003 *income* of those in the middle fifth of the economic ladder and more than *three* times the *income* of those in the lowest fifth.[5] Even more striking is the extent to which this growth was concentrated in the top 1 percent of households, whose average household incomes more than doubled in real terms over the period. The result of these changes is that the *share* of total household income accruing to the top quintile grew from 42.4 percent to 48.8 percent, and the shares of each of the bottom four fifths diminished. In fact, this redistribution benefited only an extremely narrow slice of households: only the top 10 percent saw their share of after-tax income grow; at the apex, the share of household income attributable to the highest 1 percent rose from 7.5 to 12.2 percent.[6]

A similar story can be told about earnings and wealth. Wage controls during World War II resulted in substantial wage compression, especially among high wage earners. Surprisingly, when controls were lifted, the share of wages commanded by top earners did not immediately bounce back to prewar levels. However, in the 1970s, it began to increase steadily before skyrocketing in the late 1980s and late 1990s, a development fueled in part by the inclusion of stock options in compensation packages. Between 1970 and 1999, a time when average earnings of full-time employees more or less stagnated in real terms, the average compensation of the top one hundred CEOs, as reported annually in *Forbes,* was multiplied roughly thirty times.[7]

Wealth—especially financial wealth like equities, bank deposits, or bonds—has always been more unevenly divided than either earnings or household income. Over the period since 1983, the bottom four-fifths households have never had as much as 20 percent of net worth or as much as 10 percent of financial wealth. In 1998, the top 1 percent commanded fully 38 percent of net worth and 47 percent of financial worth.[8] With respect to changes over time, the pattern for concentration of wealth has affinities to what we have seen for earnings and family income. The share of wealth owned by the top 1 percent grew during the 1920s to a peak in 1929 before falling during the Depression and continuing to decline during and after World War II. During the late 1970s concentration of wealth began to increase, reaching, by the late 1990s, levels close to that recorded for 1929.[9]

While the distribution of income is especially unequal in less affluent countries, cross-national studies concur in finding a higher level of inequality in disposable income in the United States than in other developed democracies.[10] It is important to note that, before taxes and government benefits, income inequality in the United States is not notably high. One study shows relatively little variation among eleven developed countries—and no particular distinctiveness for the United States—when it comes to inequality in pretax and pretransfer family income. However, in the United States, government benefits are not particularly generous, and taxes are not especially redistributive. The result is that the diminution in inequalities in market incomes is less substantial in the United States than in other developed countries, even countries like Belgium and France, where pretax and pretransfer income is less equally distributed than it is in the United States.[11] Moreover, while there has been a general trend over the last generation toward greater income inequality in wealthy democracies, in no na-

TABLE 1.   Growing Economic Inequality: After-Tax Household Income by Income Group

	Average After-Tax Income (in 2003 dollars)				Share of After-Tax Income		
	1979	1990	2003	Change	1979	1990	2003
Lowest fifth	$ 13,500	$ 13,100	$ 14,100	$600	6.8%	5.3%	5.0%
Second fifth	27,300	27,200	30,800	3,500	12.3%	10.8%	10.3%
Middle fifth	38,900	39,900	44,800	5,900	16.5%	15.8%	15.5%
Fourth fifth	50,900	54,500	63,600	12,700	22.3%	21.9%	21.4%
Highest fifth	89,700	112,200	138,500	48,800	42.4%	47.3%	48.8%
Top 10 percent	113,500	151,100	190,400	76,900	27.6%	32.3%	33.9%
Top 5 percent	149,600	210,100	270,200	120,600	18.1%	22.6%	24.2%
Top 1 percent	305,800	520,000	701,500	395,700	7.5%	11.0%	12.2%

Source: Congressional Budget Office, "Historical Effective Tax Rates: 1979 to 2003," December, 2005, http://www.cbo.gov/showdoc.cfm?index=7000&sequence=0on, accessed on July 31, 2006.

tion except the United Kingdom has the increase in income inequality been as pronounced as it has been in the United States.[12]

Two arguments are sometimes made that blunt concerns about the level of income inequality in the United States. The first is that the high level of affluence in America—as measured, say, by per capita GDP—implies a higher, if unequal, standard of living for all. However, according to one comparative study, "low-paid workers in the United States—the most productive economy in the world—have markedly lower living standards than low-paid workers in other advanced economies."[13] Another study shows that the real purchasing power of those in the poorest tenth of the population in the United States is, in fact, below the average for that stratum in eight developed countries: below Canada, Belgium, the Netherlands, and Germany; a shade higher than Sweden and Finland; and higher than the United Kingdom. Thus, America's greater affluence is enjoyed only by those at the top. Considering the two countries for which the real purchasing power of the poorest tenth of the population most closely approximates that of their American counterparts, Sweden and Finland, in 2000 the real income gap between those in the highest tenth and those in the lowest tenth was $18,620 in Sweden, $17,780 in Finland, and $41,900 in the United States.[14]

The second argument suggesting that income inequality is less problematic in the American context focuses on the American Dream of equality of opportunity. If unequal rewards reflect talent and industry rather than family background or previous condition of privilege and if the able and hardworking, thus, have opportunities to rise above modest beginnings, then the degree of economic inequality might not occasion concern. However, recent research shows considerable correspondence in the economic deserts of successive generations.[15] Affluent, well-educated parents are able to transmit their economic status through several mechanisms: they pass along their genetic endowments; they use their income to invest in their children's health, education, and development; they create a home environment that cultivates interests, habits, and personality traits that are helpful in the marketplace; and they make direct bequests of useful resources, including family wealth and personal contacts.

It is difficult to make comparisons across nations with respect to whether these processes operate even more powerfully elsewhere. However, among developed democracies, it seems that, contrary to the expectation in the United States and abroad, the United States is not notable for high rates of class and occupational mobility across generations. Instead, along with France and Britain, the United States seems to be in the middle of the pack when it comes to the association between social origins and destinations. Canada, Sweden, and Norway have higher rates—and Japan, Germany, and Ireland lower rates—of intergenerational mobility.[16] With respect to change over the last generation, there is no definitive answer as to how these processes have been altered in an era of growing economic inequality in the United States. One piece of evidence is a study comparing high school graduates from the classes of 1980 and 1982, on the one hand, and 1992, on the other, that shows a growing advantage of affluent students in access to higher education.[17] In addition, a sophisticated cross-generational analysis of economic outcomes among adults shows that, after rates of class mobility increased during the 1960s, they have leveled off, and not reversed since then. It is too early to discern the impact of increasing economic inequality on the prospects for mobility of the next generation.[18]

Inequalities of Political Voice

As evidenced by the principle of one person, one vote, when we move from the marketplace to the level playing field of democracy, questions about equality are central. Public opinion data demonstrate that most Americans favor a high degree of political equality and seek a democracy in which people's voices weigh heavily and count equally. In fact, Americans show much less willingness to approve of unequal responsiveness in democratic governance than to accept unequal results in the economic sphere.[19]

The exercise of political voice goes to the heart of citizen accountability in a democracy, and equal political voice goes to the heart of equal protection of citizen interests. Political voice refers to the sum total of political inputs that citizens in a democracy use to control who will hold political office and to influence what public officials do. Through their political voice, citizens raise political issues, communicate information about their political interests and concerns, and generate pressure on policymakers to respond to what they hear. Although the particular mix will vary from polity to polity, citizens in a democracy have a variety of options for the exercise of political voice. They can seek indirect influence through the electoral system by voting or engaging in other efforts to support favored political parties or candidates; or they can seek direct influence through the messages they send to officeholders about their politically relevant preferences and needs. They can act individually or work with others in informal efforts, formal organizations, political parties, or social movements. They can undertake mainstream activities or challenging ones like protests or demonstrations. They can make contributions of time or money. Of course, we know that public officials act for many reasons, only one of which is their assessment of what the public wants and needs. And policymakers have ways other than the medium of citizen participation of learning what citizens want and need from the government. Nonetheless, what public officials hear clearly influences what they do.

So long as citizens differ in their preferences and interests—that is, so long as Madison's insight in *Federalist* 10 that differences of opinion are sown in the nature of humankind, especially in the unequal acquisition of property, continues to be compelling—then a concern with equal protection of interests requires that we take seriously the fact that citizens differ in their capacity, and desire, to exercise political voice. The democratic principle of one person, one vote is the most obvious manifestation of the link between voluntary participation and equal protection of interests. However, for forms of voluntary political participation beyond the vote, there is no such mandated equality of participatory input. Thus, a concern with equal protection of interests in a democracy demands that we consider the distribution of civic activity, who takes part and what they say. When aggregate participatory input is representative across all politically relevant groups and categories, then equal political voice has been realized—even if all individuals are not equally active.

To focus on equality of political voice is not to presume a populist preference for direct over representative democracy. To be concerned about inequalities of political voice is not to suggest a leveling between ordinary citizens, on the one hand, and elected and appointed political authorities, on the other. That is, our concern extends only to inequalities of political voice among members of the public and is not meant to suggest equality in political voice or public authority between ordinary citizens and government officials. Moreover, our construction of equality of political voice carries no presumption that duly constituted public authorities must act as instructed delegates and eschew the making of independent judgments in policy matters. Rather, greater equality of political voice would imply that the independent deliberations and judgments of the people's representatives would be informed by a fuller understanding of the actual circumstances and needs of citizens. When significant sectors of the public are silent, the ability of public authorities to assess the potential consequences of their policy decisions is compromised. There has long been controversy over the capacities of ordinary citizens to participate in making binding political decisions. However, equal voice requires, not that the people whose voices are being heard must be wise, only that they be able to articulate what matters to them politically and the connections they make between government actions and their personal lives, that they be able to communicate what they want and need. As Hamilton observed in elaborating on "the strong chords of sympathy between the representative and the constituent" in *Federalist* 35: "Is it not natural that a man who is a candidate for the favor of the people, and who is dependent on the suffrages of his fellow-citizens for the continuance of his public honors, should take care to inform himself of their dispositions and inclinations?"[20]

Social Class and Political Activity

Students of civic involvement in America are unanimous in characterizing political input through the medium of political participation as being extremely unequal. The exercise of political voice is stratified most fundamentally by social class.[21] Those who enjoy high levels of income, occupational status, and, especially, education are much more likely to take part politically than are those who are less well endowed with socioeconomic resources. Attendant to the class differences in political participation are disparities in political voice on the basis of both gender and race or ethnicity.

Figure 1, which uses data from the 2000 American National Election Study to present information about the political activity of groups stratified by family income, shows the extent to which political participation is structured by social class. Had we focused on level of education rather than income, the differences would be even more pronounced. The bars in the top portion of figure 1 show the average scores for each income group on an additive scale of nine political acts. The pattern is clear. With each step on the income ladder, political activity rises until it tails off insignificantly in the top income group, the roughly one-eighth of the sample with annual household incomes over $95,000. The gradient is sufficiently steep that those with family incomes over $50,000, a group that constitutes nearly half the sample, is, on average, more than twice as active as those with family incomes below $15,000.

In the bottom half of figure 1, we decompose the scale into its constituent activities: voting in 1996, voting in 2000, taking part in campaign

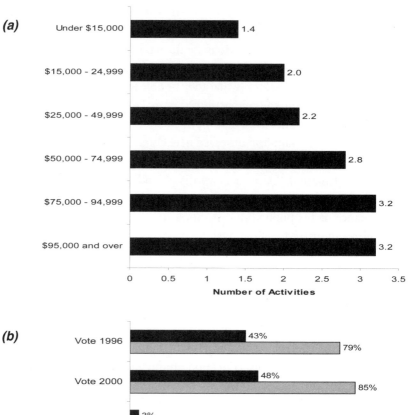

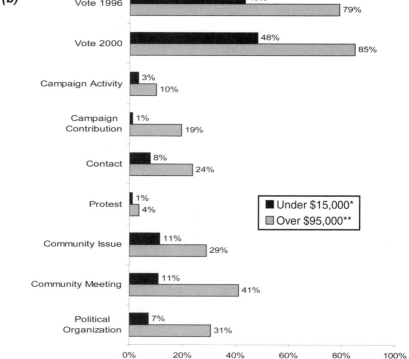

Fig. 1.   Income and political activity. *(a)* Average activity score for household income groups; *(b)* percentage undertaking various activities. (Data from 2000 American National Election Study. *Note:* * N = 179 weighted cases, ** N = 170 weighted cases.)

activity, making an electoral contribution, contacting a public official, taking part in a protest or march, working on a community issue, attending a meeting about a community issue, or being a member of an organization that tries to influence government.[22] While there are different ways to measure the magnitude of the differences, the disparity in activity between the two income groups seems especially wide when it comes to making campaign contributions. Interestingly, even protesting—which demands little in the way of skills or money and which is often thought of as "the weapon of the weak"—is characterized by the pattern of socioeconomic bias. The successes of the labor and civil rights movements illustrate the possibilities for the disadvantaged when they mobilize collectively. However, the United States also has a long tradition of middle-class protest movements ranging from abolition and temperance to environmentalism and disarmament. The bottom line is that, even when it comes to protest, the well-educated and well-heeled are more likely to take part.

In all democracies, access to the free marketplace of political ideas is stratified by income and education, a pattern that has emerged over and over in studies of citizen participation. However, the association between political activity and socioeconomic status is more pronounced in the United States than in other developed democracies.[23] There is an interesting parallel to the pattern that we described earlier for the extent of economic inequalities in developed democracies. Across polities, the association between psychological involvement with politics, one of the strongest predictors of political participation, and socioeconomic status is more or less uniform.[24] Yet there is considerable variation across democracies in the extent to which participation is stratified by social class and, therefore, in the extent to which activists are not representative of the public as a whole. The explanation for this variation derives from the way that the political linkage institutions—interest groups and, especially, political parties—in particular countries mediate the relationship between socioeconomic status and participation. In many democracies, much more than in the United States, the parties and voluntary associations, taken together, enroll citizens from across the socioeconomic spectrum, and particular linkage institutions—especially labor unions and labor or social democratic parties—bring lower SES groups into politics on the basis of shared economic concerns. Where such an institutional configuration obtains, the class bias in participation is ameliorated.

Do Class Differences in Political Voice Matter?

One important line of reasoning suggests that participatory differences among demographic groups do not really matter. In a significant analysis of the representativeness of the electorate, Wolfinger and Rosenstone demonstrate that, although the electorate is not demographically representative of the public at large, voters do not differ from nonvoters in their partisan leanings or their opinions on policy matters as expressed in surveys.[25] That is, although those who go to the polls differ from those who stay home in many ways—including their income and education—their answers to questions in public opinion polls are quite similar.

However, this finding takes on a different meaning when we take a broader view of the attributes of citizens that matter for politics—encompassing not just demographics and policy positions as expressed in response to survey questions but also other circumstances that are relevant for policy and the actual content of participatory input.[26] Political participants can be distinguished from inactives in many ways that are of great political significance: although similar in their attitudes, political activists are distinctive in their personal circumstances and dependence upon government benefits, in their priorities for government action, and in what they say when they get involved. These disparities are exacerbated when we move from the most common political act, voting, to acts that are more difficult, convey more information, and can be multiplied in their volume.

Consider, for example, economic needs and circumstances. Compared with those who are politically quiescent, those who take part in politics are much less likely to have experienced a need to trim their sails economically—to have been forced to work extra hours to get by, to have delayed medical treatment for economic reasons, or to have cut back on spending on food. Predictably, almost no one among those making large campaign donations reported having cut back financially in order to make ends meet. Not only are there differences in economic circumstances, there are differences in their need for various kinds of government assistance. Those who receive such means-tested government benefits as food stamps and housing subsidies are underrepresented among political activists, even among those who undertake participatory acts that might be expected to be especially relevant to their circumstances—getting in touch with public officials, taking part in protests, and getting involved in informal community efforts. Their inactivity has consequences for the messages sent to public officials about government programs. The government hears differentially from beneficiaries of different programs, and the ones it hears from are systematically among the more advantaged citizens; for example, Medicare recipients are *more* likely than Medicaid recipients to get in touch with a public official about their medical benefits.

Furthermore, in spite of the fact that inactive citizens do not differ substantially from activists in their responses when survey researchers choose the issues, when it comes to what political activists actually *say* when they take part, members of various underrepresented groups have distinctive participatory agendas. With regard to the issues and problems that animated their political activity, among those who engage in the kinds of participatory acts that permit the communication of explicit messages to policymakers—for example, contacting, protesting, or serving as a volunteer on a local board—more advantaged and less advantaged activists have distinctive policy agendas attached to their participation. Compared with those who are more advantaged, those who have limited income and education are considerably more likely to discuss issues of basic human need—that is, matters like poverty, jobs, health, and housing—in association with their participation. These matters, not surprisingly, figure especially importantly in the participatory agendas of those who receive means-tested government benefits like food stamps or Medicaid. However, because the disadvantaged are so inactive, public officials actually hear less about these matters from them than from more advantaged activists. In short, when we consider what policymakers actually hear, the association between socioeconomic status and participation has potential political consequences.

Changing Participatory Representation

The widespread agreement about the extent to which political voice is unequal is not matched by consensus as to whether the extent of that inequality has *changed* over the last generation. Part of the reason for the absence of agreement is that political voice is multifaceted, and developments with respect to various modes of expressing political voice—for example, campaign giving, protest, or activity in political organizations—need not operate in tandem.

Recent decades have witnessed several trends with potential—and potentially contradictory—implications for participatory inequalities. Some of them might be expected to have had an ameliorative impact on the strength of the relationship between participation and education or income. Consider, for example, a development that has received a great deal of academic and media attention: the recent decline in political activity.[27] Because those on the lowest rungs of the socioeconomic ladder have traditionally been so politically inactive, the recent decline in overall rates of political activity cannot come solely from erosion at the bottom. Thus, participatory decline might actually decrease participatory stratification. Inequality in political voice may have also been reduced by the rise in education during recent decades. Since education is such a powerful predictor of political engagement, rising absolute levels of education might be expected to facilitate the political activation of those at the bottom of the class hierarchy and produce class convergence in participation. In fact, however, it seems that increasing education does not necessarily produce commensurate increases in activity.[28]

In contrast, other developments might lead to the aggravation of inequalities in political voice. Since 1980, several factors—among them the attenuation of the labor movement and the increasing economic inequality we have discussed—have conspired to exacerbate class stratification, though not class conflict. These trends would suggest increasing inequality in political activity. Moreover, the institutions that link citizens to policymakers have been transformed in ways that have the capacity to enhance the voice of the well-off and well-educated. Reflecting a trend that characterizes many institutions of American society, the domain of citizen politics has become increasingly professionalized in the past generation. Roles in political parties and interest groups that would once have been taken on by volunteers are now assumed by professional staff with expertise in such matters as campaign management, polling, direct mail, and public relations. To keep such political operations going requires that citizen supporters provide voluntary contributions of cash rather than of expertise or sweat equity. Under the circumstances, those who have the wherewithal to write large checks would be expected to enjoy enhanced political voice. In addition, when it comes to voting, recent decades have witnessed a sharp increase in the proportion of the electorate that is disenfranchised by virtue of having been convicted of a crime—a trend with a disproportionate impact on those on the lowest rungs of the socioeconomic ladder, especially African American males.[29]

Has there been a change in whose voices are heard? Studies of various forms of participation, including voting, are unanimous in finding that the strong association between political activity and socioeconomic status has decidedly *not* been ameliorated in recent decades. Beyond that, however, there are no easy conclusions when it comes to changing inequality of political voice.

Consider, first, one of the most basic rights and responsibilities of the citizen, the vote. The enfranchisement of blacks in the South as the result of the civil rights movement and the Voting Rights Act of 1965 coupled with increasing levels of education within the public might be expected to have rendered the electorate more representative not only in racial but also in socioeconomic terms. In contrast to other forms of participation, for which those in the lowest ranks of income and education register such low rates that not much decline is possible, erosion at the bottom is possible when it comes to voting.

Scholars differ on whether voting stratification has changed over recent decades, and the numerous studies have conflicting findings.[30] In one of the most recent contributions to the literature, Richard B. Freeman concludes that, despite many efforts to expand the electorate and make voting easier, the decline in turnout since the late 1960s has come disproportionately from those at the bottom of the socioeconomic hierarchy, thus exacerbating the demographic bias of the electorate. Furthermore, whatever the disagreements among scholars, no one suggests that the U.S. electorate is *less* stratified today than it was when turnout peaked most recently in 1960.

Only rarely does an over-time study consider a broad range of activities beyond voting. The only study to encompass a variety of modes of political activity finds that the socioeconomic bias in political participation fluctuated somewhat in the two decades separating the early 1970s and early 1990s, but was more or less the same at the end of the period as at the beginning.[31] Figure 2a shows the average amount of participation as measured by an additive scale of twelve political acts for five equal groups (quintiles) ranked on the basis of education and income. For every quintile, there is an overall decline in participation between 1973 and 1994. Figure 2a also makes clear the striking degree to which political activity is structured by education and income. The five quintiles array themselves neatly in order with discernible differences between adjacent quintiles. The lines move more or less in tandem and never cross. Those at the highest level of education and income are roughly five times more active than those at the bottom—undertaking, on average, about 2.1 acts compared to 0.4 acts for the lowest quintile.

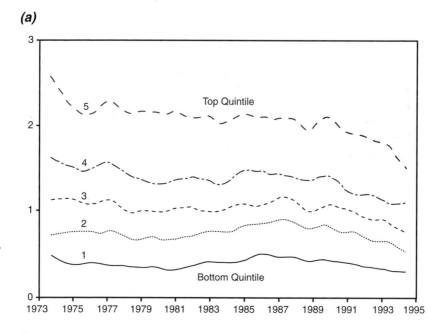

(a)

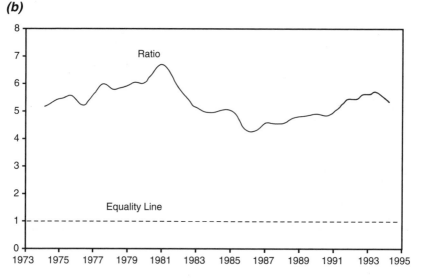

(b)

Fig. 2.   Has the class stratification of political activity changed? *(a)* Political activities, by SES quintile mean number of activities; *(b)* political activities ratio, top fifth to bottom fifth. (Data from Roper Social and Political Trends Data, 1973–94, reproduced from Henry E. Brady, Kay Lehman Schlozman, Sidney Verba, and Laurel Elms, "Who Bowls: The (Un)Changing Stratification of Participation," in *Understanding Public Opinion,* ed. Barbara Norrander and Clyde Wilcox, 2nd ed. [Washington, D.C.: CQ Press, 2002], figures 10.1 and 10.2.)

Figure 2b measures representational inequality by presenting a "representation ratio"—namely, the ratio of average participation by the top quintile to the average participation by the bottom quintile. A ratio of 1 indicates representational equality between the two quintiles (or any two groups). It is hardly surprising that the representation ratios presented in figure 2b, which range between 4 and 7, show an ongoing pattern of participatory dominance by the highest quintile in terms of education and income. What is surprising, however, is the absence of any clear trend over time. Participatory inequality rises somewhat in the late 1970s, falls during the early 1980s, and ends the two-decade period almost exactly where it started. It might be argued that the recent increase in political activity by the elderly—who do not command high levels of income or, especially, education—might obscure increased inequality on the basis of social class among younger cohorts. However, when the elderly are eliminated from the analysis, the findings are unchanged.

These data suggest that we tread carefully before assuming that greater economic inequality implies commensurate increases in class-based inequalities in political participation. However, they leave many questions unanswered. One problem with drawing inferences about changing political voice from these data is that evidence based on the enumeration of activities does not take into account how much people do when they take part. This concern is especially relevant when it comes to giving to campaigns and to other political causes. Not surprisingly, political contributors, especially those who make large donations, are the least representative of the participant publics. Studies indicate that the social characteristics of campaign contributors have not changed in recent decades.[32] At the same time, however, political contributions have become a more important component of the participatory mix over the last generation. It is well known that, even when measured in constant dollars, campaign giving has risen rapidly over the last generation at a time when other forms of political activity are declining. In particular, soft money donations, which until recently have not been subject to limits, increased especially dramatically. Although there are no longitudinal data to assess the consequences of this configuration of circumstances, there is reason to suspect that the changing mix of modes of activity—in particular, a participatory system in which large-scale campaign giving figures increasingly importantly—exacerbates inequalities in participatory input.

A second concern is that, because the additive scale in figure 2 combines numerous activities, it obscures developments with respect to particular forms of participation. The domain of organizational involvement presents particular complexities. Activity in voluntary associations is significant for political voice in two ways. First, regardless of whether the organizations in question take stands in politics—and a large share of them do not—people who are active in membership associations are more likely to take part in politics because, through their organizational involvement, they cultivate democratic habits, develop politically useful civic skills, and are exposed to political cues and to requests for political participation. Second, voluntary associations themselves are an important vehicle for the expression of political voice.

There is evidence that voluntary associations no longer do the first as well as in the past; that is, they no longer function as effectively as they once did as schools for democratic citizenship, a development that has had a disproportionate impact on the civic life of the less privileged.[33] Recent decades have witnessed not only erosion but also transformation in organizational involvement. Membership in voluntary associations has declined, and the decrease has not been uniform across different kinds of groups. Instead, organizations that traditionally enrolled both working-class and middle-class members have fared especially badly: in the period between World War II and the late 1990s, the median decrease in membership for a group of twenty-one cross-class chapter federations was 60 percent; the analogous figure for a group of seven elite professional societies was only 28 percent. Furthermore, with the erosion of the share of workers enrolled in unions, the gap between the proportion of college-educated Americans who are members of a professional society and the proportion of non-college-educated Americans who are union members has grown substantially.[34] Even though organizations like the Odd Fellows, the Fraternal Order of the Eagles, or the General Federation of Women's Clubs did not seek to influence politics and, thus, did not serve as avenues for the expression of political voice, the decline in these kinds of organizations has had particular consequences for the civic capacities of less well educated and less affluent citizens, thus exacerbating political inequalities.

Organized Interests and Equality of Political Voice

When it comes to the expression of political voice, the role of organizations as schools for citizenship is secondary to their function as conduits for political messages. Although the evidence for this proposition is not simply incomplete but impossible to gather, it is probably fair to say that, of the various forms of collective political voice, expressions of preference through organized interest activity are least likely to represent all citizens equally and that the economically advantaged speak especially loudly and clearly in organized interest politics.[35] Once again, while it is unambiguous that not all individuals—and, consequently, not all points of view—are equally well represented through organized interest politics, it is less clear whether those inequalities of political voice have been exacerbated during a period of marked increases in economic inequality among Americans.

Representation by Organized Interests

The set of organizations that represent Americans' political interests and preferences—which is not coterminous with the vast set of voluntary associations that individuals can join, many of which are not involved in politics—is remarkable in its breadth and diversity. It includes membership groups with millions of members, groups with few members, and institutions—most notably corporations, but also universities, hospitals, and think tanks—that have no members in the ordinary sense; organizations based on how people earn a living, how they spend their leisure, and how they define themselves in religious or ethnic terms; organizations, especially corporations, that have billions in assets and others that live from hand to mouth; organizations with liberal views and organizations with conservative views. In view of the stunning array of organizations that take part in American politics, it makes sense to ask: Is everyone represented? Is everyone represented equally?[36]

Although it is conceptually difficult to specify what political equality would look like when political input arises from organizations rather than from individuals, there is widespread agreement that whatever an unbiased set of organized interests would look like, it would not very closely resemble what we have ever had in the United States.[37] E. E. Schattschneider observed famously that "the flaw in the [organized interest] heaven is that the heavenly chorus sings with a strong upper-class accent."[38] He argued that what he called the "pressure system" is biased in favor of groups representing the well off, especially business, and against groups representing two other kinds of interests.

The first kind of interest that is unlikely to achieve representation is broad public interests or public goods. These are objectives like safer streets or safer consumer products, cleaner water or cleaner government, en-hanced domestic security or reduced domestic violence, that are broadly beneficial to all in society. In fact, the characteristic of a public good as defined by economists is that if it is available to some members of a society, it cannot be withheld from everyone else. Schattschneider argued that, while everyone has a stake in such broad public interests, relatively few people care intensely about them or give them the highest political priority. In many controversies, a broad public interest is opposed by a well-orga-nized private interest with a substantial stake in the outcome; for example, organizations representing steel manufacturers and electric utilities are more likely to be active in opposition to air quality regulations than are en-vironmentalists to be active in support—even though everyone shares an interest in breathing clean air and public opinion data consistently demon-strate widespread popular support for environmental preservation.

In an influential formal analysis, Mancur Olson reached the same con-clusion through logical deduction that Schattschneider had by empirical observation. Olson pointed out that large, diffuse groups lacking the capac-ity to coerce cooperation or to provide selective benefits often face severe collective action problems that prevent them from organizing on behalf of their joint political concerns.[39] According to Olson, the rational individual has an incentive not to spend scarce resources of money and time in sup-port of favored causes but rather to free ride on the efforts of others. Only when an organization has the capacity to force a potential free rider to sup-port group efforts or when it supplies benefits available only to those who assist in the collective effort will an organization emerge and prosper. Thus, Olson's logic gives a formal foundation to Schattschneider's observation that the proportion of people who take part in an organization seeking public goods is far smaller than the proportion that would benefit from those conditions.

Schattschneider predicted that a second kind of interest, that of the dis-advantaged, would be also underrepresented in organized interest politics. Not all potential constituencies are in a position to bear the costs of politi-cal organization and advocacy. Although money is surely a necessity, these costs are not simply financial. The affluent and well educated are not only able to afford the financial costs of organizational support but are in a bet-ter position to command the skills, acquire the information, cultivate the media, and utilize the connections that are helpful in getting an organiza-tion off the ground or keeping it going. In short, a group of jointly inter-

ested citizens that is reasonably well endowed with a variety of kinds of resources, for example veterans, is more likely to overcome the hurdle posed
by the logic of collective action than is a group of similar size and similar
intensity of concern that is resource-poor, say public housing tenants or
nursing home residents.

The data in table 2, which summarize the distribution of organizations
that were listed in the *Washington Representatives* directory in 1981, 1991,
and 2001, make clear that the essential outlines of Schattschneider's analysis of the pressure system still pertain today.[40] The figures for 2001 show that
the set of organized political interests continues to be organized principally
around economic matters. Over three-fifths of the organized interests in
Washington are institutions or membership associations directly related to
the joint political concerns attendant to making a living. In this domain, the
representation of business is dominant. Corporations are, by far, the most
numerous of the organizations in the pressure system. American corporations accounted for more than a third of the organizations with Washington representation in 2001.[41] Trade and other business associations, which
have for-profit corporations as members, are another 13 percent. If we add
the variety of other organizations from the business community—for example, foreign corporations and business associations, and occupational

TABLE 2. Organized Interests in Washington Politics

	Share of D.C. Organizations			Relative Increase	Absolute Increase
	1981	1991	2001		
Corporations[a]	46.0%	33.8%	34.9%	33%	1,004
Trade and Other Business Associations	15.6	14.8	13.3	49%	506
Occupational Associations	8.0	8.6	6.7	46%	249
Unions	1.6	1.5	1.0	6%	6
Public Interest	3.9	4.9	4.6	108%	279
Identity Groups[b]	2.7	3.5	3.8	147%	267
Social Welfare or Poor	.5	.7	.8	191%	61
U.S. Governments	5.0	6.9	10.4	262%	877
Foreign	8.8	10.2	7.7	54%	314
Other	6.8	12.4	15.3	295%	1,335
Don't Know	1.2	2.8	1.4	108%	86
Total	100.1%	100.1%	99.9%	75%	4,984
N	6,679	7,926	11,664		

[a]Includes U.S. corporations, U.S. subsidiaries of foreign corporations, and for-profit firms of professionals
such as law and consulting firms.
[b]Includes organizations representing racial, ethnic, or religious groups, elderly, women, or LGBT.

associations of business executives—more than half, 55 percent, of the organizations active in Washington represent business in one way or another.

Not only is business extremely well represented, but occupations that are well paid and highly skilled are much more likely than those further down the ladder to have organizational representation. Sixty-two percent of the occupational organizations and labor unions, taken together, represent professionals or managers and administrators, a figure that is roughly twice their proportion of the labor force.[42] In short, the large part of the pressure system that is organized around how people make a living is skewed sharply toward the top.

Consistent with Schattschneider's analysis, the number of public interest groups is relatively small, accounting for less than 5 percent of the organizations active in Washington. The data in table 3 show the range of public goods sought by interest organizations and make clear that these broad public interests are not inevitably liberal. Discussions of public interests often overlook how often, in any real political controversy, opposing conceptions of the public interest compete with each other: for example, wilderness preservation with economic growth, consumer product safety with low prices, or national security with low taxes.[43] It is extremely difficult to extract a bottom line that summarizes the ideological balance between competing visions of the public interest. Overall, the set of organizations representing public goods probably leans somewhat to the left. Still, table 3 makes clear that there is also considerable representation of conservative public goods. In fact, explicitly ideological public interest groups—for example, anti- or pro–gun control groups on the domestic front or pro–national security or pro-peace groups in the international domain—are bal-

TABLE 3.   Public Interest Groups

	Share in 2001	Increase from 1981
Consumer	6.0%	−3%
Environmental and wildlife	24.1	111%
Government reform	5.0	184%
Civil liberties	2.3	56%
Citizen empowerment	3.5	438%
Other liberal groups	15.3	95%
Other conservative groups	15.9	87%
Other	27.7	166%
Total	99.8%	108%
N	537	

anced between conservative and liberal organizations. Moreover, many of the public interest groups in various presumptively liberal categories are, in fact, either ideologically neutral or conservative. Examples include consumer groups like the American Automobile Association and the American Motorcyclist Association; wildlife organizations like Pheasants Forever; school choice organizations like the Center for Education Reform; or government reform organizations like Citizens Against Government Waste. Furthermore, compared to advocates of liberal public interests, conservative public interest organizations are more likely to find themselves on the same side of a policy controversy as an intense private interest—for example, a corporation or trade association representing real estate developers or the manufacturers of infant car seats.

In addition, just as they are in individual political participation, the economically disadvantaged continue to be underrepresented in pressure politics. Organizations of the poor themselves are extremely rare, if not nonexistent, and organizations that advocate on behalf of the poor are relatively scarce.[44] Less than 1 percent of the organizations active in Washington in 2001 fell into the category we label as "social welfare or poor": organizations like Goodwill Industries or Metropolitan Family Services that provide direct services to the needy or organizations like the National Alliance to End Homelessness or the Food Research and Action Center that advocate on behalf of the poor in the United States. Of the more than 11,000 organizations enumerated in the 2001 directory, *not one* was an organization of recipients of social welfare benefits—for example, jobless workers or public housing tenants—advocating on their own behalf. Furthermore, as Jeffrey Berry points out, the health and human service nonprofits that have as clients "constituencies that are too poor, unskilled, ignorant, incapacitated, or overwhelmed with their problems to organize on their own" are constrained by the 501(c)3 provisions in the tax code from undertaking significant lobbying.[45]

However, in an era when economic gains have flowed very disproportionately to those at the top, it is not simply the poor whose economic interests receive little direct representation. If they are not members of a labor union, those who work in occupations having modest pay, benefits, and status—such as hairdressers, store clerks, and auto mechanics—are relatively unlikely to have organized political representation. Less than 2 percent of all organizations are unions or organizations of people who work in "other occupations." Even these organizations are skewed in the direction of organizing those who, although not defined as professionals by the Census Bureau, pursue occupations requiring technical training: for example, shorthand reporters, insurance adjusters, travel agents, pilots, and medical technologists. Furthermore, the economic interests of many other groups that are not economically privileged—for example, students, holders of company pensions, working people without health care benefits, women at home—receive little direct organizational representation.

We should, however, note an important qualification to the generalization that the organized interest community is biased in favor of the well-off, especially business, at the expense of the economically disadvantaged and broad publics. When it comes to the sets of groups that coalesce around noneconomic axes of cleavage—for example, race, ethnicity, age, or gender—it is not the dominant groups in society that receive the lion's share of explicit organizational representation. Few, if any, groups are explicitly organized around the interests of, for example, men, the middle aged, or WASPs, but numerous groups represent the interests of women, the elderly, Muslims, Asian Americans, or African Americans. Still, for all their numbers, such groups constitute only a small fraction, about 3 percent, of the universe of organized interests. Furthermore, the interests of middle-aged, white men are surely well represented in the mainstream economic organizations—corporations, business associations, professional associations, and unions—that form the bulk of the organized interest community. When it comes to economic issues, the bias of organized interests toward the well-off seems quite clear.

Changing Organized Interest Representation

At the same time that there has been continuity, the organized interest community has also changed in important ways in the decades since Schattschneider warned about the "upper-class accent" of the "heavenly chorus." To summarize those developments briefly: recent decades have witnessed a notable increase in the numbers of organizations active in Washington politics; while that increase has brought in many organizations that challenge the strong voice of business in Washington politics, few of those organizations represent the economic interests of those further down the economic ladder.

Even though, on average, individual membership in voluntary associations has diminished, the pressure community has grown substantially.

Many new political organizations have come into being—not all of them, by any means, membership associations—and many existing organizations that were hitherto outside of politics have come to take part in politics. The 2001 *Washington Representatives* directory listed nearly 75 percent more organizations than it had two decades before. With this growth in the number of politically active organizations has come enhanced representation of groups and interests—for example, gays, the disabled, African Americans, and women—that have traditionally had very limited representation in organized interest politics.[46] This circumstance may reflect the fact that social movements in the United States often leave organizations in their wake. In contrast to protest politics in other democracies, American social movements are likely to generate an organizational legacy. Moreover, the bias against groups representing broad public interests has almost certainly been ameliorated. Organizations that advocate on behalf of such public goods as environmental preservation, national security, safe streets, durable consumer products, clean government, or low taxes have increased in numbers and in resources. The presence of all these new organizations in national politics—the result, in part, of infusions of initial resources from foundations and other patrons—has reduced the share of all organizations that represent domestic and foreign business interests and might be seen as reducing the political inequalities in the set of organized interests active in politics.[47]

At the same time, several developments have the opposite effect, shoring up the dominance of organizations traditionally well represented in organized interest politics. At least in part in reaction to the explosion in the number of consumer and environmental groups that became active in national politics in the late 1960s and early 1970s, previously apolitical corporations and professional associations began a massive mobilization into politics. Beginning in the late 1970s, large numbers of existing corporations and professional associations augmented their political efforts, often by establishing an independent office in Washington rather than relying on trade associations and lobbyists-for-hire to manage their political affairs.[48] As shown in table 2, although the rate of increase of such traditionally dominant organizations is below that of the pressure system as a whole, the *number* of such new organizations is impressive. The absolute increase in organizations is greatest for corporations. In spite of the relative rapid growth of organizations advocating on behalf of public goods, racial and ethnic minorities, women, the elderly, the disabled, gays, and the poor, the total number of such new organizations is roughly a third of the number of new business-related organizations.

Furthermore, after a union-backed measure in the 1974 amendments to the Federal Election Campaign Act preserved political action committees (PACs) as part of the campaign finance system, the Federal Election Commission issued an advisory opinion in the 1975 *Sun Oil* case that permitted corporations to use corporate funds to set up and administer PACs and to solicit voluntary contributions from managers and stockholders. Since then, there has been sharp growth in the number of PACs associated with corporations and professional associations and in the number of dollars flowing through them. Since the elections of 1994 that ended Democratic control of Congress and, therefore, the right to chair committees and subcommittees, business-related PACs have no longer had a strong incentive to channel funds to Democrats. Increasingly, they have focused their giving on Republicans.

Over the past half century, while business interests have gained new antagonists—as well, of course, as new allies—in the public interest community, their traditional adversary, organized labor, has become progressively weaker, both politically and economically. The attrition in the power of labor unions, which were traditionally part of the coalition backing egalitarian social programs, has significant consequences for the political representation of the interests of less affluent Americans.[49] In contrast to the substantial growth in the numbers of politically active organizations of various kinds—ranging from corporations to environmental groups to civil rights groups—the number of labor unions is, in contrast to every other kind of organization, essentially flat. What is even more significant than the absence of growth in the number of unions is the diminution in the share of workers who are union members. Only 12.5 percent of the workforce is unionized, a fraction of its high point during the 1950s. The erosion in union membership has come entirely from the ranks of private-sector workers. Currently, only 7.9 percent of workers in the private sector are union members, less than half the rate in the early 1980s.[50]

The implications of the weakening of labor unions are thrown into relief when we note that, while the membership associations, public interest law firms, and think tanks that represent diffuse public interests in politics broaden the perspectives brought to political contestation, they do not broaden the socioeconomic base of citizen politics. Even when they provide political opposition to the business interests that have traditionally been so powerful in pressure politics—and they frequently do not—these public interest organizations tend to be staffed and supported by the well-educated and privileged and, thus, do not diminish class-based inequalities in political voice.

Thus, recent decades have witnessed a series of opposing processes—some of which have reinforced the political voice of interests traditionally well represented in organized interest politics and some of which have strengthened less traditional interests. On the one hand, the domination of the field by business in pressure politics has diminished: many relatively marginal groups—including racial and ethnic minorities, women, gays, and the disabled—have become organized, and business has new antagonists (and allies) among public interest groups. On the other, labor unions have grown substantially weaker, and the economically disadvantaged have been left behind in the explosion of organized interest representation. The bottom line is extremely difficult to calculate. Whether these contradictory trends have had an impact in either direction on the inequalities that have long characterized organized interest politics is probably impossible to measure. What is clear is that this realm of citizen politics continues to be characterized by substantial inequalities of political voice.

Conclusion

As this essay is being written, another of Washington's periodic influence-peddling scandals is unfolding—so fresh that it does not yet have a moniker to join the annals of Abscam, Koreagate, the S&L scandal, and other recent examples. The behavior that appropriately elicits outrage from the public, the media, and untainted public officials offends the belief that persuasive public argument, not cash passed privately under the table, should win the day in making public policy. In essence, such corruption is an equality issue. The norms of democracy presume that all citizens have an opportunity to be heard in public discussion. When public policy is for sale to the highest bidder, those who object to the auction, along with those who cannot meet the winning bid and those who cannot afford to place bids at all, are frozen out.

We are perhaps naive in thinking that the nasty business currently on the front pages is not the usual modus operandi of American politics. Despite what some reformers would have us believe, such corruption is not the day-to-day political norm. But what does not command attention or generate indignation is the way that the ordinary operations of politics do violence to norms of democratic equality. This chapter, which has differed from others in this volume in both its tone and its reliance on systematic data, has shown that those at the top of the class hierarchy speak much more loudly in citizen politics. As individuals, they are more likely to go to the polls and to engage in other forms of political activity, including protest, that are richer in the capacity to convey political messages. They are more likely not only to make campaign contributions but also to write large checks when they donate. Moreover, the set of organizations that are active in Washington politics is strongly skewed in the direction of the representation of the economic interests of the affluent and well educated and their preferences with respect to public goods. We have also seen that, over the last generation, economic inequality has become much more pronounced in the United States. Political inequality has not followed a parallel path. The evidence is much more complicated and ambiguous when it comes to changing inequalities of political voice. What is clear is not so much that the level playing field of politics has tilted even further in an era of increasing economic inequality but that the playing field was slanted at the start.

We are not so alarmist as to argue that the extent of inequality in the expression of political voice portends the demise of American democracy. After all, the republic has lumbered on with ongoing political inequalities at least since we have had the technology to measure them. Nevertheless, those political inequalities constitute a serious affront to one of the foundational norms of American democracy and they result in a circumstance where republican governance takes place without benefit of a full understanding of the preferences and needs of all. So long as some people's voices register so much more loudly and clearly in our political discourse, we fail to realize an important part of the democratic promise.

NOTES

1. The significance of egalitarianism in the American ethos emerges clearly in the observations of one student of American exceptionalism:

There have been many attempts to distill the essence of American political thought into a list of themes. Huntington, for instance, says that the content of what he calls "the American Creed" includes constitutionalism, individualism, liberalism, democracy, and egalitarianism. Lipset notes in one book that the most important American values are equality and achievement; in another he observes, "The American creed can be subsumed in four words: antistatism, individualism, populism, and egalitarianism" . . . I will start with two aspects of American political thought, individualism and equality, because these two categories tend to include a lot of other ideas that scholars have identified as significant parts of American political thought.

John Kingdon, *America the Unusual* (New York: St. Martin's, 1999), 25–26 (internal references have been omitted).

2. On this theme see J. R. Pole, *The Pursuit of Equality in American History,* rev. ed. (Berkeley and Los Angeles: University of California Press, 1993).

3. On the growth of economic inequality, see Sheldon Danziger and Peter Gottschalk, eds., *Uneven Tides: Rising Inequality in America* (New York: Russell Sage Foundation, 1993); Peter Gottschalk, "Inequality, Income Growth, and Mobility: The Basic Facts," *Journal of Economic Perspectives* 11 (1997): 21–40; Richard B. Freeman, *When Earnings Diverge: Causes, Consequences, and Cure for the New Inequality in the United States* (Washington, D.C.: National Policy Association, 1997); Frank Levy, *The New Dollars and Dreams: American Incomes and Economic Change* (New York: Russell Sage Foundation, 1998); Edward N. Wolff, *Top Heavy* (New York: New Press, 2002); Thomas Piketty and Emmanuel Saez, "Income Inequality in the United States, 1913–1998," *Quarterly Journal of Economics* 118 (2003): 1–39; Gary Burtless and Christopher Jencks, "American Inequality and Its Consequences," in *Agenda for the Nation,* ed. Henry J. Aaron, James M. Lindsay, and Pietro Nivola (Washington, D.C.: Brookings, 2003), chap. 3; Robert Greenstein and Isaac Shapiro, *The New Definitive CBO Data on Income and Tax Trends* (Washington, D.C.: Center on Budget and Policy Priorities, September 23, 2003), http://www.cbpp.org/9-23-03tax.htm (accessed January 4, 2006); Lane Kenworthy, *Egalitarian Capitalism* (New York: Russell Sage Foundation, 2004); Lars Osberg, Timothy M. Smeeding, and Jonathan Schwabish, "Income Distribution and Public Social Expenditures," and Howard Rosenthal, "Politics, Public Policy, and Inequality: A Look Back at the Twentieth Century," in *Social Inequality,* ed. Kathryn M. Neckerman (New York: Russell Sage Foundation, 2004).

4. Piketty and Saez, "Income Inequality," 7–11. Updated data are available at http://elsa.berkeley.edu/~saez/TabFig2004prel.xls (accessed March 13, 2008).

5. It is interesting to note the difference between the patterns for the two decades in these data. From 1979 to 1990, real after-tax household incomes actually decreased for the bottom two groups and grew quite sluggishly for the third and fourth quintiles. Only in the top fifth was income growth steady throughout the period.

6. We should note that the end of the stock market bubble of the late 1990s did reduce incomes at the top of the economic ladder from their high in 2000. However, income inequality in 2004 matched that in 2001, which was then at its highest since the Census Bureau began calculating a summary measure of income inequality in 1967. After three years of economic recovery, median income in 2004 was still below its prerecession levels. See *Economic Recovery Failed to Benefit Much of the Population* (Washington, D.C.: Center on Budget and Policy Priorities, August 30, 2003), http://www.cbpp.org/ 8-30-05pov.htm (accessed January 4, 2006).

7. Piketty and Saez, "Income Inequality," 29–33.

8. Wolff, *Top Heavy*, 12–13.

9. Kevin Phillips, *Wealth and Democracy* (New York: Broadway Books, 2002), 122–23. An unpublished 2005 paper by Emmanuel Saez, "Income and Wealth Concentration in Historical and International Perspective," p. 17 and figure 5, describes the same temporal pattern but finds a lower level of concentration of wealth for the recent period.

10. This paragraph draws on Burtless and Jencks, "American Inequality," and on Timothy M. Smeeding, "Public Policy, Economic Inequality, and Poverty: The United States in Comparative Perspective," May 10, 2005, http://www-cpr.maxwell.syr.edu/faculty/smeeding/pdf/Public%20Policy-SSQ_5.10.05.pdf (accessed on January 4, 2006). Of the countries Smeeding discusses, only Russia and Mexico have higher levels of income inequality than does the United States. Burtless and Jencks cover a variety of issues and have an especially helpful discussion of how the seeming contradiction between highly unequal wages and relatively equal pretax, pretransfer incomes can be resolved by taking into account high rates of labor market participation, long working hours, and low rates of unemployment in the United States.

11. Smeeding, "Public Policy," table 5.

12. Smeeding, "Public Policy." Using a somewhat different set of countries and a somewhat different time span, Freeman (*When Earnings Diverge*, 15) finds that, during the 1980s and early 1990s, inequality rose more in the United States than in any other nation in a group of sixteen, except for New Zealand.

13. Freeman, *When Earnings Diverge*, 19.

14. Figures about purchasing power parity (PPP) are taken from Smeeding, "Public Policy," figure 2. Smeeding warns of the difficulties in making such comparisons across nations. Thus, these figures should be interpreted with caution. Nonetheless, the pattern is unmistakable.

15. On these themes, see Burtless and Jencks, "American Inequality"; Michael Hout, "How Inequality May Affect Intergenerational Mobility," in Neckerman, *Social Inequality*, chap. 26; and Samuel Bowles, Herbert Gintis, and Melissa Osborne Groves, "Introduction," Bhashkar Mazumder, "The Apple Falls Even Closer to the Tree Than We Thought: New and Revised Estimates of the Intergenerational Inheritance of Earnings," and David Harding, Christopher Jencks, Leonard M. Lopoo, and Susan M. Mayer, "The Changing Effect of Family Background on the Incomes of American Adults," in *Unequal Chances: Family Background and Economic Success,* ed. Samuel Bowles, Herbert Gintis, and Melissa Osborne Groves (Princeton: Princeton University Press, 2005).

16. See the summaries in Hout, "How Inequality May Affect Mobility," 971–76; and Harding et al., "Changing Effect of Family Background," 133.

17. David T. Ellwood and Thomas J. Kane, "Who Is Getting a College Education: Family Background and the Growing Gaps in Enrollment," in *Securing the Future*, ed. Sheldon Danziger and Jane Waldfogel (New York: Russell Sage Foundation, 2000), table 10.1. While the postsecondary profile of students from the lowest income quartile barely changed over the period, the educational prospects of the students from the highest income quartile were enhanced visibly. In that affluent group, 19 percent of the 1980 and 1982 graduates got no further education, and 55 percent attended four-year colleges; for

1992 graduates from the top income quartile, only 10 percent went no further and 66 percent went to four-year colleges.

18. See Harding et al., "Changing Effect of Family Background." They find interesting differences between men and women in mobility patterns. Almost every background factor has a stronger impact on outcomes for women than for men, but the period after 1971 witnessed a weakening of these effects for women.

19. For a discussion of public attitudes toward inequality in economic and political outcomes and extensive bibliographic references, see Kay Lehman Schlozman, Benjamin I. Page, Sidney Verba, and Morris P. Fiorina, "Inequalities of Political Voice," in *Inequality and American Democracy* , ed. Lawrence R. Jacobs and Theda Skocpol (New York: Russell Sage Foundation, 2005), 20–28.

20. Alexander Hamilton et al., *The Federalist,* ed. Robert Scigliano (New York: Modern Library, 2000), 212.

21. The academic literature on citizen participation in America is extensive. A number of helpful sources contain general discussions of political participation and extensive bibliographical references. Among them are Lester W. Milbrath and M. L. Goel, *Political Participation: How and Why Do People Get Involved in Politics?* 2nd ed. (Chicago: Rand McNally, 1977); Linda Bennett and Stephen Earl Bennett, "Political Participation: Meaning and Measurement," in *Annual Review of Political Science,* ed. Samuel Long (Norwood, N.J.: Ablex, 1986); Jan E. Leighley, "Attitudes, Opportunities and Incentives: A Field Essay on Political Participation," *Political Research Quarterly* 48 (1995): 181–209; Henry E. Brady, "Political Participation," in *Measures of Political Attitudes,* ed. John P. Robinson, Phillip R. Shaver, and Lawrence Wrightsman (San Diego, Calif.: Academic Press, 1999); M. Margaret Conway, *Political Participation in the United States,* 3rd ed. (Washington, D.C.: CQ Press, 2000); and Kay Lehman Schlozman, "Citizen Participation in America: What Do We Know? Why Do We Care?" in *Political Science: The State of the Discipline,* ed. Ira Katznelson and Helen V. Milner (New York: W. W. Norton, 2002). Empirical studies that demonstrate the significance of social class for political participation and explicate the mechanisms that link social class to participation include Sidney Verba and Norman H. Nie, *Participation in America* (New York: Harper Row, 1972); Raymond Wolfinger and Steven Rosenstone, *Who Votes?* (New Haven: Yale University Press, 1980); Steven J. Rosenstone and John Mark Hansen, *Mobilization, Participation, and Democracy in America* (New York: Macmillan, 1993); Sidney Verba, Kay Lehman Schlozman, and Henry Brady, *Voice and Equality: Civic Voluntarism in American Politics* (Cambridge: Harvard University Press, 1995); and Norman Nie, Jane Junn, and Kenneth Stehlik-Barry, *Education and Democratic Citizenship in America* (Chicago: University of Chicago Press, 1996).

22. Actual question wording can be found on the website of the American National Election Studies. As is ordinarily the case in surveys, these data inflate the proportion who claim to have voted. The measure of campaign activity includes either attending campaign meetings or rallies or doing other campaign work; the measure of campaign contributions includes donations to parties, candidates, or groups working for or against candidates; the measure of membership in a political organization was constructed from a series of questions in which respondents were asked whether they be-

long to any organizations and, if so, whether any of these organizations seek to influence the government.

23. The most significant cross-national study of the relationship between socioeconomic status and political activity is Sidney Verba, Norman H. Nie, and Jae-on Kim, *Participation and Political Equality* (Cambridge: Cambridge University Press, 1978). More recent evidence demonstrating the relationship between SES and political activity, and the particular strength of that relationship in the United States, can be found in Russell J. Dalton, *Citizen Politics*, 4th ed. (Washington, D.C.: CQ Press, 2006), chap. 3.

24. Verba, Nie, and Kim, *Participation and Political Equality*, 72. The remainder of this paragraph draws on Verba, Nie, and Kim's argument.

25. Wolfinger and Rosenstone, *Who Votes?* chap. 6.

26. The discussion in this section draws on Verba, Schlozman, and Brady, *Voice and Equality*, chaps. 6–8.

27. See Rosenstone and Hansen, *Mobilization, Participation, and Democracy;* and Robert D. Putnam, *Bowling Alone: The Collapse and Revival of American Community* (New York: Simon and Schuster, 2000).

28. See Nie, Junn, and Stehlik-Barry, *Education and Democratic Citizenship.*

29. See Christopher Uggen and Jeff Manza, "Democratic Contraction? Political Consequences of Felon Disenfranchisement in the United States," *American Sociological Review* 67 (2002): 777–803; and Jeff Manza and Christopher Uggen, "Punishment and Democracy: Disenfranchisement of Nonincarcerated Felons in the United States," *Perspectives on Politics* 2 (2004): 491–505.

30. Among recent works, Rosenstone and Hansen, *Mobilization, Participation, and Democracy*, 241–45, and Richard B. Freeman, "What, Me Vote?" in Neckerman, *Social Inequality*, find (on the basis of data that end in 1988) an increase in SES stratification of voters. In contrast, Jan E. Leighley and Jonathan Nagler, "Socioeconomic Class Bias in Turnout, 1964–1988: The Voters Remain the Same," *American Political Science Review* 86 (1992): 725–36; Jan E. Leighley and Jonathan Nagler, "Individual and Systemic Influences on Turnout: Who Votes?" *Journal of Politics* 54 (1992): 718–40; and Todd G. Shields and Robert K. Goidel, "Participation Rates, Socioeconomic Class Biases, and Congressional Elections: A Cross Validation," *American Journal of Political Science* 41 (1997): 683–91, do not. Those who report increased stratification of the electorate tie that change to erosion in turnout rather than to increased economic inequality. In fact, Freeman (p. 722) shows the greatest increase in the stratification of the electorate to have occurred between 1968 and 1972, *before* economic inequalities began to rise sharply. In addition, Rosenstone and Hansen (p. 243) show the 1960s to be the distinctive era with income and educational inequality of the electorate at lower levels than either before or after. See Shields and Goidel, "Participation Rates," and Freeman, "What, Me Vote?" for summaries of the relevant studies and bibliographical references.

31. Henry E. Brady, Kay Lehman Schlozman, Sidney Verba, and Laurel Elms, "Who Bowls? The (Un)Changing Stratification of Participation," in *Understanding Public Opinion*, ed. Barbara Norrander and Clyde Wilcox (Washington, D.C.: CQ Press, 2002).

32. Todd G. Shields and Robert K. Goidel, "Who Contributes? Checkbook Participation, Class Biases, and the Impact of Legal Reforms, 1952–1994," *American Politics Quar-*

terly 28 (2000): 216–33; and Clyde Wilcox, "Individual Donors in the Presidential Nomination Process," unpublished manuscript, 2003.

33. Theda Skocpol's work is central to understanding the changes in associational life and their implications for contemporary democracy. See *Diminished Democracy: From Membership to Management in American Civic Life* (Norman: University of Oklahoma Press, 2003); "Civic Transformations and Inequality in the Contemporary United States," in Neckerman *Social Inequality;* and "Voice and Inequality: The Transformation of American Civic Democracy," *Perspectives on Politics* 2 (2004): 3–20.

34. Skocpol, *Diminished Democracy,* 212–19.

35. This section draws heavily from the intellectual framework contained in Kay Lehman Schlozman and John T. Tierney, *Organized Interests and American Democracy* (New York: Harper and Row, 1986), chap. 4. The study of organized interest politics has a venerable history in political science. Important works include E. E. Schattschneider, *The Semi-Sovereign People: A Realist's View of Democracy in America* (New York: Holt, Rinehart, and Winston, 1960); Raymond A. Bauer, Ithiel de Sola Pool, and Lewis Anthony Dexter, *American Business and Public Policy: The Politics of Foreign Trade* (Chicago: Aldine, 1963); Grant McConnell, *Private Power and American Democracy* (New York: Knopf, 1966); Theodore Lowi, *The End of Liberalism: Ideology, Policy, and the Crisis of Public Authority* (New York: W. W. Norton, 1969); David Bicknell Truman, *The Governmental Process: Political Interests and Public Opinion,* 2nd ed. (orig. ed. 1951) (New York: Knopf, 1971); James Q. Wilson, *Political Organizations* (New York: Basic Books, 1973); Charles E. Lindblom, *Politics and Markets: The World's Political Economic Systems* (New York: Basic Books, 1977); and Jack Walker, *Mobilizing Interest Groups in America: Patrons, Professions, and Social Movements* (Ann Arbor: University of Michigan Press, 1991). Frank R. Baumgartner and Beth L. Leech, *Basic Interests: The Importance of Groups in Politics and in Political Science* (Princeton: Princeton University Press, 1998) present useful discussions of the political science literature and many references. Further discussion of the specific issue of the representation of interests through organized interest politics and additional bibliography can be found in Schlozman and Tierney, *Organized Interests,* chap. 4; and Andrew McFarland, "Interest Groups and the Policymaking Process: Sources of Countervailing Power in America," in *The Politics of Interests,* ed. Mark P. Petracca (Boulder: Westview Press, 1992).

36. To the extent that organizations have an impact on public policy, unequal representation by organizations may imply unequal influence upon policy. After taking many political factors into account, one sophisticated study of controversies in four policy domains found it difficult to predict which of the players will prevail in influencing policy but reported that it is essential to be at the table. See John P. Heinz, Edward O. Laumann, Robert L. Nelson, and Robert H. Salisbury, *The Hollow Core: Private Interests in National Policymaking* (Cambridge: Harvard University Press, 1993), 344–60. Absence of representation is, obviously, especially detrimental at the critical phase before policy controversies emerge—when the political agenda is being set. On the role of organized interests in agenda setting, see Frank R. Baumgartner and Bryan D. Jones, *Agendas and Instability in American Politics* (Chicago: University of Chicago Press, 1993), esp. chap. 9, who show the impact on the political agenda of the emergence of new environmental

groups. In short, although we should not equate the organizational representation of an interest with political influence, representation is fundamental.

37. On the complexities in understanding equal voice when political representation is by organized interests, see Schlozman and Tierney, *Organized Interests,* esp. chap. 4.

38. Schattschneider, *The Semi-Sovereign People,* 35.

39. See Mancur Olson, Jr., *The Logic of Collective Action: Public Goods and the Theory of Groups* (Cambridge: Harvard University Press, 1965). For discussion of the problem of organizational maintenance and the difficulties confronting someone who wishes to found a membership group or keep one going, see Wilson, *Political Organizations,* especially chaps. 2–3.

40. The directory, *Washington Representatives* (Washington, D.C.: Columbia Books), is published annually. It lists every organization that has a presence in Washington politics by virtue of maintaining an office in the capital (or surrounding area) or hiring Washington-based counsel or public affairs specialists. Collection of these data was supported by Boston College and Harvard University. This enterprise has benefited from the industry, enthusiasm, and talents of an extraordinary group of research assistants: Will Bacic, Jeremy Bailey, John Barry, Ageliki Christopher, Lauren Daniel, Sarah Debbink, Glen Feder, John Gattman, Heitor Gouvea, Gail Harmon, Kate Letourneau, Miriam Mansury, Katie Marcot, Rafael Munoz, Janice Pardue, Michael Parker, Robert Porter, Karthick Ramakrishnan, Veronica Roberts, Ganesh Sitaraman, Martin Steinwand, Emily Thorson, Clay Tousey, and Jill Weidner. For discussion of these data, and detailed description of each of the ninety-some categories into which they were coded, see Kay Lehman Schlozman, Traci Burch, and Samuel Lampert, "Still an Upper-Class Accent: Organized Interest Politics and Pluralist Orthodoxy," paper delivered at the Annual Meeting of the American Political Science Association, Chicago, September 2004. Complete data from which tables 2 and 3 are constructed can be found in appendix B of that paper.

41. For corporations—and for universities, hospitals, think tanks, and any other organization in the pressure system that does not have members in the traditional sense—there is ambiguity as to whose concerns and preferences are being represented. Whom do corporations represent politically—the stockholders, managers, employees, or customers? Surely, these constituencies often have compatible interests. Still, evidence ranging from the recent behavior of management at Enron, Tyco, and WorldCom to the diminution of employee health and pension benefits to the number of labor-management disputes before the NLRB seems to confirm the long-standing wisdom that the interests of management rarely take a backseat to those of competing corporate constituents.

42. Because it excludes from the numerator all unions and associations of public employees, this figure is, in fact, a considerable understatement. Some professionals—for example, teachers and nurses—are organized by white-collar unions rather than by professional associations. In addition, many of the organizations of government employees—ranging from state foresters to postal supervisors to district attorneys—bring together professional, managerial, or administrative personnel.

43. This point is made by Andrew S. McFarland, *Public Interest Lobbies* (Washington, D.C.: American Enterprise Institute, 1976), chap. 2.

44. See Douglas R. Imig, *Poverty and Power: The Political Representation of Poor Americans* (Lincoln: University of Nebraska Press, 1996).

45. Jeffrey Berry, *A Voice for Nonprofits* (Washington, D.C.: Brookings, 2003), 65. In his analysis of the impact of the tax code on lobbying by nonprofits, Berry points out that a tax provision of which many nonprofits are not aware, the possibility of H election, permits them autonomy in undertaking political action.

46. See Debra C. Minkoff, *Organizing for Equality* (New Brunswick, N.J.: Rutgers University Press, 1995).

47. Much of this growth occurred in the period immediately before that covered in our data. Even so, table 3 shows the rate of increase from 1981 to 2001 in the number of public interest groups to be quite high. On the implications for politics of the growth of new citizens' groups, see Jeffrey Berry, *The New Liberalism: The Rising Power of Citizen Groups* (Washington, D.C.: Brookings, 1999). On the role of foundations and other patrons in stimulating these developments, see Walker, *Mobilizing Interest Groups,* esp. chap. 5. Discussions of the role of patronage in stimulating the growth of public interest organizations have tended to focus on the cultivation of liberal groups. However, conservative advocates for broad public interests, especially conservative think tanks and legal foundations, have also benefited from analogous sponsorship from conservative foundations. See Thomas Ferguson and Joel Rogers, *Right Turn: The Decline of the Democrats and the Future of American Politics* (New York: Hill and Wang, 1986), 86–87.

48. David Vogel, *Fluctuating Fortunes: The Power of Business in America* (New York: Basic Books, 1989), chap. 8, documents the massive increase in the government relations capacity of business.

49. See, for example, Michael Goldfield, *The Decline of Organized Labor in the United States* (Chicago: University of Chicago Press, 1987); and Benjamin Radcliff and Patricia Davis, "Labor Organization and Electoral Participation in Industrial Democracies," *American Journal of Political Science* 44 (2000): 132–41.

50. Figures taken from the website of the *Statistical Abstract,* http://www.census.gov/prod/2005pubs/06statab/labor.pdf (accessed on January 12, 2006).

The Real Immigration Crisis

Peter Skerry

A couple of years ago I attended a conference in Toronto, where a colleague presented his research on the challenges of border control in Europe. He prefaced his remarks with the observation that Western democracies would be able to deal with mass migration only when they faced up to its inevitability.

Fair enough. The next day, after the conference ended, we participants were treated to a bus tour of Toronto's immigrant neighborhoods. At one point, the bus stopped in front of a Starbucks, and everyone piled out for coffee. Moving down the aisle, I noticed that the speaker from the previous day was not getting up. When I asked if he would join us, he indicated no and explained that he objected to the way such chains were coming to dominate consumer markets across the globe. I was tempted to quip, "Isn't that inevitable?" But I kept quiet, went out, and ordered my usual—a medium, nonfat latte.

More recently, I came across an article about U.S. immigration policy by Kevin Hassett, an economist at the American Enterprise Institute. Objecting to a proposal by congressional Republicans to extend the fence along the Mexican border, Hassett commented: "Building a fence is a strange move for the party of Ronald Reagan, whose call to tear down the Berlin wall ranks as one of the most memorable lines of the 20th century."[1]

Now Hassett is hardly the first to invoke this comparison. But certainly, there is a fundamental difference between a fence—a not very effective one—built by a democratic nation to exercise its sovereign right to keep unauthorized individuals out, and a barrier—manned by armed guards with orders to shoot to kill—erected by a police state to imprison its own citizens.

These two vignettes highlight the failure of our political and intellectual elites to clarify for their fellow citizens the dilemmas presented by contemporary mass migration. This abdication of responsibility spans the political spectrum from liberal to conservative. And both the dominant pro-immigration camp and the restrictionist rump have demonstrated a lack of moral leadership, as well as of political imagination.

To be sure, immigration is a particularly intractable issue. Immigration policy combines technical complexity with emotional considerations of national identity, ethnicity, and race. Narrow, well-organized business interests have much at stake in the formulation of immigration policy, but the mass of ordinary, unorganized Americans is also invested in this intensely symbolic issue. No wonder that immigration does not play out along the usual partisan and interest group fault-lines. As economic historians Timothy J. Hatton and Jeffrey G. Williamson note, "There are several characteristics of immigration policy that makes it especially prone to political illusion."[2]

This is precisely why this issue cries out for strong leadership. But few among our elites have struggled to make sense of, much less engage, widespread popular disaffection with immigration. As a result, ordinary Americans have been left to sort out this nettlesome issue for themselves. Not surprisingly, they have come up with some downright silly and at times offensive claims about what could be the largest influx of immigrants in American history. Silly, offensive, or not, these views constitute political facts that must be reckoned with. Instead, our leaders have either dismissed popular discontent with current policy, or pandered to it.

The most powerful illusion at work here is our preoccupation with illegal immigration, which has been on full display since 2006, when the issue moved to the center of the national political stage. There are currently at least 12 million illegal immigrants in the United States. This *is* a problem, but the public's preoccupation with it is overwrought and misinformed. To judge by recent events, Americans are now more alarmed by Mexican day laborers than Islamist terrorists. On the other hand, proponents of "comprehensive immigration reform" offered less than they promised. Their package of a temporary worker program combined with a de facto amnesty for millions of illegal immigrants was neither "comprehensive" nor "reform." It certainly would not have addressed what is bothering millions of Americans.

The result is continued stalemate and confusion. Even if a Democratic Congress and a lame duck Republican president manage to enact an amnesty, the basic dilemmas will remain unresolved. Yet the real crisis here is not the strains from record numbers of immigrants. Despite dire predictions of an emergent helot class of immigrants and of weakened national cohesion, we will almost certainly muddle along. But we are witnessing a revealing test of our political and intellectual elites: specifically, their inability and unwillingness squarely and honestly to address a complex and emotional issue of direct and growing importance to millions of anxious Americans.

The Opinion Gap

Not all Americans are upset with current levels of immigration, but many are. One recent analysis of the survey data concludes that "a plurality or majority of Americans want fewer immigrants coming into the country."[3] Hatton and Williamson make the same point more forcefully: "For most of the past fifty years, at least half of the Americans surveyed thought there were too many immigrants."[4]

Nevertheless, newcomers—both legal and illegal—have continued to arrive here in ever increasing numbers. Analysts working with the restrictionist Center for Immigration Studies conclude that the gap between public opinion and policy is wider here than in just about any other policy domain.[5] Hatton and Williamson agree: "The evidence is quite clear that the gap between public attitude and government policy is far greater for immigration issues than it is for war, inflation, unemployment, gun control and abortion."[6]

Underlying this gap are divergent views about immigration across social and economic strata. Economists Kenneth Scheve and Matthew Slaughter note that "less-skilled people prefer more restrictive immigration policy, and more-skilled people prefer less restrictive immigration policy." As they sum up their statistical analyses: "If you could put a high school dropout with roughly 11 years of education through both high school and college, ending up with about 16 years of education, then the probability that this individual supports immigration restrictions would fall by some 10 to 14 percentage points."[7]

These findings are corroborated by surveys sponsored by the Chicago Council on Foreign Relations. In its 2002 report, the council notes that immigration elicits much stronger reactions from the public than from elites: "The public is substantially more alarmed by immigrants and refugees coming into the United States as a critical threat to U.S. interests by a 46 point margin (60 of the public versus only 14 percent of leaders)."[8] Indeed, the council's research indicates that this gap has been at least this wide for more than a decade.[9]

With regard to illegal immigration, 70 percent of the public believes "controlling and reducing illegal immigration" to be "a very important foreign policy goal of the United States,"[10] while only 22 percent of U.S. leaders agree.[11] This forty-eight-point gap is one of the widest documented by the council, only slightly smaller than the gap between leaders and the public over the importance of protecting American jobs.[12]

The Popular Response

On the popular side of this divide, one does encounter perceptions that are wide of the mark. For example, a frequently heard complaint is that immigrant families are not learning English. Yet while immigrants themselves may not be learning as much English as desirable, their children and grandchildren certainly are.[13]

Another commonly voiced concern is the threat to American jobs and wages posed by immigrants. Indeed, Hatton and Williamson cite one recent poll that more than three-quarters responding "thought that immigrants robbed jobs from natives."[14] Other polls report somewhat lower figures.[15] Either way, a large proportion of the American public consistently expresses concerns about the negative labor market impacts of immigration.[16]

For these labor-market worries, there *is* some social scientific support. Harvard economist George Borjas reports that between 1980 and 2000 immigration had its biggest negative impact on the low-skilled, reducing the wages of native-born high school dropouts by 9 percent.[17] This is troubling. But overall, immigration has a relatively small negative impact on Americans' wages.[18]

The public is also concerned about the demands immigrants put on government services. In their recent study of racial, ethnic, and class tensions in four Chicago neighborhoods, William Julius Wilson and Richard P. Taub document that working- and lower-middle-class Americans tend to regard immigrants as freeloaders who don't contribute to the common good. They cite a typical letter to the editor of a local newspaper: "Americans born and raised here better wake up! . . . many of you or most of you are not entitled to the same benefits as many of the immigrants who never paid a dime in taxes."[19]

Again, this complaint has *some* factual basis. Researchers report that immigrants typically arrive planning not to remain, but to work hard, save as much money as possible, and then return home. And while many, probably most, do end up staying, their decisions are often hedged by dreams of eventually going home.[20] Native-born Americans pick up on such lack of commitment and conclude that immigrants may not be reliable neighbors.

From there, it is but a short leap to concluding that "immigrants don't pay taxes." This is not true, of course. Even illegal immigrants pay taxes, for example sales and property taxes. Many also contribute to Social Security and to federal and state income taxes.[21]

But the relevant question is whether immigrants, with their disproportionately low skill and education levels, contribute as much in taxes as they claim in public services. Because they have more children than natives, and because their households earn less, immigrants tend overall to receive more in public benefits than they pay in taxes. To be sure, this is not the case at the federal level. But at the state and local levels, where the relevant benefits—schools, hospitals, and social welfare programs—are overwhelmingly paid for and delivered, immigrants do constitute a net fiscal drain. This negative impact at the state and local levels certainly occurs in the short run and, as economist Gordon Hanson emphasizes, in the long run as well. Taking all three levels of government into consideration, the same conclusion appears to be true: immigrants definitely represent a net drain in the short term, and, some economists estimate, over the long term as well.[22] Thus, while the perception of immigrants as freeloaders who contribute nothing to America's coffers is a gross distortion, the widespread anxiety that immigrants cost more than they contribute is hardly misplaced.

Of course, immigrants also contribute to economic growth. But the overall increase is slight, about one-tenth of 1 percent of U.S. gross domestic product (GDP). More to the point, this is less than the percentage of GDP attributable to the fiscal costs of immigrants.[23]

Beyond these fiscal considerations, the transient situation of many immigrants contributes to social strains that are difficult to quantify but visible and vexing to many Americans. Immigrants intent upon saving money cram into overcrowded apartments. Frequently unattached males, separated from family and loved ones, they can be noisy and troublesome neighbors, whose run-down cars jam streets and end up parked on what used to be tidy plots of grass. Across the nation, local jurisdictions have enacted ordinances and implemented programs to address such concerns. Yet these initiatives invariably antagonize immigrants or their advocates, resulting in still more friction.

Even efforts to find work can foment controversy. For many Americans today, the image of immigrants that most readily comes to mind is not shadowy figures running across the border, but male laborers hanging out near a Home Depot, waiting to be hired by contractors or homeowners. To some passers-by, such scenes are evidence of ambition and hard work. But to others, they represent the annoying, even threatening behavior of unkempt men leering at passing women, darting out into traffic to negotiate with potential employers, drinking and urinating in public, perhaps dealing drugs, and sometimes worse.

The difficulties posed by immigrants are generally rather mundane annoyances, which is why complaints about them are readily dismissed, especially by those affluent enough to insulate themselves from such problems. But to entrenched residents of neighborhoods undergoing change, these seemingly small matters loom large. Wilson and Taub quote a longtime resident of one Chicago neighborhood:

> You know, just on this street, we've had a couple people move in and they're not, you know, they don't understand about block clubs, you know . . . we have people they trying to work on they cars on the street. And this may sound really trivial, but if you don't maintain standards . . . We have garages and alleys, that's where you do that stuff, back there, okay.[24]

Noteworthy here is that this is not a white resident (as the reader with an ear for language might have noticed), but a lower-middle-class black woman concerned about the arrival of less affluent blacks in her neighborhood.

The Elite Response

Despite their pro-immigration bias, elites have not always been aggressive advocates for generous immigration policies. They did not have to be. In part, this was because political and intellectual elites could free ride on the efforts of discreet but well-organized business interests who made sure their labor needs were met. Even as immigration levels began to rise during the 1970s, these elites were able to keep immigration substantially off the political agenda by framing it in the narrowest and most technical terms, typically as an aspect of labor market policy. Even when researchers began to document some limited labor market competition between immigrants and low-skilled, native-born Americans, pro-immigration advocates managed to avoid talking about the many other arenas where immigrants appeared to be competing with Americans.

Undergirding this flaccid but pervasive disposition in favor of immigration has been the conviction, articulated by my Starbucks-contesting colleague, that in the contemporary world high levels of immigration are inevitable. But inevitability is in the eye of the beholder. Then, too, such smugness and confidence are buttressed by self-interest. Economists agree that the owners of capital, business entrepreneurs, and well-educated professionals benefit overwhelmingly from immigration.[25] While many ordinary Americans see immigrants as potential competitors for jobs, neighborhood turf, or public resources, the wealthy and merely affluent see them as employees—the nannies, gardeners, dishwashers, maids, and laborers who help to get things done.

Still, there is much more at work here than crude self-interest. Deeply held convictions about openness and diversity are just as important in this respect as sheer economic self-interest. But like the influence of oil on U.S. policy in the Middle East, the direct benefits to elites of mass immigration should be neither ignored nor exaggerated.

Only as immigrants' numbers have continued to grow and their presence spread throughout the nation have elites felt constrained to articulate a stronger and more explicit defense of their pro-immigration stance. One response has been to dismiss the growing backlash as the work of media demagogues. For liberals, a good candidate for this role has been CNN's Lou Dobbs, whose nightly news program has single-mindedly, almost obsessively, focused on the negative impact of illegal immigrants on the lives of ordinary Americans—and on the federal government's failure to solve the problem.[26] On the right, pro-immigration conservatives have suggested that talk radio has been stirring up anti-immigrant sentiment.[27]

Yet the recent history of immigration politics demonstrates quite the opposite: years before media personalities took on this issue, an outraged citizenry was pressing it on reluctant and unresponsive politicians. During the 1980s and into the 1990s, it was extremely difficult to get any public officials—even in California—merely to raise the topic of immigration. To do so was to risk denunciation as a bigot. Such was the situation that led to passage of Proposition 187, the 1994 California ballot initiative that would have banned virtually all public services to illegal immigrants. That draconian measure was eventually gutted by the federal courts. Even so, it was supported by 58 percent of California voters, including almost one-fourth of Latino voters, who correctly felt that no one was listening to them.[28]

Confronted by political facts like Proposition 187, pro-immigration elites have typically responded by characterizing them as expressions of bigotry and intolerance. It is tempting to come to this conclusion, given the degree of crankiness, meanness, and irrationality among anti-immigration activists. Yet as I have been arguing, such widespread popular discontent should not be so readily dismissed.

Guidance through this thicket is available from a surprising source. John Higham was perhaps the leading student of American ethnic and immigrant history during the second half of the twentieth century. His first book, *Strangers in the Land: Patterns of American Nativism, 1860–1925,* was published in 1955 and remains the classic reference on the irrational forces that culminated in the restrictive immigration legislation of the 1920s.[29] Higham's oft-cited work laid down the template for subsequent efforts to understand and interpret Americans' negative reactions to immigrants in the past and in the present. As he put it:

> Nativism cut deeper than economic jealousy or social disapproval. It touched the springs of fear and hatred; it breathed a sense of crisis. Above all, it expressed a militantly defensive nationalism: an aroused conviction that an intrusive element menaced the unity, and therefore the integrity and survival, of the nation itself.[30]

Yet just two years after *Strangers in the Land* first appeared, Higham modified his position: "I propose that research on the conflicts associated with foreign elements in American society should take a new line. The nativist theme, as defined and developed to date, is imaginatively exhausted."[31] Over the next forty years, in a series of remarkable but neglected essays, Higham developed this critique of his own original perspective.[32]

Specifically, Higham argued that analysts exploring the origins of hostility to immigrants needed to focus less on irrational passions and abstract ideologies and more on structures and institutions, where quotidian but concrete conflicts of status and interest could be analyzed. Moreover, Higham insisted that the scope of inquiry should include not merely conflicts between dominant or established groups and newcomers, but between different groups of newcomers as well. As he put it: "We must assume, I think, that in a competitive society everything which differentiates one group from another involves a potential conflict of interest."[33]

The Economists Weigh In

As I have suggested, while *Strangers in the Land* continues to be cited with approval, Higham's mature insights have been uniformly ignored. Yet recent work by economic historians supports the later Higham. Kevin H. O'Rourke and Jeffrey G. Williamson have investigated the origins of restrictive immigration policies in the United States and other New World countries during the early decades of the twentieth century. They report that the huge influx of unskilled immigrants arriving here between 1870 and World War I substantially lowered the real wages of American workers and led to rising inequality. As they summarize their findings:

> Although the size of the immigrant flow did not seem to have any consistent impact on New World policy up to 1930, its low and declining quality certainly did, provoking restriction. Racism or xenophobia do not seem to have been at work in driving the evolution of policy (which is not to deny that they existed). Rather, it was immigrant quality, labor market conditions, and policies abroad ... that mattered most for policy. New World countries acted in a way that revealed an effort to defend the economic interests of unskilled labor.[34]

Turning back to the contemporary situation, Higham's revisionism again finds support. As indicated earlier, economists report that the current influx has a narrow, negative impact on American workers, specifically high school dropouts who compete directly with unskilled immigrants. At the same time, restrictionist policy preferences correlate with low skill levels. Does this not suggest that Americans who want to curtail immigration are acting rationally in defense of their economic self-interest? No—and yes.

No, because the proportion of Americans expressing restrictionist views is greater than the relatively small segment of the labor force competing directly with immigrants. Yes, because, as Scheve and Slaughter point out, high-skill workers have benefited from substantial wage premiums, while "the majority of the US labor force has had close to zero or even negative real-wage growth for about 25 years."[35] In fact, it is striking that this period of wage stagnation coincides roughly with the steadily increasing numbers of immigrants arriving since the United Stated reopened its doors in 1965.

Not surprisingly, then, many Americans attribute their economic woes to immigration. Yet the evidence is that immigration, trade, and other aspects of globalization have contributed only modestly to growing wage inequality. For example, productivity gains and wage increases have been the most sluggish in service sectors, which are relatively insulated from global economic forces. More to the point, premiums to skilled labor are attributable primarily to technological change.[36]

Before concluding, though, that popular concerns about immigration and globalization are misplaced, it is worth noting that the economists who have examined the evidence do *not* come to this conclusion. Scheve and Slaughter observe that "it seems plausible that amid poor real and relative-wage performance, less-skilled US workers have blamed globalization for these outcomes and thus have been more likely to oppose policies aimed at further liberalization." They also note: "These perceptions do not simply reflect ignorance about the economic benefits of liberalization. On the contrary, the majority of those surveyed acknowledge gains from international transactions."[37]

Hatton and Williamson respond similarly to "the divergence between public attitudes toward immigration and what the evidence seems to show":

First, small [labor market] effects aren't zero effects. Second, the public may agree with academics that technological change is the main driving force in labor markets, but it may also believe that while policy has little impact on technical change, it can have a big impact on immigration. Third, the public is forward-looking and anticipates big effects in the future.

Finally, Hatton and Williamson point out that "the public may have a counterfactual in its head when it expresses anti-immigrant attitudes." They go on to suggest: "Even though immigration may not account for much of observed labor market experience over the past three decades, a world without immigration might have improved that experience quite a bit."[38]

According to such analysts, then, anxieties about immigration are not easily dismissed as irrational or racist. In a period of dramatic and profound economic change, there is enormous uncertainty. The fact that some relatively narrow segment of the populace is directly harmed by these changes signals to others that they too are vulnerable. So Americans turn to their government to do something to protect them—at their jobs, in their neighborhoods, and at schools, hospitals, and other public institutions. Prudent leaders will avoid nitpicking, listen carefully, and craft responsible policies.[39]

Illegal Immigrants: Neither Victims nor Criminals

But why is the ongoing debate not about immigrants, but about *illegal* immigrants? Answering this question is a challenge. For as I suggested earlier, while the public's fixation on illegal immigrants is not without some factual basis, it is not entirely rational. More to the point, the terms of this debate again reflect the failure of elites to clarify the dilemmas posed by contemporary migration. While pro-immigration elites condescend to or just ignore the outrage many Americans feel about illegals, restrictionists cater to it. Neither has engaged the American public constructively on this topic.

More than a decade ago, in the mid-1990s, opinion polls demonstrated that Americans greatly overestimated the number of illegal immigrants in our midst.[40] Today, there is no reason to believe that that misperception has diminished. Yet it is also true that the number of illegals here has continued to grow, and at an increasing rate.[41] As illegals have dispersed around the United States, what was once a regional concern has become a national one.[42]

Still, the debate over illegal immigration remains a curious one. Were it possible to stop illegal immigration tomorrow, most of the concerns expressed by so many Americans would remain unaddressed.[43] In fact, because legal immigrants outnumber illegals, they are a greater source of those concerns. The evidence suggests that the real challenges here do not stem exclusively or even primarily from illegal immigration. Rather they involve the social strains and disorder attendant on the movement of large numbers of unskilled, poorly educated immigrants into and out of American neighborhoods, whatever their legal status. Nevertheless, virtually all participants in this debate—regardless of their political orientation or substantive views on immigration—share the same unchallenged assumption: that legal immigration is uniformly benign or even beneficial, while illegal immigration is uniquely problematic.

In other words, I am suggesting that popular concerns about immigration are actually broader and deeper than anyone has bothered to notice, or admit. This is because the dominant frame—illegal immigrants, bad; legal immigrants, good—serves the interests of skittish politicians and other elites of diverse persuasions, all of whom find this simple dichotomy a relatively safe way to address a technically complex, emotionally charged issue that they would prefer to avoid completely.

On the defensive since the mid-1990s, pro-immigration advocates have learned that by retreating tactically and talking tough about illegal immigration, they bolster their case for legal immigration.[44] Restrictionists have gone through the obverse process and learned how to narrow an array of objections to immigration in general down to illegal immigration in particular. At some point, restrictionists figured out that it is less costly politically to inveigh against illegals than against Hispanic immigrants.

The upshot is that pro-immigration elites depict illegal immigrants as victims. Consider the rhetoric one hears across the political spectrum. Liberal columnist Ron Brownstein describes illegals as "living in the shadows." Conservative Linda Chavez refers to them as a "huge, subterranean population" that exists in fear of one day being "whisked away by government agents." Cardinal Roger Mahony bemoans their exploitation at the hands of "unscrupulous employers" who know they "are reluctant to seek legal recourse." Finally, President Bush has characterized undocumented workers as dwelling "in the shadows of American life—fearful, often abused and exploited."[45]

From this perspective, illegals are not seen as agents who have made choices and are responsible, at least partially, for their consequences. But of course they are. As mentioned earlier, immigrants—including illegals—typically come to the United States with plans to amass savings and eventually return home. Anthropologist Leo Chavez points out that such strategies help explain why illegals put up with substandard living conditions and at least in part why they endure exploitative, even dangerous work situations.[46] But as we have also seen, immigrants' plans change, and even illegals end up staying and putting down roots. Hundreds of thousands of illegals manage to buy houses.[47] Others join labor unions.[48] They also succeed in educating their children, some of whom are now knocking on the doors of state universities demanding to be charged in-state tuition like other residents. In a recent *New York Times* article, Veronica, an illegal Mexican immigrant living in San Antonio, complains about Mexican Americans deriding her as a *mojado* (wetback), but then recounts how the nurses and doctors at a nearby hospital saved her son when his appendix burst. As Veronica concludes: "Living here without papers is still better than living there."[49]

But if illegal immigrants are not just victims, neither are they mere criminals—as they are routinely referred to by restrictionist politicians. Illegals are in fact well integrated into the warp and woof of American society. As Moises Naim, editor of *Foreign Policy* magazine, points out, there is no distinct, isolated underground economy, for the simple reason that the mainstream relies so heavily on illegal labor.[50] These are, after all, *our* laborers, gardeners, and cleaning ladies.

Beyond the labor market, the line between legal and illegal remains blurred. To begin with, many currently legal immigrants did not start out that way. Over the decades there have been several amnesties. The last one, in 1986, legalized some 3 million aliens. More recently, as many as one-third of those acquiring residence papers have had prior experience here as undocumented immigrants; *two-thirds* of adult legal immigrants from Mexico have.[51]

The pervasive media image of people sneaking across the Mexican border is only half right. As many as 45 percent of undocumented persons now in the country entered *legally* through a port of entry—as shoppers, workers, tourists—and then overstayed their visas.[52] Between 1 and 1.5 million illegals are in "twilight status," which typically means being caught in processing delays, waiting to be made a "lawful permanent resident." Most of these individuals typically gain that permanent status.[53]

In other words, a nontrivial number of immigrants are here illegally for reasons not entirely of their own making. Indeed, errors and delays by immigration bureaucrats are notorious, and arguably contribute to undermining the rule of law as much as the presence of millions of illegals. Immigration law is a complicated maze of exceptions and deadlines carved out by Congress to accommodate diverse constituencies. These are not only difficult for bureaucrats to administer; they are hard for individuals to comply with and easy to run afoul of.

So the popular understanding of illegal immigrants as a distinct class of flagrant lawbreakers hardly accounts for all the facts on the ground. As Naim concludes about the broader problem of illicit flows, of which illegal immigration is but one facet, "To think of a clean line between good guys and bad guys is to fail to capture the reality of trafficking today. The fact is that illicit trade permeates our daily lives in subtle ways."[54] In the United States today, it is a crime to work without proper papers; but so is it a crime to hire such individuals.

More to my point, there is a symbiotic aspect to the way elites on both sides of this debate benefit from the bright line they maintain between legal and illegal immigrants. Whether talking tough or trying to gain sympathy for illegals, pro-immigration advocates depict them as part of "the underground economy" or "the black market." Yet just such images fuel the claims of restrictionists that illegals constitute a distinct—and threatening—caste.

The Protectionist Possibility

There is one response to Americans' anxieties that I have not discussed, but that avoids the problems I have been describing: protectionism. As journalist Thomas B. Edsall recently noted, the 2006 midterm elections benefited an emergent protectionist wing in the Democratic Party.[55]

One of the most visible and aggressive spokesmen for this perspective is Jeff Faux, founder of the Economic Policy Institute, a labor-oriented think tank. Faux has not embraced restrictionism, but he has argued that U.S. trade and immigration policies serve the interests of an ascendant class of capitalists who may profess allegiance to the United States but in fact have a globalist agenda that transcends any national loyalty.[56]

As indicated above, one objection to this analysis is that economic research does not support it. According to Scheve and Slaughter, "Most academic researchers have concluded that technological change, not globalization, has been the major force affecting US labor markets in recent decades."[57]

Another problem is that Faux seems intent on fighting the last class war. Harvard political economist Torben Iversen has observed that if the old paradigm of class politics ever made sense, it no longer does, even in European societies. Contrary to those who emphasize postindustrial value conflicts, Iversen argues that distributive economic politics and conflict are still very important. But he also explains:

> Distributive conflict is no longer mainly between capital and labor, but rather between workers owning different levels and types of human capital. . . . Levels of skills determine income and hence redistributive preferences, whereas the specificity of those skills determines exposure to labor risks and hence preferences over social insurance.[58]

Exactly so. America's expansive immigration policy is hardly attributable to global firms alone. It is supported by small and medium-size businesses, to say nothing of the Catholic Church, human rights organizations, and minority groups. It is also sustained by the sympathy and support of large numbers of middle- and upper-middle-class citizens whose economic self-interest dovetails with genuine convictions about the importance of openness and diversity to the fulfillment of American national ideals. Policy entrepreneurs like Faux will have a difficult time fitting all these elements into their global class analysis.

Conclusion

Leftists like Faux have hardly been the only critics of our elites. Their chorus has been joined by analysts as varied as Christopher Lasch[59] and Samuel Huntington.[60] My emphasis has been less on elites' self-interest and more on their smugness and self-indulgence; less on their disloyalty and more on their detachment and disdain. At the same time, the challenge involves more than character flaws or personal failings. As Lasch has persuasively demonstrated, elites in America have been shaped by pervasive and entrenched notions of progress.[61] There are deep historical and cultural forces at work here, as well as structural factors at both the national and the international levels.

Yet nothing is written in stone. There are enormous opportunities here for elites, existing or emergent, to play a critical role in a policy area marked by great complexity and powerful symbols. If elites fail to seize them, these opportunities will be thrust upon them—upon all Americans—by the political realities generated by immigration. Immigrant numbers cannot keep rising independently of public opinion without major political repercussions. Pro-immigration advocates cannot keep whistling past the graveyard, hoping that the public doesn't notice the ever-increasing influx. And political leaders will no longer be able to convince themselves that the status quo is acceptable—just because voters don't find immigration to be the most salient issue on which to vote, or because aggressive restrictionists get rebuked at the polls.

Economic historians O'Rourke and Williamson draw an explicit parallel between our situation today and that at the beginning of the twentieth century. They argue against the conventional understanding that that earlier wave of globalization was stopped by exogenous events such as World War I. Indeed, they argue that interwar deglobalization was the result of oppositional forces generated by globalization itself. Regarding immigration specifically, O'Rourke and Williamson conclude:

New World immigration controls were erected to combat the increased inequality to which the mass migrations gave rise, or were thought to have given rise. The record suggests that unless politicians worry about who gains and who loses, they may be forced by the electorate to stop efforts to strengthen global economy links, and perhaps even to dismantle them.[62]

In this era of mass air travel and instantaneous global communication, such a scenario may be difficult to imagine. It may well be that pro-immigration elites are correct in asserting the inevitability of worldwide migration. Even so, there is nothing inevitable about its consequences and aftermath. These must be attended to and managed, not passively endured or ignored. The concerns and anxieties of the American people need to be addressed now, not when we are in the midst of the next Proposition 187 furor.

The stakes are high, but probably not what we have been warned about. For all the challenges of contemporary immigration, national cohesion is probably not at risk. A less dramatic but more likely outcome, if we do not pursue genuine immigration reform, is that Americans will have one more reason to feel disaffected with our political institutions and the electoral process, finding in this failure of leadership another excuse for retreat into sullen skepticism.

If we continue to do nothing, we might also begin to see the emergence of an Hispanic, largely Mexican-origin, underclass—of which there are already some signs.[63] The existence of just such a group could be what political entrepreneurs use to mobilize those disaffected Americans against immigration. In any case, the unresolved tensions and animosities around immigration will certainly not make it easy to build a constituency to address the needs of such an emergent underclass.

These scenarios may be too gloomy. The future is always difficult to predict. What seems certain is that without more perseverance, clarity, and wisdom from our elites, America's immigration dilemmas will not soon be resolved.

NOTES

1. Kevin A. Hassett, "'City on a Hill' Is No Place for a Border Fence," http://www.aei.org/publications/filter.all,pubID.24966/pub_detail.asp (accessed March 13, 2008).

2. Timothy J. Hatton and Jeffrey G. Williamson, *Global Migration and the World Economy* (Cambridge: MIT Press, 2005), 342.

3. Kenneth F. Scheve and Matthew J. Slaughter, *Globalization and the Perceptions of American Workers* (Washington, D.C.: Institute for International Economics, 2001), 44.

4. Hatton and Williamson, *Global Migration,* 348–49.

5. Roy Beck and Steven A. Camarota, *Elite vs. Public Opinion: An Examination of Divergent Views on Immigration* (Washington, D.C.: Center for Immigration Studies, December 2002), 1.

6. Hatton and Williamson, *Global Migration,* 362.

7. Scheve and Slaughter, *Globalization,* 69, 71.

8. *Worldviews 2002: American Public Opinion and Foreign Policy* (Chicago: Chicago Council on Foreign Relations, 2002), 72.

9. See *Worldviews 2002: U.S. General Population Topline Report* (Chicago: Chicago Council on Foreign Relations), 92; and *Worldviews 2002: U.S. Leaders Topline Report* (Chicago: Chicago Council on Foreign Relations), 22.

10. *Worldviews 2002: U.S. General Population Topline Report,* 112.

11. *Worldviews 2002: U.S. Leaders Topline Report,* 39.

12. To be sure, these are foreign-policy leaders, who are likely to be more pro-immigration than less cosmopolitan domestic-policy elites. Nevertheless, the gap between elites and nonelites on this issue generally is robust.

13. Richard Alba and Victor Nee, *Remaking the American Mainstream: Assimilation and Contemporary Immigration* (Cambridge: Harvard University Press, 2003), 217–30.

14. Hatton and Williamson, *Global Migration,* 350.

15. CBS News Poll, October 3–5, 2005.

16. Scheve and Slaughter, *Globalization,* 35–36.

17. George Borjas, "The Labor Demand Curve Is Downward Sloping," *Quarterly Journal of Economics* 118, no. 4 (2003): 1335–76.

18. Scheve and Slaughter, *Globalization,* 85.

19. William Julius Wilson and Richard P. Taub, *There Goes the Neighborhood: Racial, Ethnic, and Class Tensions in Four Chicago Neighborhoods and Their Meaning for America* (New York: Alfred A. Knopf, 2006), 24–25.

20. Douglas S. Massey et al., *Return to Aztlan: The Social Process of International Migration from Western Mexico* (Berkeley and Los Angeles: University of California Press, 1987), 254–56.

21. Gordon H. Hanson, *Why Does Immigration Divide America? Public Finance and Political Opposition to Open Borders* (Washington, D.C.: Institute for International Economics, 2005), 17–18.

22. Hanson, *Why Does Immigration Divide America?* 36–40.

23. See Hanson, *Why Does Immigration Divide America?* 36–40, and George Borjas, *Heaven's Door: Immigration Policy and the American Economy* (Princeton: Princeton University Press, 1999), 87–104.

24. Wilson and Taub, *There Goes the Neighborhood,* 155–56.

25. Borjas, *Heaven's Door,* 87–104; Hanson, *Why Does Immigration Divide America?* 36–38.

26. Ken Auletta, "Mad As Hell: Lou Dobbs's Populist Crusade," *New Yorker,* December 4, 2006, 67–73.

27. Linda Chavez, "The Realities of Immigration," *Commentary*, July–August 2006, 34–40.

28. "Demographic Profile of the Electorate: November 8, 1994," *Los Angeles Times Election Poll.* For an incisive analysis of this episode, see Peter H. Schuck, *Citizens, Strangers, and In-Betweens: Essays on Immigration and Citizenship* (Boulder: Westview Press, 1998), 149–62.

29. John Higham, *Strangers in the Land: Patterns of American Nativism, 1860–1925* (New York: Atheneum, 1975).

30. Higham, *Strangers in the Land,* 162.

31. John Higham, "Another Look at Nativism," in *Send These to Me: Jews and Other Immigrants in Urban America,* ed. John Higham (New York: Atheneum, 1975), 103.

32. John Higham, "Instead of a Sequel, or, How I Lost My Subject," in *The Handbook of International Migration: The American Experience,* ed. Charles Hirschman, Philip Kasinitz, and Josh DeWind (New York: Russell Sage Foundation, 1999), 383–89. See also Higham, "Ethnic Pluralism in Modern American Thought" and "Another American Dilemma," in Higham, *Send These to Me.*

33. Higham, "Another Look at Nativism," 111.

34. Kevin H. O'Rourke and Jeffrey G. Williamson, *Globalization and History: The Evolution of a Nineteenth-Century Atlantic Economy* (Cambridge: MIT Press, 2001), 203.

35. Scheve and Slaughter, *Globalization,* 10.

36. Scheve and Slaughter, *Globalization,* 10. See also Jagdish Bhagwati, "Technology, Not Globalisation, Is Driving Wages Down," *Financial Times,* January 4, 2007.

37. Scheve and Slaughter, *Globalization,* 92, 9.

38. Hatton and Williamson, *Global Migration,* 342.

39. Broadly similar policy advice about trade is offered in Alan S. Blinder, "Offshoring: The Next Industrial Revolution?" *Foreign Affairs* 85, no. 2 (2006): 113–28.

40. Seth Mydans, "Poll Finds Tide of Immigration Brings Hostility," *New York Times,* June 27, 1993.

41. Jeffrey S. Passel, *The Size and Characteristics of the Unauthorized Migrant Population in the U.S.* (Washington, D.C.: Pew Hispanic Center, March 2006), 2–3.

42. Jeffrey S. Passel, *Unauthorized Migrants: Numbers and Characteristics—Background Briefing Prepared for Task Force on Immigration and America's Future* (Washington, D.C.: Pew Hispanic Center, June 2005), 11–13.

43. This point gets elaborated in Peter Skerry and Devin Fernandes, "Citizen Pain: Fixing the Immigration Debate," *New Republic,* May 8, 2006, 14–16.

44. This point is made forcefully in Kenneth K. Lee, *Huddled Masses, Muddled Laws: Why Contemporary Immigration Policy Fails to Reflect Public Opinion* (Westport, Conn.: Praeger, 1998), 144–45.

45. Ronald Brownstein, "Bush Needs to Imitate Clinton to Solve Immigration," *Los Angeles Times,* July 23, 2001; Linda Chavez, "Legalizing Immigrants Just Makes Sense," *Chicago Sun-Times,* July 18, 2001; Cardinal Roger Mahony, "Immigrant Workers Deserve Legal Status and Respect," *Los Angeles Times,* June 8, 2000, quoted in Edward Alden and Scott Heiser, "A Border War: Why America Is Split over Its Rising Numbers of Illegal Immigrants," *Financial Times,* August 29, 2005.

46. Leo R. Chavez, *Shadowed Lives: Undocumented Immigrants in American Society* (Fort Worth, Tex.: Harcourt Brace College Publishers, 1992), 25–26, 98, 132–33.

47. Rob Paral, "The Potential for New Homeownership among Undocumented Latino Immigrants," report prepared for the National Association of Hispanic Real Estate Professionals, no date; Roberto Suro, *Survey of Mexican Immigrants—Part One: Attitudes about Immigration and Major Demographic Characteristics* (Washington, D.C.: Pew Hispanic Center, March 2005), 10, 23.

48. Ruth Milkman, "Immigrant Organizing and the New Labor Movement in Los Angeles," *Critical Sociology* 26, nos. 1–2 (2000): 59.

49. Lizette Alvarez, "Fear and Hope in Immigrant's Furtive Existence," *New York Times*, December 20, 2006.

50. Moises Naim, *Illicit: How Smugglers, Traffickers, and Copycats Are Hijacking the Global Economy* (New York: Doubleday, 2005), 17, 240–41.

51. Douglas S. Massey and Nolan Malone, "Pathways to Legal Immigration," *Population Research and Policy Review* 21, no. 6 (2002): 474, 477–79, 484–86.

52. "Modes of Entry for the Unauthorized Population," *Fact Sheet* (Washington, D.C.: Pew Hispanic Center; May 2006), 1.

53. David A. Martin, "Twilight Statuses: A Closer Examination of the Unauthorized Population, Policy Brief, Migration Policy Institute; June 2005, 6.

54. Naim, *Illicit*, 240–41.

55. Thomas B. Edsall, "Speed Bump at the Border," *New York Times*, November 28, 2006.

56. Jeff Faux, "Flat Note from the Pied Piper of Globalization," *Dissent*, Fall 2005; "How NAFTA Failed Mexico," *American Prospect*, July 3, 2003; *The Global Class War: How America's Bipartisan Elite Lost Our Future—And What It Will Take to Win It Back* (New York: John Wiley and Sons, 2006).

57. Scheve and Slaughter, *Globalization*, 86.

58. Torben Iversen, "Class Politics Is Dead! Long Live Class Politics! A Political Economy Perspective on the New Partisan Politics," *APSA-CP Newsletter* 17, no. 2 (2006): 3.

59. Christopher Lasch, *The Revolt of the Elites and the Betrayal of Democracy* (New York: W. W. Norton, 1995).

60. Samuel Huntington, *Who Are We? The Challenges to America's National Identity* (New York: Simon and Schuster, 2004).

61. See Christopher Lasch, *The True and Only Heaven: Progress and Its Critics* (New York: W. W. Norton, 1991).

62. O'Rourke and Williamson, *Globalization and History*, 287.

63. Joel Perlmann, *Italians Then, Mexicans Now: Immigrant Origins and Second-Generation Progress, 1890 to 2000* (New York: Russell Sage Foundation, 2005).

Religion and Polarization

James Q. Wilson

Today America is divided over religion to a degree we have not seen since the anti-Catholic efforts of the Know-Nothing Party in the nineteenth century and the Ku Klux Klan in the twentieth. And in those earlier conflicts, the struggle was at least between two religious traditions, Protestantism and Catholicism. Now the struggle is between people of any faith (Catholic, Protestant, or Jewish) and secularists who worry that political leaders who express a religious commitment, such as President Bush, are the enemies of freedom.

The split between the religious and the secular is large and has grown. In 2004, white voters who attended religious services at least weekly were three times as likely as those who seldom or never went to church to oppose abortion and twice as likely to object to gay marriage and to describe themselves as conservative. When I was an undergraduate, I was taught that income chiefly explained the difference between Democratic and Republican voters. When I was a graduate student, I was told that education now explained more of these differences than did wealth. Today, religious identification is more closely associated with the presidential vote of white voters than is age, sex, income, or education.[1]

The importance of religion was emphasized by editorial comment after the 2004 election. A series of angry statements accused President Bush of having led a "jihad" against the American people by attempting to found a "theocratic" state in which "Christian fundamentalists" will use their "religious energy to promote divisions and intolerance at home and abroad."[2] Pundits eagerly looked for evidence that the election was settled by voters who had embraced "moral values," presumably the wrong ones.

My argument is that America is a religious nation, but not one in which religion threatens politics, restricts human freedom, or seeks theocratic rule. The critics of religious leaders, especially those in the liberal media, have misjudged the relations between religion and American democracy.

The Historical Legacy of Religion

One does not have to be a close student of American history to recall that religion has animated both worrisome and desirable causes. Religious differences animated the objections of the Know-Nothing Party to the presence of American Catholics, but it also supplied the moral outrage against the ownership of human beings. The civil rights movement was led by the Rev. Martin Luther King, Jr., and his appeal was essentially religious in nature. Southern white Protestant churches, though they had long been a part of a segregated society, did not resist King's claims. Though many churches were passive or silent, some, such as the Southern Baptists and Southern Presbyterians, publicly supported desegregation.[3] And those who opposed the war in Vietnam rarely, if ever, complained that the Rev. William Sloane Coffin appealed to God to argue against American involvement there.[4]

When Jimmy Carter ran for the presidency in 1976 he brought to his candidacy the support of many evangelicals. But at the time only about one-third of them described themselves as Republicans. Carter, and then Clinton after him, carried several southern states with some evangelical help. By 1996, however, matters had changed. White Protestant evangelicals had become much more conservative, more Republican in party identification, and more likely to vote for the Republican presidential candidate. In 1976 these voters made up only one-sixth of all Republican supporters; by 1996, they made up one-third of that support.[5] In 2006, born-again or evangelical Christians gave 58 percent of their votes to Republican House candidates; among white voters with these attitudes, 70 percent of their votes went to Republicans. The conversion of evangelicals from being Democrats to becoming Republicans may be the result of their view that liberals had become zealous secularists who defended a court-ordered right to abortion and denounced school prayer. (A clue to this was the name of an early evangelical group: the Moral Majority.) But we have no direct evidence on this matter.

Though the great majority of Americans believe in God and life after death, secularists (by which I mean people for whom religion plays no role in their lives whether or not they believe in God or an afterlife) are rising in number. They tend to live in big cities on the Pacific Coast or in the Northeast and to have been much more likely to vote for Al Gore in 2000 and for John F. Kerry in 2004.[6] Religion is not a trivial factor in presidential elections. America's secular voters tend to live in Blue counties, whereas America's religious ones live in Red ones.

In 2004, nearly two-thirds of the people who said they attended church more than weekly voted for Bush and only one-third voted for Kerry. But these voters make up only one-sixth of the electorate. Of the voters who said they never attend church, two-thirds voted for Kerry and only one-third for Bush, but these voters make up only one-seventh of the electorate. And between 2000 and 2004 Bush gained support among people who said they attended church rarely or never. In short, religion makes a difference, but very religious (and very irreligious) voters are only a minority of the electorate. But they are an especially important minority because secularists are, I think, overrepresented among the mass media.

Traditional evangelical Protestants made up over one-fourth of all the voters who supported Bush. If you add to that share the votes of traditionalist Catholics and Protestants and other evangelicals, you account for over one-half of his vote. Atheists, agnostics, and secularists made up one-sixth of all of the supporters of Kerry, and if you add to that the votes of Jews and black Protestants, you get almost half of Kerry's vote. Between 2000 and 2004, Bush gained support among traditional religious groups, while the Democratic candidate gained support among modernist religious groups, atheists, and agnostics.[7]

Religion Abroad

In 1998, the proportion of people attending religious services once a week or more often was 5 percent in France, 4 percent in England and Denmark, and at comparably low levels in other Protestant nations. Even in Catholic Italy and Spain, no more than a third of all adults frequently attended church. Only in Ireland is church attendance high, involving about two-thirds of the people.[8] After the Second World War, religious affiliation was probably more important than social class in explaining why French and German voters supported either Catholic or Socialist parties, but by the 1980s politics had lost most of its religious basis.[9] By contrast, frequent religious attendance in the United States is about the same today as it was in 1981, and involves, by some contested estimates, nearly half the population.[10] Moreover, a much higher percentage of Americans pray than is true in any European nation except, again, Ireland.[11]

We want to know why America is more religious than Europe, and especially England. After all, England settled the American colonies with people who were, in most cases, deeply religious. Both countries were among the first to practice representative government and both celebrated individual rights; indeed, as I and others have argued elsewhere, England invented individualism.[12] Despite individualism, religious activities were alike in both countries up to about a hundred years ago. Scholars have estimated that in the second half of the nineteenth century, about half the adult English population was in church on Sunday, and something like that fraction was true of the United States.[13] In 1860, one-fifth of all of the adult males in New York City served on the boards of Protestant organizations, and about half of all adult Protestant males were members of at least one church-related voluntary association.[14] In the late 1820s over 40 percent of young children in New York City and about half of those in England attended Sunday schools.[15]

America and England were alike in the nineteenth century but by the middle of the twentieth had become completely different. America continued to be a nation of churchgoers, while England stopped being one. Today almost half of American adults go to church, but less than one-twentieth of English adults do.[16]

The Persistence of Religion in America

There is no single or simple explanation for America and England becoming so religiously different. One possibility is that America was settled by millions of immigrants who brought their religion with them,[17] but that can only be part of the story. Churchgoing is especially strong today in counties with relatively few immigrants. Moreover, the great increase in American religiosity occurred long before the Irish and Italians arrived in large numbers. Professors Rodney Stark and Roger Finke, reanalyzing data first published in the 1930s, estimate that there was a dramatic growth in church congregations and membership between 1776 and 1850, long before European Catholics began arriving, and that the largest increases were among Baptists and Methodists.[18] The increase in membership continued right into the 1980s (except for a brief decline during the Civil War years). In addition, the rapid growth in the number of Mormons, a faith that, at least in America, has not emphasized recruitment among immigrants, suggests that immigration cannot be the entire explanation for American religiosity.[19]

Moreover, German immigrants when they first move to America have been like Germans still living in their homeland: that is, most are Lutherans who do not go to church frequently. But third-generation Germans here are much like other Americans: that is, they have joined the Baptist, Methodist, or some evangelical church and attend services as frequently as most Americans.[20]

A second explanation that also has some importance is one advanced by Professor Jose Casanova: Europe was governed by "caesaropapist churches," while America was not.[21] If I may translate from Casanova's sociological jargon, I believe he means by "caesaropapist" that Europe was for centuries ruled by nations or principalities that combined church and state into an absolutist rule (though after the Protestant Reformation it seems a bit misleading to call Calvin's Geneva or Luther's Sweden "papist").

His central argument, if not his language, is, I believe, correct. Where the state enforced religious orthodoxy, both the church and the state were vulnerable to popular revolts. The hostility to liberalism expressed by Pope Pius IX meant that European states had to choose between obedience and rebellion. Sometimes, as with the *Kulturkampf* in Germany in the nineteenth century, the state attacked the status of the Catholic Church. The demand for representative government was inevitably linked to the demand for religious freedom. One could not endorse the French Revolution without attacking the Catholic Church that had for decades been protected by the state. And even when the church lost its monopoly power, many European states continued to participate in its management in ways that made political dissent equivalent to religious dissent. In France, the state must still approve the appointment of Catholic bishops.[22] In Scandinavia, where the official churches are Protestant, these religious bodies were not disestablished so much as converted into instruments of the welfare state. In Sweden, the government supports a state church with tax revenues; church laws are passed by parliament, and all bishops are appointed by the state. At the same time Sweden abolished all religious requirements for serving on church governing boards, a step that allowed church control to be placed in the hands of atheists. In virtually every European nation, there is a tax-supported state church.[23]

When this is the case, political and religious affiliations tend to coincide. In much of Europe, Catholic political parties arose after the First World War; in countries such as Belgium, Germany, Italy, and the Netherlands these parties governed the country for many years. Religiously defined parties helped bring voters into representative government, but rule by Christian Democrats did nothing to strengthen Christianity. On the contrary, people who opposed Christian parties learned to oppose Christianity. A liberal or socialist party (or in France, a Gaullist one) became almost by definition a non-Christian one.[24]

Tocqueville explained the advantages of a separation of church and state in 1835: In nations where religion forms "an alliance with a political power, religion augments its authority over a few and forfeits the hope of reigning over all." When this alliance exists, as it has in Europe, the "unbelievers of Europe attack the Christians as their political opponents rather than as their religious adversaries."[25]

England, like continental Europe, has had a state church. For centuries Catholics ruled but then were replaced by Anglican rule; for a brief period the Puritans ruled. Beginning in the later part of the seventeenth century, officeholders had to subscribe to Anglicanism, and students matriculating at Oxford and Cambridge had to sign the Twenty-Nine Articles of Anglican faith. Marriages and burials had to follow Anglican rites. When a liberal political movement emerged in the nineteenth century, nonconformist sects were part of its animating spirit; as William Gladstone said, nonconformity was the "backbone" of the English Liberal Party.[26] The efforts by Anabaptists, Catholics, Jews, Methodists, Quakers, and Unitarians to carve out religious freedom were, of necessity, focused on the state and its traditional religious authority.

Religion, Politics, and Markets

These close ties between state and church have no counterpart in the United States. It is true, of course, that many colonies in America had important religious policies. Six required their voters to be Protestants, four said their citizens must believe in the divine inspiration of the Bible, one required belief in the Trinity and two in heaven and hell, and five had an officially established church.[27] But when the United States was created out of these colonies it could only be done by adopting a federal Constitution that left all of these matters to the states. The Constitution said nothing about religion except to ban religious tests for office, and the First Amendment made it impossible ever to have a national church. (Just what else the amendment means by its ban on any law "respecting an establishment of religion" is unclear, but that it banned a national religion or church is indisputable.) The reason for official national silence on religious matters owes something to the writings of John Locke, Roger Williams, James Madison, and other defenders of religious tolerance, but it owes even more, I think, to the fact that no national union was possible if the federal government had any religious powers. Americans were worried that a national government with religious powers would persecute dissenters here just as they had been attacked in England. Religion was felt to be a state matter, and remained so until the Supreme Court changed the rules in 1947.[28]

Though the newly united American states took religion seriously, the people did not define themselves by their religious or ethnic identity, but by the American Creed as set forth in the Declaration of Independence.

Despite federal silence on religious matters, in America there have been many political movements linked to religious ideas. Indeed, the nation became, as Mark DeWolfe Howe put it, a de facto Protestant state, with local schools teaching religious beliefs, state governments enforcing the Sabbath with blue laws, and many political efforts to mobilize anti-Catholic sentiment. In Oregon, the Ku Klux Klan and other groups obtained passage of a law that would have banned Catholics from running their own schools, a policy that was struck down by a unanimous Supreme Court.[29]

One of the reasons that a policy of separating church and state found so many Protestant supporters is that the chief virtue of separation was its tendency to prevent the Roman Catholic Church from achieving a unification of church and state. This was the theme of many Protestant demands, some based on describing the pope as the Antichrist, and found constitutional expression in the demand for the passage of the Blaine Amendment in 1874. The amendment, banning direct government aid to religious schools, was never ratified nationally, but copies of it found their way into many state constitutions.

There was, of course, never much evidence that Catholics wanted to merge state and church. Indeed, Protestant demands that public schools teach Protestantism led many Catholic leaders to endorse the principle of separation and favor locally controlled school districts as ways of preventing anti-Catholic programs.[30] In short, in a religiously diverse nation pressure came from several religions to avoid state influence on churches.

Despite the many state efforts to benefit or attack religion, the absence of any federal policy on the matter has made America fundamentally different from England. American churches find themselves in a free market where their existence and growth depends entirely on their own efforts.

They get no tax money and confront federal officials who are indifferent to any demands for support. The churches and synagogues that grow are the ones that offer people beliefs of great value; the ones the decline are those that offer people relatively little except such social status as may come from being seen at services.[31] Privatizing religion has generated religious growth just as privatizing business has encouraged economic development.

In England religion was closely linked both to political authority and to social status. Into the twentieth century, Protestantism was associated with the monarchy and the empire, and religion was linked at first with aristocratic hierarchies and then with radical theologians, neither of whom earned much respect from the average Briton. Even today, the archbishop of Canterbury is appointed by the prime minister. In England the Anglican Church offered aristocratic bravado and then Christian Socialism, later renamed Christian Sociology.[32] England had no local governments nor local units of political parties that could be controlled by religious groups, and scarcely any local media that could represent religious preferences. Methodism in England began as a dissenting group among Anglicans, and for many years Methodists sought to maintain their status as an especially devout but not rebellious part of the Church of England, and so surrendered much of their evangelical zeal.[33]

The contrast with America could not be sharper. In an influential book, Dean Kelley, a member of the liberal National Council of Churches, observed the growth of religiously demanding churches and the decline of religiously undemanding ones. What we now call the mainline Protestant churches—the Episcopalians, Methodists, Presbyterians, and the more theologically liberal Lutheran churches—are losing members, while the more ardent, evangelical, and fundamentalist churches—the Southern Baptists, Mormons, Seventh-day Adventists, Jehovah's Witnesses, Assemblies of God, and the Salvation Army—are growing in membership.[34] He explained this difference: not because mainline churches are politically liberal, but because they do not offer a compelling set of religious incentives, namely, finding salvation through Christ, supplying meaningful worship services, and providing religious instruction.[35] The churches that are losing out are, in Kelley's words, "reasonable" and "sociable," while those winning out are "unreasonable and unsociable." They are "unreasonable" in that they refuse to recognize the validity of the teachings of other churches, observe unusual rituals and peculiar dietary customs, practice temperance, and disregard what some people, especially secularists, would call the decent opinions of mankind.

These arguments by a religious leader have been supported by the work of empirical scholars. Laurence Iannacone and his colleagues have shown that strict Protestant churches grow more rapidly than lax ones because strictness raises the level of membership commitment, increases the benefits of belonging, discourages participation in rival organizations, and reduces the number of free riders who go to church but pass on the costs of attending to others. Compared to mainline churches, strict ones grow more rapidly and have higher rates of participation, and these relationships exist independently of the age, sex, race, income, region, or marital status of the members. Church growth abroad is also most rapid in nations that do not have a state church.[36] Adam Smith was not only correct about what produces economic prosperity, he was correct about what produces religious success.[37]

Matters are more complicated in nations that have dictatorial political regimes, as did the old Soviet Union and some Muslim states today. Where there is political freedom, the absence of a state church facilitates the growth of religion; where political freedom is lacking, state churches may either require participation or a secular regime may make public displays of religion undesirable. These are contested issues, and one should compare the work of Iannacone and others who stress markets with that of Pippa Norris and Ronald Inglehart, who emphasize cultural values.[38]

Religion Constrained by Politics

One must begin by recognizing that both secular and religious groups can do undesirable or even terrible things. Churches in America have supported blue laws, but secularists have supported the more extreme forms of political correctness. Some religious extremists have murdered abortion workers, but the Weather Underground and the Symbionese Liberation Army, both totally devoid of any religious sentiments, murdered people and blew up buildings. Evangelical and fundamentalist religions have opposed abortion and rejected homosexual marriage, but secular courts have created these issues by authorizing abortions and homosexual marriage without any democratic support. Religious leaders encouraged the Crusades that resulted in looting and death, but Fascism and Stalinism killed millions of innocent people. Fanaticism is an equal opportunity employer.

My central argument is that in the United States, unlike in England or continental Europe, religion has had a remarkably democratic character.

Protestant churches organized people on the basis of their consent, endorsed cultural but not political conflicts within the state, and acquired status locally because in this country political authority was decentralized. American churches created problems, of course. Protestantism, though democratic, was not always liberal (by "liberal" I mean disposed toward personal freedom). Though it was preoccupied with cultural rather than political issues, Protestantism was often anti-Catholic and sought political power to enforce blue laws. Protestantism, though decentralized, could use local political authority to do unwise things, such as to attack evolutionary biology.

But taken as a whole, rising church movements here were compatible with and even encouraged an open society by supporting personal choice, not arguing for a state-supported church, and limiting their actions to local governments rather than trying to manage the nation as a whole.

Religion has, of course, had an impact on American public policy. Because it is powerful in certain localities, it carries weight when it tries to block congressional votes going toward causes it rejects. This is true for both Democratic and Republican administrations, and means that organized religion can provide vetoes much as can Planned Parenthood and the National Rifle Association.

But as with other organizations with strong local constituencies, religion must compete with rival interests to obtain whatever new legislation it wishes. Despite the presence of conservative presidents, scarcely any bill favored by what is now called the Christian Right has been passed by Congress. Protestant leaders could not prevent the creation of Catholic schools, and religious activists could not legally install school prayer, maintain a ban on abortion, or obtain meaningful bans on pornography.[39] Despite the efforts of the Moral Majority and the 700 Club, conservative religious voters could not nominate a presidential candidate. And several religious leaders have suffered, just as several political ones have, from various scandals.[40] The factors that encourage religious organizations (free markets, a decentralized government, a localized media) are the very things that discourage religious activists from having a large impact on policy.[41]

In England, by contrast, the existence of an alliance between Anglican ministers and political authorities, the need for nonconforming sects to struggle against a state church, and the deep social class basis of religion meant that either religion would be imposed from above or it would vanish for lack of success. As England became more tolerant, no enforced religion could be imposed, but as England remained centralized, religion lacked the "unlimited social space"[42] that it enjoyed in America. And so religion in England collapsed while in America it grew.

The Constraints of Political Life

Christian political activists have responded to this reality by adapting to the constraints of American politics more than have their secularist opponents. I am persuaded that religious leaders, like many political and economic ones, adjust to the opportunities and barriers our political and legal system has created. To reach these conclusions one first has to wade through and then overcome the rhetoric with which Christian political leaders and their critics surround themselves. When Rev. Jerry Falwell founded the Moral Majority in the 1970s, he claimed that it had four million members with two million active donors, and some liberal critics were worried that it was a "disciplined, charging army."[43] In fact, it was neither disciplined nor an army and had vastly fewer members than its leaders proclaimed; by 1987 it had closed down for want of any influence. It was replaced by several organizations, including the Christian Coalition led by Ralph Reed, but the Coalition adapted to past failures by moderating religious rhetoric and identifying reasonable goals it could attain by working in parallel with the Republican Party. For example, Coalition leaders tried to restrict rather than outlaw abortion and worked toward obtaining a child tax credit. The most extreme religious activists were kept out of Coalition leadership posts.[44] In Virginia the Coalition worked with secular conservatives, such as Republican governor George Allen in his 1993 campaign. Allen refused to argue for a ban on abortion, but conservative Christians backed him because they had learned to settle for half a loaf.[45]

These constraints arise, as Robert Wuthnow has pointed out, from living in a culture that has for many decades struggled with the tension between Christianity and civility, the need to cope with political resistance, and the ecumenical efforts of such organizations as the National Conference of Christians and Jews.[46]

The constraints imposed by America's culture and constitution affected many faiths. During the nineteenth and early twentieth centuries, Roman Catholicism was under attack here because it was based on a hierarchical church that had attacked liberalism. But that claim about American Catholics was never true; Alexis de Tocqueville and Harriet Martineau had both pointed out early in the nineteenth century that, as she put it, "the Catholic religion is modified by the spirit of the time in America."[47] Despite her view, the attacks on Catholics increased so that by 1949 Paul Blanshard's book, *American Freedom and Catholic Power*, was a best seller, warmly endorsed by John Dewey, Lewis Mumford, Reinhold Niebuhr, and Bertrand Russell.[48] They seemingly had good grounds for their concerns: Catholic leaders had endorsed autocracy in Spain and Portugal and the pope had signed a concordat with Hitler.

But at the very same time, Catholics theologians such as Jacques Maritain in France and John Courtney Murray in this country were modifying Catholic philosophy in order to accommodate it to American sensibilities. They set forth an American Catholic position based on a concern for democracy and individual rights. Their views, however much they may have irritated the Vatican, fit nicely with the actual experience of American Catholics, and, after John F. Kennedy won the presidency in 1960, anti-Catholic sentiment began to evaporate. Catholics behaved in much the same way as conservative Protestants: to persuade Americans, you must be American.

Identifying Religious Voters

Liberal critics of Christian conservatives would have you believe that the Christian Right consists of fundamentalist evangelicals who, lacking much education and living in small southern towns, are conspiring under the direction of their ministers to take over the nation.

To address this argument one first has to sort through the rhetoric. First, some distinctions: Fundamentalists are not necessarily (or even often) evangelists; neither movement was born in the South; the leaders of these movements have often been people of considerable education; and the great majority of churchgoers attend services where politics is not mentioned. Fundamentalists believe in the accuracy of the Bible and often work hard to maintain the correctness of their view against other Protestant denominations. Evangelists may or may not have a fundamentalist view; their mission is less to defend the faith than to recruit new members to it. Both movements were created, not in the South, but in Boston, Chicago, and New York City, and their intellectual sponsorship was at the Princeton Theological Seminary and the Yale Divinity School. Most of the early leaders were affluent and well educated, and on many political issues these groups have either endorsed liberal views or worked in concert with progressive leaders on such matters as restricting immigration.[49] In the 2004 elections, 87 percent of church ministers never mentioned a candidate, and of those that did the majority did not urge a vote for either candidate.[50]

Fundamentalists and evangelicals were not always allies and on occasion became bitter opponents. Some fundamentalists, having failed to defeat the liberal Social Gospel, turned away from all alliances and often departed their own churches to found new, doctrinally pure ones. Fundamentalists emphasized their rejection of worldly delights, which often meant rejecting the world itself. Evangelicals, on the other hand, were eager to spread the word without abandoning their churches. Such leaders as Charles Fuller and Billy Graham wanted to save souls more than they sought doctrinal purity. When it was founded, the National Association of Evangelicals invited Pentecostals and Anabaptists to join them, much to the horror of fundamentalists. (One early fundamentalist minister called Pentecostals "the last vomit of Satan.")[51] The split between fundamentalists and evangelicals became vivid when, in 1957, Billy Graham asked the liberal Protestant Council of New York City to help organize his crusade.[52]

Analyzing fundamentalists and evangelicals is difficult because public opinion surveys are not very good ways of measuring deep subjective states. As Professor Christian Smith has pointed out, when the Gallup poll defines evangelicals, it asserts that they believe that the Bible is literally true, have had a "born again" experience, and have recruited others to Christianity. But his own detailed interviews show that self-identified evangelicals often differ from these Gallup traits: some doubt that the Bible is literally true, some have not been born again, and some never recruit anyone. If you use the Gallup definition of an evangelical, you discover that they do not have much education. But if you let people define themselves as evangelical, they turn out to be very well educated.[53] Self-identified evangelicals tell pollsters that they are more educated than nonreligious respondents.[54]

Christian evangelicals and fundamentalists are alike in having become conservative. But that statement is not much different from noting that secular voters have become liberal. The Princeton Theological Seminary and the Yale Divinity School may once have encouraged evangelical Christianity, but today they are barely able to endorse Christianity.

If you use the best surveys to compare conservative Protestants to all other Americans, one discovers that they differ in some ways and are alike in others. Conservative Protestants, unlike most Americans, believe morality is based on an absolute standard, that religion should play a role in public life, and that salvation can only be found through Jesus Christ. But conservative Protestants are like all other Americans in supporting the civil liberties of people with whom they disagree, respecting Jews, and allowing people to live by their own morality even when they disagree with it.

The Apparent Benefits of Religion

Religion is also important in a deeper, nonpolitical way. There is a growing body of evidence that suggests that, other things being equal, people with a strong religious faith are more likely to live in two-parent families, achieve upward economic mobility, resist the lures of drugs and crime, overcome health problems, and give money to charity (including to nonreligious charities). Religious liberals are more likely to donate money and time, even to nonreligious programs, than are secular ones, and religious conservatives are more likely to donate than secular conservatives, even after controlling for race, education, and income.[55] I use the word "suggests" very deliberately, for when scholars look at the effects of religion "other things being equal," it is obvious that other things are not entirely equal. After all, people who take religion seriously are likely to differ from those who do not in some important but unmeasured way. We cannot fully control for unmeasured difference by statistical manipulations. It would be nice to assign religious beliefs to a random sample of people and then observe their effects, but happily that is impossible.

Nevertheless, there are many studies that find these religious effects independently of the sex, age, race, and income of people, and so together they create an important argument that ought to be taken seriously.

In 1998 a review of several dozen studies of religion and health concluded that "religious commitment may play a beneficial role in preventing mental and physical illness, improving how people cope with mental and physical illness, and facilitating recovery for illness."[56]

In 1979–80 a survey was conducted by the National Bureau of Economic Research (NBER) among black males ages sixteen to twenty-four living in the poorest neighborhoods of Boston, Chicago, and Philadelphia. Religiosity was measured by statements about the strength of religion in the lives of respondents and the frequency of church attendance. Crime was measured by whether respondents said that they had committed any of several illegal acts in the last year. Scholars have found an association between religiosity and low levels of delinquency, after controlling for other factors, such as age, education, gang membership, or living in public housing or with a single parent.[57] Essentially the same findings emerge from a study that uses a different source of data (black respondents in the National Youth Survey) and takes into account the effect of neighborhood disorder on crime. Crime rates are lower when the respondents attend church frequently, and church attendance tends to immunize people from the hostile effects of disorderly neighborhoods, and these effects exist even after controlling for sex, age, single-parent families, and links to deviant peers.[58]

There is also evidence of an association between religious affiliation and the extent to which women cohabit rather than marry; the least religious are more likely to cohabit, the most religious are more likely to marry.[59] Similar findings suggest that suicide rates, alcoholism, and drug abuse are less common among religious than among nonreligious people.[60] Comparable findings have been produced for marital happiness, low rates of illegitimacy, and the absence of depression.

All of these arguments have to be placed into context. There are many nonreligious people who are healthy, happy, free of alcohol or drug abuse, not likely to kill themselves, and philanthropic to a fault. But among people at risk for these problems because they are poor or live in bad neighborhoods, religion may buffer the otherwise harmful effects of their environment.

This is a hard argument to sustain before an academic audience because many professors and intellectuals are the creatures of detached reason for whom religion is a sign of personal failure, low self-esteem, or pure ignorance. The chasm of repugnance and dislike that separates Americans who are secular from those who are religious is a great pity. Professor William J. Stuntz of the Harvard Law School has tried to bridge that chasm: he describes himself as an evangelical Protestant who works at a secular university. He is a Red State voter in a Blue State university. He has fretted in an important essay about how much each side has to learn from the other. Both sides—those in churches and those teaching at universities—struggle to understand difficult texts, worry about important ideas, and share a concern for helping the poor. Instead, each side is preoccupied with abortion and views the other with deep suspicion. Professor Stuntz recounts the remarks of a faculty colleague who said Stuntz was the first Christian he had ever met who wasn't stupid, and of a member of Stuntz's church who thought that being a Christian lawyer was like being a Christian prostitute.[61]

Our Shared Obligations

Both sides could use a bit more humility. Evangelical Christians often forget that it was the Enlightenment and its commitment to scientific learning that helped create a prosperous modern world, while secular professors seem to ignore the unease and uncertainty that necessarily afflicts everyone who wishes to understand the human condition.

As Alan Wolfe has made clear, American democracy has shaped American religion just as much as religion has influenced our democracy. It is easy to overlook this mutual effect. Liberals often wrongly think that what religious people say about their beliefs is an accurate guide to how in fact they behave, just as religious people sometimes think that secular people must lead lives of unrestrained dissipation.[62] Neither view is correct. Both sides have come to share in the American political ethos with its commitment to toleration and moderation.

In the United States, a weak central government and a proliferation of diverse and independent local governments has produced a condition, as Tocqueville said 170 years ago, in which public action requires the mobilization of private motives. In Europe, where any public action is government action, private motives are less important. In America a legacy of personal freedom has made private motives very important, and for many people religion supplies those motives.

Apart from whatever beneficial effects religion may have on health or happiness, American preoccupation with religion, especially since the emergence of the so-called Christian Right, has helped improve the level of political participation. The emergence of countless religious sects that are both self-governing and compete for members in a theological free market has expanded human involvement in democratic rule. Various advertisements and government programs seek to encourage participation, but what encourages it the most, especially among people who are not well off, is their religious beliefs.

The country today is more divided by religion than by income, and often that division is passionate. But the legacy of America is that we must live together; we must, in the words of David Brooks, recognize that there is no one vocabulary we can use to settle great issues. Some religious conservatives demand that we replace teaching evolution with teaching creationism, or its latest substitute, "intelligent design." Some secular liberals want to defy the laws of the State of California and authorize gay marriages. One can support a student having choices about what to study or a law authorizing gay civil unions, but the passions that are aroused by premature efforts to impose one view or the other without following the due process of the law are harmful. Even worse is the tendency of the mass media to say that rallying to support Terri Schiavo or defending heterosexual marriage will "ignite a culture war," while violating state law on behalf of a secular goal is only an affirmation of human rights. There is a culture war, but unfortunately our press only informs us about one side of it.

If the left wing of the Democratic Party is to become once again a national rather than a regional organization, it must enter into a new dialogue with faith communities. This means discussing, not simply defending, abortion and embracing a commitment to life that extends beyond opposition to the death penalty so that the commitment includes people in a persistent vegetative state. It means taking seriously not only gender but also obscenity, not only racial diversity but black crime, not only gay marriage but marriage generally, not only barriers to the advancement of women but differences between women and men. If the right wing of the Republican Party wishes to remain a national party, its supporters cannot attack abortion doctors, use legislative fiat to usurp scientific knowledge, or say that judges must be held accountable for doing what an independent judiciary is supposed to do.

The effect of religion on political polarization in America is unmistakable. Religious conservatives have become an influential part of the Republican Party and secular liberals an important part of the Democratic Party. Polarization, thus, reflects more than merely preferences; it embraces deeply held beliefs. That division is worrisome because it reawakens in America a deep tension that we can observe in many earlier periods, such as those when hostility to Catholics and Jews was politically salient. After the Second World War, we largely overcame that tension. The great strength of this country is that we have learned to live together despite our deepest passions.

NOTES

This essay has been revised and updated for this volume. It was first printed in volume 27 of the Tanner Lecture Series, 2007. This essay was first delivered in 2005 as the Tanner Lecture on Human Values at Harvard University. It is printed here with the permission of the Tanner Lectures on Human Values located at the University of Utah. I am grateful for financial aid from the Earhart Foundation, the research assistance of Bryan

O'Keefe and Karlyn Bowman, and the comments from Peter B. Clark, John DiIulio, Roger Finke, Morton Keller, and Jon A. Shields.

1. Alan Abramowitz and Kyle Saunders, "Why Can't We All Just Get Along? The Reality of a Polarized America," *The Forum* 3 (2005): 15–16.

2. These comments were written by Maureen Dowd, Sidney Blumenthal, Robert Kuttner, and Thomas Friedman. A convenient summary can be found in Ramesh Ponnuru, "Secularism and Its Discontents," *National Review,* December 27, 2004, 32–35. These views are not simply those of pundits. For an uncommonly silly book that expresses these views, see Sam Harris, *The End of Faith* (New York: Norton, 2004).

3. Wilfred McClay, "The Church of Civil Rights," *Commentary,* June 2004, 45, and David L. Chappell, *A Stone of Hope: Prophetic Religion and the Death of Jim Crow* (Chapel Hill: University of North Carolina Press, 2004), chap. 6.

4. On these matters, see Stephen L. Carter, *The Culture of Disbelief* (New York: Basic Books, 1993), esp. 49, 59–60, 227–28.

5. John C. Green et al., "Bringing in the Sheaves: The Christian Right and White Protestants, 1976–1996," in *Sojourners in the Wilderness,* ed. Corwin E. Smidt and James M. Penning (Lanham, Md.: Rowman and Littlefield, 1997), 80.

6. Green et al., "Bringing in the Sheaves," 94, 197.

7. John C. Green et al., "The American Religious Landscape and the 2004 Presidential Vote: Increased Polarization," Fourth National Survey of Religion and Politics, sponsored by the Pew Forum on Religion and Public Life, 2005.

8. Pippa Norris and Ronald Inglehart, *Sacred and Secular: Religion and Politics Worldwide* (Cambridge: Cambridge University Press, 2004), 72.

9. Richard Rose and Derek Unwin, "Social Cohesion, Political Parties, and Strains in Regimes," *Comparative Political Studies* 2 (1969): 7–67; Arend Lijphart, "Religious vs. Linguistic vs. Class Voting," *American Political Science Review* 73 (1979): 442–58; Russell J. Dalton, *Citizen Politics: Public Opinion and Political Parties in the United States, Great Britain, West Germany, and France* (Chatham, N.J.: Chatham House, 1988), 161–69.

10. Gallup Poll, March 2, 2004, and Michael Hout and Andrew M. Greeley, "The Center Doesn't Hold: Church Attendance in the United States, 1940–1984," *American Sociological Review* 52 (1987): 326. But as Norris and Inglehart point out, other studies suggest that actual church attendance in the United States is lower than these figures imply. See note 16.

11. Norris and Inglehart, *Sacred and Secular,* 85.

12. James Q. Wilson, *The Marriage Problem* (New York: HarperCollins, 2002), chap. 4; Alan Macfarlane, *The Origins of English Individualism* (New York: Cambridge University Press, 1978).

13. Steve Bruce, "The Strange Death of Protestant Britain," in *Rethinking Ethnicity,* ed. Eric P. Kaufmann (London: Routledge, 2004), 121.

14. Gregory H. Singleton, "Protestant Voluntary Organizations and the Shaping of Victorian America," in *Victorian America,* ed. Daniel Walker Howe (Philadelphia: University of Pennsylvania Press, 1976), 49–50.

15. Paul Boyer, *Urban Masses and the Moral Order in America, 1820–1920* (Cambridge: Harvard University Press, 1978), 41; Thomas W. Laqueur, *Religion and Respectability:*

Sunday Schools and Working Class Culture, 1780–1850 (New Haven: Yale University Press, 1976), 44; Callum G. Brown, *The Death of Christian Britain* (London: Routledge, 2001), 161–62.

16. There is a spirited debate among scholars as to what level of church attendance exists in this country. For an argument that attendance is less than half of what the polls suggest, see C. Kirk Hardaway, Penny Long Marler, and Mark Chaves, "What the Polls Don't Show: A Closer Look at U.S. Church Attendance," *American Sociological Review* 58 (1993): 741–52; Robert D. Woodberry, "When Surveys Lie and People Tell the Truth: How Surveys Oversample Church Attenders," *American Sociological Review* 63 (1998): 119–22; Stanley Presser and Linda Stimson, "Data Collection Mode and Social Desirability Bias in Self-Reported Religious Attendance," *American Sociological Review* 63 (1998): 137–45. Criticisms of these views are in Theodore Caplow, "The Case of the Phantom Episcopalians," *American Sociological Review* 63 (1998): 112–13; Michael Hout and Andrew Greeley, "What Church Officials' Reports Don't Show: Another Look at Church Attendance Data," *American Sociological Review* 63 (1998): 113–19, and Hout and Greeley, "The Center Doesn't Hold: Church Attendance in the United States, 1940–1984," *American Sociological Review* 52 (1987): 325–45.

17. The immigrant argument is made in Steve Bruce, *God Is Dead* (Oxford: Blackwell, 2002), 219–20.

18. Rodney Stark and Roger Finke, "American Religion in 1776: A Statistical Portrait," *Sociological Analysis* 49 (1988): 39–51; Finke and Stark, "Turning Pews into People: Estimating 19th Century Church Membership," *Journal for the Scientific Study of Religion* 25 (1986): 180–92.

19. By 1980, Mormons were the fifth-largest denomination in the United States. See Rodney Stark, "The Rise of a New World Faith," in *Latter-Day Saint Social Life*, ed. James T. Duke (Provo, Utah: Brigham Young University Press, 1998), 16. Mormons are recruited, not in areas where religiosity is strong, but where it is weak. Cf. Rodney Stark and William S. Bainbridge, *The Future of Religion* (Berkeley and Los Angeles: University of California Press, 1985).

20. Rodney Stark, "Germans and German-American Religion: Approximating a Crucial Experiment," *Journal for the Scientific Study of Religion* 36 (1997): 182–93.

21. Jose Casanova, *Public Religions in the Modern World* (Chicago: University of Chicago Press, 1994), 29.

22. David Barrett et al., *World Christian Encyclopedia,* 2d ed. (Oxford: Oxford University Press, 2001), 284.

23. Rodney Stark and Roger Finke, *Acts of Faith: Explaining the Human Side of Religion* (Berkeley and Los Angeles: University of California Press, 2000), 228–30.

24. Tom Buchanan and Martin Conway, eds., *Political Catholicism in Europe, 1918–1965* (Oxford: Clarendon Press, 1996), esp. 30–33; Stathis N. Kalyvas, *The Rise of Christian Democracy in Europe* (Ithaca: Cornell University Press, 1996), 258–64.

25. Alexis de Tocqueville, *Democracy in America,* ed. Phillips Bradley (New York: Alfred Knopf, 1945), 1:310, 314.

26. Andrew C. Gould, *Origins of Liberal Dominance: State, Church, and Party in Nineteenth-Century Europe* (Ann Arbor: University of Michigan Press, 1999), 121–22.

27. James Q. Wilson, "The Reform Islam Needs," *City Journal*, Autumn 2002, 29–30; Donald G. Swift, *Religion and the American Experience* (Armonk, N.Y.: M. E. Sharpe, 1998), 13.

28. *Everson v. United States*, 330 U.S. 1 (1947), made the religious clauses of the First Amendment applicable to the states via the Fourteenth Amendment.

29. *Pierce v. Society of Sisters*, 268 U.S. 510 (1925).

30. Phillip Hamburger, *Separation of Church and State* (Cambridge: Harvard University Press, 2002), chap. 8 and pp. 297–98.

31. The free-market view of church activities is developed at length in Roger Finke and Rodney Stark, *The Churching of America, 1776–1990* (New Brunswick, N.J.: Rutgers University Press, 1992) and Stark and Finke, *Acts of Faith*. I believe they are correct about the United States, but I am not convinced that their theory explains differences among countries in religious affiliations. There are too many specific political and cultural differences that must be taken into account to make any single theory useful in comparative religious politics.

32. David Martin, *Tongues of Fire: The Explosion of Protestantism in Latin America* (Oxford: Blackwell, 1990), 21; E. R. Norman, *Church and Society in England, 1770–1970* (Oxford: Clarendon Press, 1976), 314–16, 364–75, 418–74.

33. David Hempton, *Methodism and Politics in British Society, 1750–1850* (London: Hutchinson, 1984), esp. 58, and *The Religion of the People* (London: Routledge, 1996), 6–27. I am grateful to Roger Finke for these references.

34. Dean M. Kelley, *Why Conservative Churches Are Growing* (New York: Harper and Row, 1977), chap. 1. Finke and Stark, *Acts of Faith*, agree with Kelley's views but give evidence that the decline in mainline church membership began, not in the 1960s as he argued, but at least by the 1940s (p. 248).

35. Kelley, *Why Conservative Churches Are Growing*, ix, 91–94.

36. Laurence R. Iannacone, "Why Strict Churches Are Strong," *American Journal of Sociology* 99 (1994): 1180–211. See also Laurence R. Iannacone, Roger Finke, and Rodney Starke, "Deregulating Religion: The Economics of Church and State," *Economic Inquiry* 35 (1997): 350–64.

37. Laurence R. Iannacone, "The Consequences of Religious Market Structure," *Rationality and Society* 3 (1991): 156–77. Indeed, Smith made exactly this prediction; see *The Wealth of Nations*, ed. R. H. Campbell and A. S. Skinner (Oxford: Clarendon Press, 1976), II, 788–89.

38. Norris and Inglehart, *Sacred and Secular*, chap. 10.

39. For a summary of what the Christian Right has or has not accomplished, see Steve Bruce, *Conservative Protestant Politics* (Oxford: Oxford University Press, 1998), 164–89.

40. On the scandals afflicting Pat Robertson and various televangelists, see Steve Bruce, *Pray TV: Televangelism in America* (London: Routledge, 1990), 172–73, 198–212.

41. J. Christopher Sopher, "Divided by a Common Religion: The Christian Right in England and the United States," in *Sojourners in the Wilderness* (Lanham, Md.: Rowman and Littlefield, 1997), 186.

42. Hempton, *Religion of the People*, 16.

43. Laura Berkowitz and John C. Green, "Charting the Coalition: The Local Chapters

of the Ohio Christian Coalition," in Smidt and Penning, *Sojourners in the Wilderness*, 42–45; Frances FitzGerald, "A Disciplined Charging Army," *New Yorker*, May 18, 1981, 53–141.

44. Mary E. Bendyna and Clyde Wilcox, "The Christian Right Old and New," in Smidt and Penning, *Sojourners in the Wilderness*, 53–55.

45. Mark J. Rozell and Clyde Wilcox, *Second Coming: The New Christian Right in Virginia Politics* (Baltimore: Johns Hopkins University Press, 1996), 216–21. This view is reinforced by a fine-grained study of conservative Christian rhetoric and actions reported in Jon A. Shields, *The Democratic Virtues of the Christian Right* (Princeton: Princeton University Press, forthcoming). Robert Wuthnow wrote that "religious conservatives have accommodated to the norms of secular rationality" in *The Restructuring of American Religion* (Princeton: Princeton University Press, 1988), 302.

46. Robert Wuthnow, *America and the Challenges of Religious Diversity* (Princeton: Princeton University Press, 2005), 32, 188, 198.

47. Harriet Martineau, *Society in America*, vol. 2 (London: Saunders and Otley, 1837), 323.

48. John T. McGreevy, *Catholicism and American Freedom* (New York: W. W. Norton, 1993), 166–70.

49. Christian Smith et al., *American Evangelicalism* (Chicago: University of Chicago Press, 1998), 1–7.

50. "Mobilizing the Faithful," Gallup Poll, December 21, 2004.

51. As quoted in Rozell and Wilcox, *Second Coming*, 10.

52. Rozell and Wilcox, *Second Coming*, 14.

53. Christian Smith, *Christian America? What Evangelicals Really Want* (Berkeley and Los Angeles: University of California Press, 2000), 10.

54. Smith, *American Evangelicalism*, 77. See also Wuthnow, *Challenges of Religious Diversity*, 210.

55. Arthur C. Brooks, "Religious Faith and Charitable Giving," *Policy Review* 121 (2003): 39–50. See also Brooks, *Who Really Cares* (New York: Basic Books), 2006.

56. Dale A. Matthews et al., "Religious Commitment and Health Status," *Archives of Family Medicine* 7 (1998): 118–24.

57. Byron R. Johnson, et al., "Escaping from the Crime of Inner Cities: Church Attendance and Religious Salience among Disadvantaged Youth," *Justice Quarterly* 17 (2000): 377–91. See also Richard B. Freeman, "Who Escapes?" in *The Black Youth Employment Crisis*, ed. Richard B. Freeman and Harry J. Holzer (Chicago: University of Chicago Press, 1986).

58. Byron R. Johnson et al., "The 'Invisible Institution' and Black Youth Crime," *Journal of Youth and Adolescence* 29 (2000): 479–98. See also Charles R. Tittle and Michael R. Welch, "Religiosity and Deviance," *Social Forces* 61 (1983): 653–82.

59. Arland Thornton, William G. Axinn, and Daniel H. Hill, "Reciprocal Effects of Religiosity, Cohabitation, and Marriage," *American Journal of Sociology* 98 (1992): 628–51.

60. William T. Martin, "Religiosity and United States Suicide Rates, 1972–1978," *Journal of Clinical Psychology* 40 (1984): 1166–69; Steven Sack, "The Effect of Domestic Reli-

gious Individualism on Suicide, 1954–1978," *Journal of Marriage and the Family* 47 (1985): 431–47; David B. Larson and William P. Wilson, "Religious Lives of Alcoholics," *Southern Medical Journal* 73 (1980): 723–27; Robert H. Coombs, David K. Wellisch, and Fawzy I. Fawzy, "Drinking Patterns and Problems among Female Children and Adolescents," *American Journal of Drug and Alcohol Abuse* 11 (1985): 315–48; Richard L. Gorsuch and M. C. Butler, "Initial Drug Abuse," *Psychological Bulletin* 3 (1976): 120–37; Ron D. Hays et al., "Multistage Path Models of Adolescent Alcohol and Drug Use," *Journal of Drug Issues* 16 (1986): 357–69; M. Daum and M. A. Lavenhar, "Religiosity and Drug Use," National Institute of Drug Abuse, ADM 80–939 (1980).

61. William J. Stuntz, "Faculty Clubs and Church Pews," *Tech Central Station* (web log), November 29, 2004.

62. Alan Wolfe, *The Transformation of American Religion* (New York: Free Press, 2003), 252.

PART FOUR

Dilemmas of Self-Government

The End of Savings

Peter Rodriguez

Introduction: Loman Still Connects

In late 1999, as the world prepared to welcome the new millennium, many were looking back at the twentieth century and wondering which of its many creations would endure. From the heart of Manhattan, Broadway looked back on myriad triumphs and failures and in this last year of the century had real cause to celebrate. The year marked the fiftieth anniversary of Arthur Miller's classic tale of the American Dream, *Death of a Salesman.* Through the desperate and tragic story of his protagonist, Willy Loman, Miller questions the foundations of American culture and grates on the exposed nerve of capitalism. Debuting just twenty years after the Great Crash of 1929, with memories of a twelve-year economic depression still fresh, Loman's sad story so disturbed and moved audiences for reasons that are easy to see. More surprising, and far harder to explain, is why fifty years later, in its revival and return to Broadway, Miller's play connected just as it had a half-century earlier.

To appreciate the oddity of millionaire money managers, fifty years later, in tears at the fate of poor Willy Loman, we should think about the state of the economy in 1999. Booms have come and gone before, but the boom of the 1990s was extraordinary even among its sister periods of growth. Nearly every economic measure sped past what were considered normal limits in the 1990s. The national unemployment rate fell well past 5 percent, a rate that was considered "full employment" and a sure sign of pending inflation. Traditionally, this would mark the moment when the Federal Reserve Board would apply the brakes by pushing up interest rates. But to everyone's surprise, inflation lay dormant and stayed that way even as the unemployment rate fell to 4 percent. Growth was so robust that a combination of low outlays for items like unemployment benefits and high tax revenues delivered a surplus to our federal government for the first time in a quarter-century.

While favorable events outside the United States were beneficial, it was nothing short of a technological revolution that delivered the fantastic economy of the 1990s. If one looks back, it is easy to recall the "irrational exuberance" that punctuated the end of the age, but the Internet boom was much more than hype. So transformational was the impact of the tech revolution that it is difficult to recall a period without online banking, iPods, and the *verb* google. Today we're miffed when someone *doesn't* have an e-mail address, when something *isn't* online. Nowadays in elementary schools no child can imagine the need for a set of encyclopedias, paper maps, or a camera with film. Through digitalization, cell phones, and an explosion of access to information, the tech boom rewrote many rules of the game, created wonderful new products, razed some stalwarts of the "old" economy, and erected virtual replacements. The tech boom of the 1990s profoundly changed the way we lived, and it did so quickly. We now live in an instant economy.

In all the excitement and change, many, many people grew suddenly richer. Stock indices soared to levels hardly imaginable before. New companies blossomed in weeks and, without profits or even customers in many cases, made their founders and investors wildly rich. More Americans than ever before seemed in on the gains as stock ownership grew wider and wider with no apparent drag on stock prices. Despite the recklessness of some, the value of the age wasn't all fueled by unfounded speculation. The technological transformation delivered real and substantial productivity enhancements on a scale not experienced in decades. Yes, there were appealing reasons to believe that this time, the old rules should be tossed aside and replaced with new ones we had yet to fully understand. The label that seemed to strike the right chord was "The New Economy," signifying an economy without hard rules about recessions, inflation, and unemployment.

The apex of the age came in 1999, which would seem to have made the story of Willy Loman a complete anachronism. But it did not. At the dawn of the new economy, the story of a weary and desperate salesman, fearful of his sons' futures and unwilling to await his own, connected with giddy investment bankers and Internet billionaires alike. The successful revival of Miller's masterpiece suggests that the uneasiness and anxiety so artfully expressed in 1949 remained just beneath the surface in the brilliant economy of 1999. Loman has been employed and rewarded, but also used up and coldly discarded by the system to which he had attached all his dreams. Perhaps the fear that never quite fades is the fear of obsolescence—the fear of living on borrowed time.

On a broader scale of time, history reminds us of the impermanence of great advances. Especially with regards to the global economy, we can look back and appreciate that gains such as those made in booms like that of the 1990s can be recalled by human forces. John Maynard Keynes, writing of the tumult caused by the Great War, reminds us of the incredible shifts in mind-set that accompanied the onset of the "first" global economy a century ago.

> What an extraordinary episode in the economic progress of man that age was which came to an end in August, 1914. . . . The inhabitant of London could order by telephone, sipping his morning tea in bed, the various products of the whole earth, in such quantity as he might see fit, and reasonably expect their early delivery upon his doorstep; he could at the same moment and by the same means adventure his wealth in the natural resources and new enterprises of any quarter of the world, and share, without exertion or even trouble, in their prospective fruits and advantages. . . . He could secure forthwith, if he wished it, cheap and comfortable means of transit to any country or climate without passport or other formality . . . and could then proceed abroad to foreign quarters, without knowledge of their religion, language, or customs, bearing coined wealth upon his person, and would consider himself greatly aggrieved and much surprised at the least interference. But, most important of all, he regarded this state of affairs as normal, certain, and permanent.[1]

The horrors of war and the geopolitical shifts like the ones of the interwar period are sensible reasons for continued anxiousness. But in the economy of the early twentieth century, some comfort could be taken in the palpability of progress. Keynes's economy may have been beset with much more frequent and pronounced downturns, but it possessed a clockwork quality with obvious linkages, visible moving parts, and a beguiling simplicity. We cannot say the same in the twenty-first century. Our instant economy is rooted as much in cyberspace as in plants and factories and is an increasingly invisible system of commerce. It is no less real or valuable than its twentieth-century predecessor. In fact it is far more valuable and, so far, stable. But it too can be expected to wax and wane, and this seems enough to sustain a latent anxiety that connects 1949 to 1999.

Listen to the Sunday morning pundits and there is no shortage of issues to worry over. (Indeed, thanks to the wonders of the new economy, you are not constrained to listening to them on Sundays anymore—they are always available and just as accessible on your computer or cell phone as on your television.) Among their most prominent concerns are internal economic risks: Social Security, Medicare, the budget deficit, international competitiveness. Mostly, we discuss these issues with a healthy backdrop of morality and warnings about our collective profligacy. For each of these issues, I shall argue, the problems are all linked to a common frailty and sense of impending doom. For each, the proximate cause, it seems, is a lack of savings by households and the government. The warnings sometimes have a partisan tone, but they do come from all quarters. It is not just blustering and newsmaking; we really do not save much for the future anymore.

Through the pundits and elected or self-appointed leaders, we speak through the airwaves as if lecturing our teenage selves on a frightening future when all the bills will at last come due. And yet, somehow, nothing seems to change. Unscathed and untested by the tumult of the markets, we cannot convince ourselves that more should be done. Thus our anxiety grows as we await the elusive reckoning that belies our current state of unprecedented growth. This is perhaps the big story, the big anxiety that is acknowledged explicitly by bankers, pundits, and policymakers as well as average citizens who don't so much know it as believe that it must be true. What may in fact be the big risk to the U.S. economy is already its great anxiety—it's the day the well runs dry and our teenage selves wake up to the harsh reality of adulthood.

The End of Savings—the Beginning of Risk

In the simplest of terms, the great risk to the American economy proceeds from a lack of savings. Though it may seem a narrow concern, the savings issue alone connects fears over the trade deficit, runaway government spending, growing foreign ownership of U.S. assets, competition with Chinese manufacturing, and the growing concern that foreign lending will dry up and our overdue day of reckoning will finally arrive. Understand the implications of low savings and you understand perhaps the greatest risk to the U.S. economy. Connecting all of these issues seems complicated, and it is at first, but it is also remarkably simple once the whole story is presented. Knitting these concerns together is the main undertaking in this chapter. The beginning is an issue anyone can appreciate: personal savings.

Since at least the beginning of the 1980s Americans have grown accustomed to regular reprimands about our high-spending consumer culture and the corresponding fall in personal savings. The warnings have the collective tone of a sage foretelling a slow slide into decline. Nothing has come of any of it. Year in and year out since about the mid-1980s, Americans have saved a smaller and smaller fraction of their personal income (see figure 1). Since the early 1960s and for a couple of decades thereafter, personal savings oscillated around about 10 percent of disposable income. Personal savings would rise a bit during recessions, but usually fell back in line thereafter. Even putting back 10 percent of disposable income may seem risky to the generation of Americans that weathered the Great Depression and World War II, but saving a dime from every dollar signals at least some efforts to build up for investments in homes, college educations, and a rainy day.

Twenty years ago the personal savings rate (i.e., the percentage saved from every dollar of income after taxes) dropped to the lowest level in decades. In fact it dropped to the lowest level anyone could remember in the United States, and no one is really sure why. Perhaps more important, the drop in personal savings did not revert upward toward 10 percent as it had before. The U.S. personal savings rate fell by about 25 percent between 1985 and 1990, plateaued during the recession of the early nineties, and fell further still throughout the decade. By the end of the millennium the personal savings rate hovered between 1 percent and 3 percent of disposable income, and, remarkably, it would fall even further. What was already an alarmingly low level of savings seemed to be giving way to a milestone of sorts: zero savings—a nation that spent absolutely everything it earned. We crossed that milestone in April 2005 when the personal savings rate fell below zero for the first time. For all of 2006, the personal savings rate was negative, indicating that Americans now take on a little debt for every dollar of their disposable income, which they spend in full. Saving a dime from every dollar seems positively miserly nowadays.

Savings and Investment in a Global Economy

For the moment, ignore what lies behind the steady and dramatic fall in the personal savings rate and, instead, ask if it matters. Ask whether it is a cause for concern not just for individuals, but for the country as a whole. It is easy to argue that every individual should be in the habit of saving for long-term needs like homes and education and for the uncertainties of life. At the

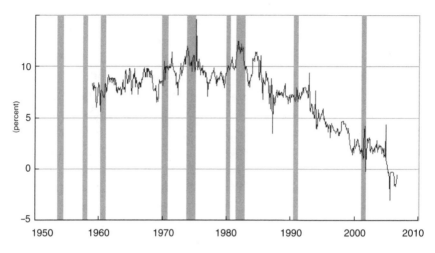

Fig. 1.   The U.S. personal savings rate. (Data from U.S. Department of
Commerce, Bureau of Economic Analysis. Shaded areas indicate recessions
as determined by the NBER. Federal Reserve Bank of St. Louis, 2006,
research.stlouisfed.org.)

same time, it is clear that most of us encounter periods when we draw down
savings to pay for homes, college, or needs in recessions or emergencies. So
individuals needn't always save part of their income and may have good
reasons to draw down savings for some events. But what does it mean if savings is low or negative for all individuals combined?

The not-so-surprising answer is that it all depends. It may not matter at
all that an entire nation is not saving or is, as a whole, wading deeper into
debt, which is precisely what is implied by a negative personal savings rate.
Then again, it may matter a lot. Whether America's dissavings (i.e., its growing indebtedness) matters depends in part on how it affects our nation's
ability to grow for the long term, which in turn depends on our ability to invest in ourselves and in our economy. Indeed, our national angst over the
steady decline in savings is misplaced, if only slightly. It is a fall in investment that deserves our worry, because a fall in investment would limit our
economy's ability to develop and learn to use new technologies, to increase
our productivity and thereby to create jobs and produce rising living standards. Without sufficient investment our economy, any economy, eventually stagnates and fails to maintain stable living standards, much less raise
them. It takes resources to educate and train, to put capital in the hands of
capable workers, to build physical and cyber infrastructures. Without

sufficient and indeed regular substantial investment, economies do not grow. And to invest, some financial resources must be saved.

It is important to be clear about just what we mean by investment. In this line of argument, investment refers not to the buying of stocks and bonds and such, but to the purchase of "hard" assets that augment or sustain our productive capacity. Think of investments as building new manufacturing facilities, improving or expanding infrastructure like ports, roads, and high-speed Internet lines, buying computers for small businesses, and funding R&D. Investments like these secure a nation's future by growing its productivity, thereby increasing output per person. Growing output per person is the way we raise material living standards and is usually what we're asking for when we hope for a better future for our children. A high and steady rate of investment is a *sine qua non* condition for a better economic future. If low savings matters, it is because low savings go along with low investment, which is a sure way to mortgage the future. We can return now to the question of whether America's dissavings matters. The answer is that it does if it lowers investments that will grow our economy for the future. So does America's growing indebtedness lower the all-important investment into our economy?

At first blush, the answer appears to be, How could it not? Savings and investment are directly linked. If we spend 100 percent of our disposable incomes on consumables like food, clothes, and entertainment, there is nothing left to go into banks and other financial institutions where our savings may wend their way into investments in infrastructure, new facilities, and R&D. In an economy isolated from the rest of the world, the only way to invest for the future is to save from today's income; savings must equal investment. If personal savings falls to zero (or even becomes negative as it did in the United States in 2006), it must follow that no investment is taking place. If investment falls to zero and stays that way, growth will stagnate and fall and the future will bring harder economic times and falling living standards. Whether or not all this is fully appreciated, the gut feeling that we should be in the habit of saving is linked to higher living standards through investments. In an isolated economy, savings fund the investments that make for a better tomorrow; so if savings go away, they take a better future with them.

Fortunately for the United States, a low personal savings rate need not be a death sentence, forcing the economy to go without vital investments. Even if citizens choose to save nothing and in fact to go into debt, their government may save for them and finance the investments that they cannot. To put it simply, the government may take income away from its citizens via taxes and use these funds to finance the investments the economy needs. In this way the government may compel its citizens to save by lowering their disposable income. It is also possible that the government could run a budget surplus and send the surplus into banks and capital markets where the funds could wend their way to individuals and firms who would make investments in the economy. For funding the investments the economy needs to grow, it is *national savings* that matters—the sum of savings by citizens out of their disposable income and savings out of the amount government collects in the form of taxes. Considering both pieces of total income—the disposable piece controlled by individuals and the tax piece controlled by government—gives us a view of all the economy's income and the two possible sources of savings.

We have established that personal savings cannot be the source of funding for the investments the U.S. economy needs, because personal savings have fallen below zero. Could government savings fund the investments the U.S. economy needs? Some might call government savings an oxymoron, and since about 1980 that characterization would ring true. Governments in general and the U.S. federal government in particular rarely run surpluses and have typically gone into debt, especially in periods of war. The 1980s, however, marked the beginning of enduring and pronounced peacetime deficits. The accumulation of sizable deficits in almost every one of the past twenty-five years catapulted the federal government's total debt (aka the National Debt) from just over $900 billion to more than $8 trillion by fall of 2006.[2] By spending more than it collects in taxes year in and year out, the federal government, like U.S. citizens, has been adding a little bit of debt for each dollar it collects in taxes, which it spends in full. Putting the two pieces together, U.S. citizens are spending more than 100 percent of their disposable income, and the federal government is spending more than 100 percent of that part of Americans' incomes that it collects. The federal government is compelling dissavings by spending more than it collects in taxes and obliging the U.S. citizens to pay for this increased debt. Our nation is growing more and more indebted through the actions of citizens and their governments.

A quarter-century of falling savings rates and increasing indebtedness would seem to imply falling investments in the U.S. economy. But this is far from the truth. In fact, the U.S. economy has seen steadily strong rates of investment, particularly for a wealthy economy already rich in physical capital. Perhaps we can conclude that the great risk to the American economy is not as great as we have imagined it to be. If low savings matters because it can lead to low investments, and the low investments haven't materialized, then low savings doesn't matter and we may rightly call our anxieties overblown. Crisis averted?

The connections between our anxieties and the true risks to our economy begin with the way that investments are funded in the United States. If our economy is being sustained by a healthy rate of investment that neither personal nor governmental savings can fund, it must be that foreigners (i.e., funds from the savings pools of other countries) are financing investments in the U.S. economy. In an isolated economy, savings must equal investment and dire consequences would result from savings rates as low as the United States'. But the United States is far from an isolated economy, and so our low savings rate need not imply falling investments. By being open to foreign trade and investment we avoid the constraint of funding our own investments and of limiting our spending to our level of income. Although personal and governmental savings rates have fallen sharply, investments have remained steadily high, funded by imported savings. Rather than limiting our nation's investments to the level we could fund from domestic savings, the United States has increased its dependence on loans from foreigners. Along the way, U.S. citizens have grown accustomed to higher debt payments; since 1995, household debt service payments as a percentage of personal income have risen by more than 40 percent (see figure 2). Only the willingness of foreigners to lend to the United States has made possible the concurrent growth in personal indebtedness, government deficits, and the maintenance of steady rates of investment.

Almost all of the above discussion serves to expound why and how the U.S. economy has financed its future through debts owed to foreign citizens and their governments. Even when presented in the guise of other concerns, like the trade deficit, the great risk to the U.S. economy is a story of debts owed to foreigners. Our increasing indebtedness to foreigners has most often been discussed in reference to the ownership of U.S. Treasuries, the financial instruments that fund government deficits. Given the lack of savings by U.S. citizens, it must be that federal deficits have been increasingly financed by foreigners. Foreigners now hold more than half of the outstanding stock of U.S. Treasury securities.[3] Similarly, foreign financing has

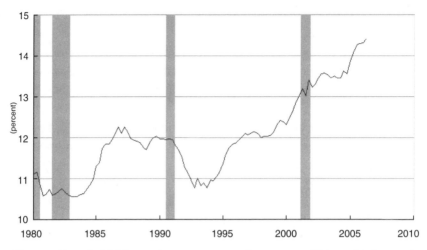

Fig. 2. Household debt service payments as a Percentage of Disposable Personal Income (TDSP). (Data from Board of Governors of the Federal Reserve System. Shaded areas indicate recessions as determined by the NBER. Federal Reserve Bank of St. Louis, 2006, research.stlouisfed.org.)

made possible a steady rate of investment in hard assets that have kept the U.S. economy growing.

The flow of foreign financing has been more than adequate to fill the void left by the evaporation of our personal and governmental savings. Our economy's easy reception of foreign monies is testament to the benefits of financial openness and evidences the perceived creditworthiness of the U.S. economy. Moreover, the diversification of ownership of U.S. Treasuries reflects a broadening of the investment pool that should bring about lower financing costs and greater financial stability. And while a rapidly growing national debt is disquieting, our national debt as a percentage of GDP remains below that of peer nations. Our debts and spending have risen markedly in the past two decades, but our wealth has too. Nevertheless, foreign financing of our investments and our spending culture is a significant and in many ways worrisome development that is the key to why the loss of national savings is the great risk to the U.S. economy.

Dependence and Its Guises

To plausibly contend that the loss of saving is the one great risk to the American economy, one must show that other prominent risks do not merit equal concern. Alternatively, one can argue as I will that other prominent risks are all entwined in the risks that stem from the great fall in national savings. Worrying about the fall in national savings is in fact worrying about the other big risks too. In particular, concerns over competitiveness, our burgeoning trade deficit, and weakness in the value of the dollar all revolve about the disappearance of American savings. To see this, it helps to think about the foreign exchange market and what motivates people to buy and sell U.S. dollars.

Plainly, people want to hold U.S. dollars, or any currency, so that they can buy things. We use money to undertake financial transactions, and we want to hold our money in a particular currency to buy things that are sold via that currency. We can separate all the things that people may want to buy with a currency into two broad buckets: (1) assets, or (2) goods and services. That is, U.S. dollars can be used either to buy financial assets like stocks and Treasury bonds or to buy goods and services. Conversely, people exchange one currency for another when they want to buy something that is sold in that other currency. The more purchases Americans want to make from London shopkeepers, the more dollars will need to be exchanged for British pounds. At the same time, it must be the case that whoever accepts the dollars in exchange for the pounds must either want the dollars for their own purchases or in order to sell them to someone else in the market who wants dollars. Just as before, the motivation for holding the dollars must be to finance the purchase of dollar-denominated assets or goods and services sold in dollars (i.e., sold by U.S. merchants).

Writ large, the preceding paragraph about foreign exchange, and the motivations to hold money and to hold it in a particular currency, connect the issues of competitiveness, the trade deficit, and the value of the dollar with the pronounced fall in national savings. Low national savings leads to the other risks, too. Start from what we know about our country's experience in world markets for goods and services. For a quarter-century or more, the value of imports into the United States has exceeded the value of exports from the United States (i.e., we have run trade deficits). In 2006, the United States will import nearly $800 billion more of goods and services from the rest of the world than the rest of the world will import from us. This imbalance has important implications in the foreign exchange market. Put another way, we seek to sell more dollars on foreign exchange markets than the rest of the world needs to buy in order to pay for the goods and services they want from us—$800 billion more this year. And yet we are able to buy these goods and services from the rest of the world, which means that we are somehow able to sell all of the dollars we push out into the foreign exchange market for other currencies.

Why would the holders of other currencies accept dollars that they don't need for buying our goods and services? The only possible motivation for accepting many more dollars than are needed to buy goods and services is to buy assets, specifically to buy U.S. dollar-denominated assets. In other words, the United States is a net buyer of the rest of the world's goods and services (i.e., we run a trade deficit) and a net seller of assets. In the parlance of economics, the United States runs *current account deficits*, which means that it is a net importer of financial resources from the rest of the world. We're a net borrower, whereas countries like Japan and China are net lenders (i.e., they run current account surpluses). Currently running at about 6 percent of GDP, the U.S. current account deficit—the level of its borrowing relative to the value of yearly production—is the highest in our history.[4]

It would seem that emphasizing that our economy is a net borrower merely reestablishes what we learned above: U.S. citizens and our governments are growing more and more indebted. But recall that the paragraphs above began with an examination of our trade deficit. Starting from the observation that the United States imports much more than it exports, we found that this is possible only if foreigners are willing to buy U.S. assets. Thus, our trade deficit, itself a source of anxiety about the competitiveness and strength of the U.S. economy, is directly related to our indebtedness and position as a net borrower in the world. We Americans don't save, but we do buy more from the world than the world buys from us, and this is all possible because the world lends us the money to do so. The world's purchases of U.S. assets, which are made with some of the dollars we exchange in order to import from the rest of the world, finance our trade deficit. The larger the trade deficit, the more we must borrow from the rest of the world, and the more of our assets they must be willing to buy. Add to the trade deficit a few other areas of exchange between the United States and foreigners, such as net receipts on foreign-owned assets, to get the value of the U.S. current account, which is also in deficit. The financing of the U.S. current account deficit shows how our slide into debt has allowed us to run trade deficits. The worry that we cannot compete and sell goods competitively, that we run trade deficits, is exactly like seeing an old problem, growing indebtedness, from a different angle.

At least one other perennial worry about the U.S. economy is also bound up in the lack of national savings story: the value of the U.S. dollar. Whether it is viewed as too high or too low, it seems that there is always some reason to be concerned about the value of the dollar. Seeing how the value of the dollar matters is not easy. Some seem to see it as a measure of the strength of the U.S. economy. High demand for the dollar, implying a strong demand for U.S. assets or goods and services, will strengthen the dollar, meaning it will take more units of foreign currency to buy a dollar. This is good in the sense that a strengthening dollar suggests that demand for U.S. assets and goods is growing. However, a strong dollar also makes U.S. goods and assets more expensive to foreigners. Given that the United States runs persistent trade deficits, a weak dollar might be welcomed by exporters. Conversely, a weak dollar would also make U.S. assets cheaper in terms of foreign currency, making them more attractive to foreign savers. Regardless of one's view of it, the value of the dollar is just another of the prices determined in the market, and its level, in and of itself, does not imply strength or weakness. Only when contextualized by other events in the economy can the value or direction of change in the dollar be meaningful.

An important contextualizing factor related to movements in the value of the dollar is the amount of U.S. borrowing—its current account deficit. Here we return to the old issue of national savings and net borrowing. When U.S. assets are attractive, meaning investors expect them to earn relatively high rates of return, foreign demand for the dollars needed to buy U.S. assets will be high, and so the value of the dollar should rise as a result. If foreigners expect the U.S. assets to grow in value, they will drive up the value of the dollar. When a rush of foreign investors seek to buy U.S. assets, borrowers in the United States will find it easy to borrow and may be able to do so at low rates. That is, U.S. borrowers won't have to offer a high rate of return because so many investors will be competing for their assets. With foreigners happy to hold U.S. assets, borrowing is less costly. But when U.S. assets are unattractive, for whatever reason, foreign investors won't want to buy them, and so demand for U.S. dollars will fall. As the need for U.S. dollars falls, so to will the value of the dollar. With fewer foreigners willing to invest in the United States, borrowing will be harder to come by, so lending rates should be expected to rise.

Another way to view the prospects for the value of the U.S. dollar is to consider its relationship to our nation's current account deficit and growing indebtedness. It turns out that this relationship is rather important and will remain a key issue for the United States. As a net borrower nation, we depend on foreigners' willingness to invest in the United States. Furthermore, as described above, foreigners' willingness to invest in the United States drives the value of the dollar. Thus, the value of the dollar depends on foreigners' willingness to finance our borrowing. In periods such as the late 1990s, when the values of U.S. stocks were growing rapidly, foreigners couldn't get enough of U.S. assets. They needed dollars to buy U.S. stocks, and so demand for the dollar was high, its value was rising, and borrowing was easy. Perhaps, then, it is no wonder that Americans and their governments have been borrowing so much and saving so little as of late. If foreigners are willing to lend and to do so at low rates, why not borrow?

Most of us reason that borrowing should be avoided because we know that it isn't free. Borrow too much today, and the pain will come eventually in the form of high interest payments. Indeed, if almost everyone is borrowing more and more at the same time, lenders should be able to charge more and more interest. Consequently, the downside to growing indebtedness should be rising borrowing costs. Given what we have established about the precipitous fall in the personal savings rate and the rise in government debt, it seems clear that those who lend to us should be charging us more and more for our borrowing. Amazingly, they are not. This fact alone offers yet another curious twist in our story.

The Falling Cost of Borrowing

For the most part, everyone who thinks about the issue agrees that a protracted borrowing habit (i.e., large and persistent current account deficits), even one considerably smaller than our nation's current habit, can pose a great risk to our economy and to future living standards. What is not agreed upon is whether our growing debts actually do represent a serious risk. A key issue dividing those who see our heavy borrowing as a serious risk from those who don't is the cost of borrowing. As discussed above, if Americans are, as a group, borrowing more and more each year, so much so that we actually spend more than 100 percent of our disposable income, we should expect the cost of borrowing to rise. But in fact, borrowing costs are not rising—they are falling.

The cost of borrowing for indebted Americans has fallen rather steadily since the mid-1990s. More remarkably, during the first years of the new millennium, when personal savings rates were nearing zero, interest rates on home mortgages, personal loans, credit cards, business loans, and government bonds were nearing their lowest levels in decades. The yield on U.S. Treasury bonds—a benchmark rate that all borrowing costs follow—has steadily fallen and in recent years has dipped below 5 percent (see figure 3). It is straightforward to explain why some see this trend in borrowing costs as comforting. If we know that our nation's borrowing is financed by foreigners who, evidently, don't require high rates of return on their lending, it must mean that they are happy to lend to the United States. For many foreign investors, the United States is seen as a stable, steadily growing, world-leading economy with efficient capital markets and some of the most transparent and effectively regulated financial institutions in the world. The willingness of foreigners to fund our borrowing at historically low costs is proof of this and suggests that the fall in savings is not so much driven by a spendthrift American consumer culture as it is by a public that has quite reasonably concluded that now is a great time to borrow.

The Risk of Not Saving

Relative to previous periods, the early years of the twenty-first century are indeed a period of very low borrowing costs. Increasing demands for borrowing, alongside falling interest rates, make it reasonable to conclude that the fall in savings in the United States is a rational reaction to foreigners' growing willingness to lend to us. The coincidence of low interest rates and low savings is consistent with an American public choosing to borrow more because it is cheap, which suggests that the situation would reverse if interest rates were to rise. If in fact the recent and remarkable fall in savings in the United States is merely an adaptation to market conditions, Americans are merely taking advantage of a worldwide vote of confidence in U.S. assets. Once the willingness to lend falls, savings will reappear, we will return to putting back a dime for every dollar, and investment will once again be funded by Americans.

Others are less sanguine about our heavy dependence on foreign lending and regard the rise in borrowing as worrisome even though borrowing costs are so low. The reason for the worry, even amid cheap lending, is a lack of faith in our ability to adapt to a sudden reduction in foreigners' willing-

Fig. 3.   Historical yields on 10-year U.S. Treasury bonds: 10-Year Treasury Constant Maturity Rate (GS10). (Data from Board of Governors of the Federal Reserve System. Shaded areas indicate recessions as determined by the NBER. Federal Reserve Bank of St. Louis, 2006, research.stlouisfed.org.)

ness to lend. Most of the deepest concerns over our dependence on foreign borrowing center on this lack of easy adaptability, and for good reason. How quickly would Americans react to a fall in foreign lending? Would we still be able to fund the high level of investments necessary to maintain and grow our living standards?

In some ways the real risks of our dependence on foreign borrowing depends on whether a twenty-first-century American consumer culture accustomed to spending every dime it earns could begin to save again if it needed to. And assuming it could, how fast could it do so? If our heavy borrowing is really just an optimal behavioral response to cheap borrowing, then we'll start to save again when foreign lending goes away. Investments need not fall, at least not too much. In fact, so long as the savings foreigners send to us don't plummet, the response could be rather smooth, and the economy may get by without marked disruption in investment or growth.

A strong case can be made for the argument that Americans are borrowing so much because foreign savings have been made so readily available. It is far harder to argue that the fall in savings could be easily reversed. To begin with, adaptation would require Americans to begin to save out of their disposable incomes, which are presently too low even to meet their spending desires, much less fund savings. Such an adjustment doesn't seem likely to occur without notable pains, and even this presumes that the economy would remain stable during the transition to homegrown savings. If the fall in foreign lending reduced spending, which it should, the economy could falter or worse, further depressing disposable income and making the adjustment even tougher. Moreover, the likely rise in interest rates that would accompany a fall in foreign savings would raise the costs of our mounting debt service payments and further reduce our disposable income. The belt-tightening that would be needed could be quite a shock to Americans, to say nothing of state and federal governments accustomed to deficit spending.

How likely is a sharp fall in foreigners' willingness to finance our current account deficit? Wouldn't some of the world's savers step in to fill the void left by those exiting the U.S. market? Eventually, yes; but the real question is how much they would charge us to step in. If fewer are willing to lend, those who remain willing will charge us more for the privilege, and interest rates will begin to rise. Alternatively, the value of the U.S. dollar could fall, as it likely would along with foreign demand for U.S. assets. A fall in the value of the dollar would effectively make U.S. assets cheaper to foreigners whose home-country currencies would now buy more dollars than before. Some combination of both a rise in interest rates and a fall in the value of the dollar may occur. In any event, the great risk is that a sharp fall in foreign willingness could lead to a sharp rise in interest rates, a fall in the dollar, depressed spending, and a recession. If adjustment in Americans' spending patterns doesn't occur quickly, or if the foreign flight from U.S. assets is pronounced and enduring, the long-term investment rate in hard assets could fall sharply, with dire consequences for long-term growth. It may not be likely, especially in a world flush with savings outside the United States, but it is possible that a sharp fall in lending to the United States could topple our economy. Even low-probability events deserve deep consideration if their consequences are severe, and these certainly are.

Will the Good Times Last?

The remaining question seems to be, Are our creditors, the large pool of foreign investors who readily fund our debts, likely to stop lending to us soon? In some ways this question is the most disquieting of all, for while we can easily rationalize Americans borrowing when money is cheap, understanding why foreigners lend when rates are low is much tougher. Perhaps the most important development in our now deeply global economy is the sharp increase in growth rates in the world's two most populous economies, China and India. Along with respectable growth in most of the world, the amazing ascent of these emerging giants has dramatically raised the global savings pool and the availability of funds for Americans to borrow. The rising incomes of the growing middle classes in China and India have initiated the possibility of savings to a generation whose parents never had a yuan or a rupee to spare. And so they do save a very high proportion of their disposable incomes.

But why would comparatively poor countries lend to one of the very richest, and how long should that continue? The current flow of world savings from poor countries to rich ones strikes many observers as odd, as unsustainable, and as firm evidence of an imbalanced world economy. World financial markets should not be expected to continue channeling money from poor countries to rich ones. The incredible needs of emerging markets, to build infrastructure, grow firms, and provide for the needs of a richer middle class, suggest that these markets will offer high financial returns and should therefore attract investors' funds. Instead, world savings have flowed to safe havens like the United States with remarkably low but comparatively stable returns. This investment pattern is sensible to a degree, but it shouldn't stay this way. To begin, the investment needs of these emerging economies are very high, and sending savings to the United States only delays badly needed local projects. Furthermore, no one expects poorer economies to put all their financial eggs into one basket, even if that basket is as large and appealing as the U.S. economy. Eventually, when they are sated with exposure to U.S. assets, or when the security and opportunity in local markets improves, the tide should begin to turn. Foreign investors will become less and less willing to send monies our way. When they do, they'll need more inducement to continue as our lenders, and the costs of borrowing for Americans will rise, perhaps sharply. Already, the Chinese central bank, the People's Bank of China, holds more than $700 billion in U.S. Treasury bonds.[5] How much more are they willing to buy?

Our dependence on foreign financing is the great risk to the U.S. economy, although it may prove to have attracted more worry than it deserves. A manageably smooth transition to higher personal savings rates is a possibility but not a certainty, and in any case a day of reckoning of sorts seems quite likely. Still, all of this suggests that our lack of savings is not yet a problem—when in fact it is. Our lack of savings is already an important risk precisely because we are more vulnerable to just about any economic or political shock than we would be if savings were higher, or at least positive. It's true that our fluid global capital markets make the management of economic shocks much easier, but markets sometimes dry up very quickly and have a tendency to cascade in an unwelcome direction. What if China, the new engine of world growth, stumbles to half its current rate of growth or even experiences a recession? What if war or political instability sends oil prices soaring? What if just about anything makes the global savings pool significantly less available to Americans? The adjustment to higher interest rates, lower borrowing, and higher savings will test our adaptability and resolve. Though we may make the adjustment without losing our future for potential growth, the risk that we'll move on to a notably dimmer future is uncomfortably high.

Perhaps what is most alarming about our dependence on foreign borrowing is not the risk it poses to our future living standards, which is both real and appreciable, but rather that it all seems so unnecessary. With global savings at an all time high and interest rates very low, our choice to grow more and more indebted is easy to rationalize. Would not any financially astute, forward-looking borrower with a ballooning house price do the same? Yes, they would, and we are borrowing at a time when in some ways it makes sense to do so. But, then again, it does not appear that, as a nation, we have been disciplined about our spending or tried hard to save. Rich as we are, particularly relative to world standards, we have put most of our borrowing toward rather uninspired uses—larger homes, second homes, consumption goods that make life easier, all of which are enjoyable creature comforts. Observing our spending patterns, it is hard to argue that our growing indebtedness has served to enhance our nation's financial stability or its long-term productive capacity. Rich as we are, a brighter future still requires steady investments in our technological capabilities, and we continue to provide that through loans readily financed by foreigners. But at the same time, we have piled on a rather thick layer of lifestyle debt to buy things that will not matter or help much if the time to tighten our belts comes soon. The real risks we face due to our debt dependence seem to carry with them the uncomfortable reminder that we need not have faced them at all.

Conclusion

Worrying about the risks to the U.S. economy in the early years of the twenty-first century is a bit like worrying about losing a marathon when you're leading by a mile. You must recognize how wonderful and rare it is to be in such a comfortable position, while at the same time acknowledging that the race is long and victory is never guaranteed. Looking back at our economy's course in the twentieth century, we see that no period has been so steadily munificent as the one that began in the early 1990s. Jobs are plentiful, money is cheap, and the recessions we stretch our memories to recall hardly merit the term. Much remains to be addressed, and the good times have passed by too many, but we have traveled far more challenging roads before. Still, we seem far too relaxed to keep our lead. With a great wind at our backs, speeding along the flat soft ground in recent years has seemed almost too easy. Perhaps we are merely conserving our strength and will have the will to keep our pace when the road ahead grows steeper. Or maybe we have grown too fond of the easy money to deal with tighter times. For most of us, having never before run against the wind, who knows how we would fare should the weather turn harsh?

Perhaps the figure that best depicts the great risk to the American economy is not Willy Loman, but Jay Gatsby. Lately, it seems the American Dream has been democratized through plentiful jobs and positively generous bankers. Once again they lead us, willingly, off into an era of materialism that is positively Jazz Age in depth and twenty-first-century global in breadth. Has our trek into borrowing been a thoughtful progression? Do the joys of our many new things exceed their full price? Have we wisely leveraged ourselves or have we grown mindlessly acquisitive? Whether our modern gilded age ends as Gatsby's did, which seems too pessimistic by half, or merely fades slowly into a new and unfamiliar scene, we will have only ourselves to hold responsible. Unlike so many of the profound risks that may befall our society, this one we can never hope to escape, for it proceeds directly from us.

NOTES

1. John Maynard Keynes, *The Economic Consequences of the Peace* (New York: Harcourt, Brace and Howe, 1920), 11–12.

2. In November 2006 the public held approximately $5 trillion of the $8.63 trillion

U.S. national debt, with the balance being held by agencies of the federal government (www.publicdebt.treas.gov).

3. This data can be obtained via the U.S. Treasury website, or from the Treasury's Office of Public Affairs at http://www.treas.gov/press/releases/js2221.htm (accessed March 13, 2008).

4. Among other places, these figures can be found in official comments of Federal Reserve Board Vice Chairman Roger Ferguson, April 20, 2005, http://www.federalre serve.gov/boarddocs/Speeches/2005/20050420/default.htm (accessed March 13, 2008).

5. Steve Schifferes, "China's Trillion Dollar Surplus," BBC News, November 2, 2006, http://news.bbc.co.uk/1/hi/business/6106280.stm (accessed March 13, 2008).

Rational Control, or Life without Virtue

Harvey C. Mansfield

In what follows I shall make a very small beginning to describe a danger that appears, at first blush, to be an irritation at worst and at best, an actual benefit. It arises from what appears, again at first blush, to be a benign intent to improve the lot of not just one individual or another, or this society or that, but of everyone and all humanity. It employs the noblest faculty of man in tandem with the lowest, most spontaneous bodily reactions—both ends against the middle, where virtue resides. Reason, which is above virtue, makes friends with interest, which is beneath virtue. In itself proud and innocent, reason conceals something innocent-looking and bland but sinister. Modern reason has an agenda and an accomplice, with which it will expose our virtue as incompetent and naive.

The reader will not find policy implications drawn from my analysis announcing and urging that we—or the government—do this or that. The reason is that almost all of what we today call "policy" is rational control of one kind or another. Almost every policy is designed to make society more rational and virtue less necessary. The "failed policies" that our political parties denounce at election time are countered with new policies having the same general aim, sure to be attacked by the opposing party for similar failings. Of course there are things we could do to support virtue, but one would have to attend to the difficulty that they too might be *policies*, presupposing the possibility and desirability of rational control. So, instead of offering policy implications from "philosophy," I will draw philosophical implications from policy. The first requirement for deciding what to do is to see where we are going.

In the brand-new building where I work the lights go on and off, the shades go up and down, and the toilets flush, automatically, without your having to turn a switch or push a handle. Rational control has replaced individual virtue, which is subject to vagaries and may not be active or awake. The old building where I used to work was shared with economists, who, living the sort of life they describe, had no incentive to flush and sometimes failed to do so.

Such virtue is so minimal that it hardly deserves the name, but even actions that are very obviously in your self-interest may be done for you if there is a chance that you might not perform them. As instruments of rational control the seat belts in your car are inferior to air bags because the former you have to buckle up on your own and the latter save you without your having to lift a finger. In this case your life is involved (though one wouldn't say at stake), and the point is to save you the inconvenience of having to be mindful. All are treated as if they were absent-minded on the chance—of course, the good chance—that some of us might be.

These examples are small matters of convenience, but they add up. In the first set of building controls you might save a lot of money; in the second, a good number of lives. But as intrusions into your privacy, your own control over your life, your virtue, they also add up. In their very minuteness they reveal the comprehensiveness of rational control. And another thing too: they often don't work. This is particularly true of the automatic flush, just one measure in the never-ending war against the human smell. That the tools and formulas of rational control often don't work, that we must constantly have recourse (first, to husbands and then) to repairmen, does not, for us, cast doubt on the whole idea of rational control. With undaunted optimism we just try something else of the same kind.

What is rational control? The examples I have given are the tail end of something very big, the idea of modernity. That idea requires subjecting our entire lives, holding nothing back—which means holding nothing sacred as exempt—to an examination by our reason as to whether we can live more effectively. What this means Francis Bacon said best: "The enlarging of the bounds of human empire, to the effecting of all things possible." This single idea was conceived and promoted by a group of philosophers, or rather, as I will suggest, first by one philosopher, who held the grand ambition of using philosophy or science to change the world. This idea would be stated and restated in different versions that would compete with one another, and partly by intent, partly by accident, it would develop in its own inner history as later philosophers criticized, but far from abandoning, perfected the earlier versions. The inner history of the modern idea, the idea of modernity, has been told by Hegel, but his history was spoiled by too much sympathy for modernity. Most ordinary historians underestimate the power of the modern idea because they do not try to see it as a whole. They do not recognize the method of indirectness in its various strategies; so they do not firmly grasp its agenda of reform. They have read of the Enlightenment but they have not thought it through.

Rational control certainly makes use of technology, as in the examples above, which means that it depends on science, modern science. But modern science and technology serve the end of "social engineering," as we say when we designate certain, often clumsy and narrow-minded, attempts to affect behavior. These attempts need to be understood broadly as "enlarging the bounds of human empire." Technology is the means to that end, and science, hardly distinct from technology, adds together the various technologies and states more general principles.

But why enlarge human empire? Science and technology take for granted that such an end is necessary and inevitable. But it is not; the idea of rational control was a choice, made at a certain moment and for reasons that are moral and political, not merely technological. The spirit of modern science antedates modern science. The spirit does not have to be formulated mathematically, though to be sure the most characteristic modern science is mathematical physics. Nor does it have to be serious. It can be seen in literary form, as a comedy.

Let's have a quick look at Machiavelli's comic play *Mandragola*, first shown in 1518. Machiavelli arranged to publish after his death his two main works, *The Prince* and the *Discourses on Livy*, which contain the amazing novelties in morals and politics that earned him his evil reputation (for merely by dying he did not escape the consequence of publishing). But in *Mandragola* we can find all the elements of the spirit of modern science without any of its apparatus.

While in Paris, Callimaco, a young blade, hears of the Florentine beauty Lucrezia, and begins a conspiracy to seduce her. But as Lucrezia is a pious, married woman, how will he manage it? It turns out that Lucrezia and her husband, Messer Nicia, want to have a son but cannot because Messer Nicia is impotent. Here are two desires—Callimaco's for adultery, which is evil, and the couple's for a child, which is good. At the end of the play both desires are satisfied. Callimaco gets to enjoy Lucrezia with her consent and not just for one night but for the indefinite future, and Messer Nicia and Lucrezia get a son (we learn in the sequel play) so that their family can continue and maintain its political standing. Now by the ruling morality of that time, that of the Christian Church, it is wrong to try to save a family by resorting to adultery. Having children is good, but adultery is wrong, and you are not permitted to do evil to get a good result. This doctrine means that "family values" might lead to the extinction of a family; a very pious couple might not be able to "be fruitful and multiply" as the Bible wants it to do.

Machiavelli conveys to us, without telling us, that this situation is irrational. The solution in his play is to relax the moral prohibition against adultery in order to save the family. The Bible, seeming to oppose the solution, in fact contradicts itself by commanding the end (reproduction) while forbidding the necessary means (adultery). In the play, Lucrezia's conscientious refusal is overcome by the argument of a crooked priest, Brother Timothy, who points out to her that God permitted Lot to have intercourse with his daughters because they believed he was the last man on earth. So, if incest, why not adultery? And if to repopulate the world, why not to satisfy Messer Nicia and herself with a son? When confronted with necessity God finds a way around morality, and this is just what His creatures should do.

Those who follow the old way of piety and morality do good but receive evil; those who follow the new way do evil—but is it so evil?—and secure good. By following the new formula, one can in principle make the family perpetual, so as to reduce or eliminate our dependence on the chance of reproduction and thus increase both human power and human liberty. The family, of course, is not a sovereign body, but Machiavelli in his *Discourses on Livy* refers to the possibility of securing a perpetual republic that would have a remedy for every risk of dissolution or defeat. All it has to do is to adhere to the new formula: Lower the moral standard to improve your chances and secure better results. Of course, as we shall see, it is also necessary to apply certain devices in the operation of this formula.

The idea of rational control was begun by Machiavelli and continued by a series of modern philosophers who followed him and constituted themselves as a movement. It was a "movement" rather than merely a school such as the Socratics, the Epicureans, and the Stoics because it had an agenda of things to be done for the sake of increasing human empire. The agenda had two aspects—liberation and reform, deconstruction and reconstruction. Regarding the first, why would one say "liberation" rather than "liberty"? Liberty in the movement of modernity appears as liberation, a liberation from irrational control. Modernity did not begin from chaos but from a certain order, an irrational order, the order of custom. (No doubt it suited modern philosophers to contrast their order with no order, so that they could begin anew and thus conceal the order they had destroyed.) Custom is what you learn from your parents. Where did they learn it? From their parents. For the ultimate source one must go back to their ancestors, who descended from gods, from God. God is the foundation of the irrational order. Modern liberation is liberation from God as the source of irrational custom.

Yet modern liberation is not total because men still need a guide, having rejected the guide of irrational tradition. Liberation is a release from prejudice and superstition, but these sources of irrational control must be replaced by something better, by forms of rational control. That is why the religious question is central to modernity. It was the first and fundamental question because human rights must be asserted against divine right, against the principle that God is in some way our ruler. All premodern regimes are more or less based on divine right, on appeal to a principle that says men do not control themselves, that they are controlled by a higher power. To liberate us from subjection, modernity must show that men can control themselves. For if men cannot act effectively on their own, they will have to return to divine right notwithstanding the objections that philosophers might propose. Liberation leads to reform. Liberation is not merely skeptical or negative; it is positive and progressive.

It appears then that the two aspects of modernity are liberty and progress, and that the two are linked. Liberty means liberation from unreason, which is progress; progress means expanding the scope of liberty. Is there no difficulty here? Yes, there is, and not a small one. There is no liberty to be irrational or to be satisfied with less liberty. For example, women today are equal to men, or much more equal than they used to be. Men, however, are less free to be their old sexist selves. No doubt this is all for the good, but men are still less free in a sense. Moreover, having abandoned the "traditional stereotypes," we have set in place new, nonsexist stereotypes. These are to be taught to children by parents and to parents by the mainstream media. Recently, on a CBS nightly news program after an eventful day, the largest segment was devoted to portraying women who were deputy general managers of professional sports teams, and who were poised to become the first women to be named a general manager of one. Progress was called for and touted before it came. This is the kind of convention promoted for rational control, one that gives women a gentle push ahead instead of holding them back, like the traditional convention that frowned on women general managers. Liberation in society is never hands off the persons being liberated; it is always accompanied by a gentle or not-so-gentle push in the direction of the end for which they were liberated. Liberated women are not left free to enjoy what they used to do under compulsion.

Progressives have a problem, then, in dealing with conservatives, who resist rational control. How should these resistors be treated? Should they be repressed or tolerated? It's clear that those who show racial prejudice should be repressed, their sentiments condemned, their arguments denied a voice. But what of sexist or antigay conservatives? Their prejudice seems at the moment less grave just as it is more widespread. Your grandfather, even your father, might be one of them. Advocates of equality for women and gays try to give such prejudice the same disrepute as racial prejudice, but they have not yet succeeded. In a recent instance of resistance to this analogy, blacks and Hispanics slated to occupy a new diversity center at a major American university themselves refused to share it with gays, thus slamming the door that had been opened for them. Liberals, believing in progress, are less likely to tolerate conservatives than vice versa because liberals are impelled to believe that those in the way of progress (racists) are prejudiced and do not deserve respect. At the same time, liberals are inclined to relativism, wishing not to judge others (sexists, perhaps). In this mood they maintain that all values are equal, forgetting the superiority of their own; the values of oppressors are held to be equal to those of liberals. As progressives liberals are too hard, as relativists they are too soft.

Progress toward rational control requires innovation—the new toilets that flush on their own. Progress thus requires receptivity to innovation, the willingness to give up the old way of custom and prejudice. Francis Bacon said that science proceeds by its light and by its fruits. Those who benefit from innovation—the plumbers who fix the automatic toilets—will welcome them; others who have to use them will probably tolerate them, wryly and with an occasional kick. "Standing in the way of progress" is not a respectable stance these days. In morals, however, progress is not so easy to obtain or accept. Looking again at Machiavelli's *Mandragola*, we note that the (allegedly) biblical excuse given to adultery is intended to shock the audience by its effrontery. We are expected to laugh at the gravest prohibitions of society and religion. Yet of course the audience will not be shocked if it does not believe in the Bible as God's Word.

Machiavelli's provocative blasphemies in this play and elsewhere in his writings imply a certain protection for the dominant religion even as it is made fun of. In *Mandragola* the institution of marriage is improved and therefore retained, its conventional character altered but not abandoned. Rational control in this case does not require a rational marriage that can withstand every objection to marriage, such as the open marriage of our day to which you are obliged only so long as you can find evident reason for being obliged. Machiavelli contemplates that conservative resistance to his monumental change will exist and continue—*and even contribute to progress.*

Conservatism in the form of prejudiced opposition to innovation ensures that there will be risk to every advance of progress, hence that there will be virtue in the new prince (as Machiavelli calls him) who promotes that advance. Machiavelli says in *The Prince* that nothing is more difficult or dangerous than to be an innovator, for the innovator "has all those who benefit from the old orders as enemies, and he has lukewarm defenders in all those who might benefit from the new orders." Yet the beneficiaries of the old orders can be won over to the new ones, "satisfied and stupefied" as Machiavelli says, precisely if they are shocked. Most such beneficiaries are filled with wonder at a person or a deed that is bolder than they are. Despite their conservatism they attend to their fears and welcome whatever, whoever, can awe them with seeming power over them. In his political works, Machiavelli recommends periodic sensational executions as a way for a regime to gain attention from its people and make them obey.

Aristotle argues that innovations are bad because they undermine the good effects of habit, and habit is necessary because people do not always see an evident reason for doing what they should. Machiavelli replies that disrupting the habit, say, of marital chastity, can renew its original purpose of providing both sexual satisfaction and reproduction. Perhaps, as in *Mandragola,* you cannot always have them together, but the action of the play is intended to freshen our appreciation of the advantages of marriage. Marriage, while still conventional, becomes more rational than it has been traditionally. Chastity becomes more attractive as well as more reasonable if it admits of necessary exceptions of the kind that impatient males have always pleaded for.

In our time progress itself has become a habit, and we all—conservatives as well as liberals—expect to be excited if not shocked by next year's car. Human beings are creatures of habit and at the same time desirous of novelty, and the idea of progress appeals to both sentiments while improving them. Habit is no longer arbitrary and reactionary, and novelty is progressive, building on past innovation rather than merely new.

With the idea of progress, novelty takes the form of conquest. To do something new is to be the first, to be a pioneer. Machiavelli, a man of thought, compared himself to the explorers of the New World. He was another Columbus, supposedly sent by a prince, actually acting on his own and for himself. His new undertaking *(impresa)* was an adventure introducing the idea of adventure. Others will follow in his path, he believed, because, though he had the idea, he left something for them to do, adventures for them, too, together with the glory that results. That rational control could be an adventure is not what we would expect from a notion that seems to remove adventure from our lives, leaving us with nothing to do and no virtue to practice. Rational control locates all reason in the controller, none in the nature and fortune that he controls. The universe is open, and so is the future. Nature, being subject to chance, has a bemusing regularity, an off-and-on intelligibility, that you cannot depend on. It's in our nature to be sexually potent, but as with Messer Nicia in *Mandragola*, sometimes nature is thwarted. Abandoning reliance on nature, and adopting the mood of seeking security, you fasten on yourself, your reason, as the only thing dependable. Security must be perfect, unnaturally perfect like life insurance, which makes you secure in some respects against your own death. You transform your search for perfect security into an adventure into the unknown. "I think, therefore I am"—there's an intrepid spirit in that.

Still, the consequence of adventure brings routine, and is intended to do so. "A trip to the moon on gossamer wings" is just one of those crazy things, but a NASA mission to the moon is intended to make a "giant leap for mankind." The path of the pioneer is accessible to the rest of us, not right away, but in principle, some time in the future. Today with a little money you can take an African safari, a trip to the Himalayas, once fairly recently a feat of adventure. The reason for this is the simplification that is at the heart of rational control.

Lucrezia and Messer Nicia *simplified* their problem of having children without committing adultery. They did it in a way that typifies modern science. They looked at the extreme statement of their problem to see whether it would ever be permitted to commit adultery and found, with the aid of Machiavelli's "judicious" (i.e., devilish) reading of the Bible, that incest (a greater extreme than adultery) would be allowed in the extreme case when it was necessary to repopulate the world. This necessity in the extreme case is universalized to cover all cases, so that the natural or the normal is newly defined by, or swallowed up in, the extreme as opposed to the usual case. Instead of having to think prudentially about the circumstances of your situation to see whether you really deserve an exception from the moral rule, you can act on a principle that has been stretched by appeal to a rather (comically) contrived "necessity" so as to do away with the truer, more challenging human necessities of thinking and sacrifice. The thought behind this inflation of necessity is of course self-serving but also, when understood as part of Machiavelli's plan for mankind, very ambitious. It resembles the scientific method of judging the whole of things by a crucial experiment of an extreme case, if possible a controlled case under laboratory conditions. *Mandragola* is a laboratory test of the truth of Christianity, which it fails.

The simplification accomplished by rational control issues in a number of devices of governing we can recognize as characteristically modern. Before mentioning them we should note their common spirit of indirectness. Rational control does not care to reason with you. It does not want to explain why you should flush the toilet or, more comprehensively, develop your character so that you will do it habitually or with a flair. It wants results. Its method is not to argue or to educate but to make a bargain with your unreason to shut out the interference of your reason that comes from forming opinions. The opinions of your faulty, boastful reason will be replaced by incentives to your passions, to your self-interest (a modern concept). In *Mandragola* all the characters get what they really want, both material satisfaction and public respectability. What they do not receive is any satisfaction proceeding from the activity of virtue as formerly understood, done for its own sake.

From this bypass of your opinions you are satisfied behind your back, as it were, through the motives that really move you, by contrast to those you profess. These motives are forcible rather than hortatory; they persuade without argument or rhetoric by "using psychology" as we say. Rather than appeal to your reason with argument or compel you with open force, they avoid direct confrontation and work on you indirectly. Rather than rule you, they make you think you are ruling yourself. There are two general ways to do this: by bureaucracy and through pluralism. Bureaucracy is the administration of scientific reason to unreason. As we have seen with the automatic toilets, bureaucracy seeks to replace your reason with rational control, which is superior to your reason because it is unfailing and considers the problem from more angles (cost, water use, offensiveness) than you could or would. True, it never asks your view of the matter, but you won't object because your reason is included in the reason of the controller whose scientific reason supersedes yours. Supposedly.

The fact that people do object to the superiority of scientific reason and hence to bureaucracy, sometimes strenuously, suggests the need for another, less obvious, pluralistic method of rational control. Rational control can often succeed better by tolerating irrationality than by replacing it with rational bureaucracy. The best example is the free market. The market does not prevent you from getting what you want but merely compels you to pay for it—and the compulsion takes the form of a trade-off within your mind as you figure out your "preferences." The automatic toilet that seems bureaucratic has actually been bought voluntarily by my employer, and if I liked it I could buy one for myself or make one for others. The latter requires taking a risk; so we see that rational control sometimes allows for risk rather than always suppressing it. Instead of suppressing risk, and with it virtue, one can discount risk, using the science of economics. Just as Machiavelli's politics posits a contrived "necessity" to do evil, modern economics is based on an exaggerated, universal "scarcity," as if God had given us nothing. We need a noneconomic—a political—view of economics to show how close it is to Machiavelli's indirect government. The Marxists used to say that the market allowed capitalists to rule liberal society through exploitation, but the truth is the contrary. The market gives capitalists the opportunity to exercise their ambition and love of risk in economic ventures so as to *prevent* them from ruling.

Representative government is a fundamental device of rational control. Such government claims merely to represent the people, never to rule them. All modern governments, even the totalitarian ones, confine themselves to this modest boast, which signifies that the government merely gives you what you ask for, or would ask for if you were rational. Any demand that the government lays upon you, such as for your life or your money, is for what you have consented to. Quite voluntary, don't you see? All constraint is indirect because its origin is in yourself. The psychology of this point is again well stated by Machiavelli (*Discourses on Livy*, I 34.4): "For wounds and every other ill that a man does to himself spontaneously and by choice hurt much less than those that are done to you by someone else." The same wound hurts more if it is also a slight to your self-esteem.

Rational control saves itself from the worst scientific tyranny when it accommodates our irrational self-esteem, our resistance to being condescended to by those of superior rationality. Self-esteem serves both the people and their leaders. In the people it nourishes love of liberty as opposed to liberation; in the leaders it gives a boost to public-spiritedness and laudable ambition. In this way rational control does not merely replace virtue but has virtues of its own. The trouble is that these virtues appear irrational because they are based on resistance to rational control rather than acquiescence. We must discern them and let them flourish despite their disagreement with our modern genius. With this conclusion my argument has escaped rational control and become an argument on behalf of conservatism, not a scolding conservatism but one suitably restrained, in touch with human nature, and still in love with virtue.

NOTE

This essay has been revised and updated for this volume. It was first published in *The New Criterion*, September 2006. Reprinted by permission.

The Corruption of Democratic Leadership

Hugh Heclo

A great danger is something that is more than merely important or atten-
tion-grabbing. Such a danger reaches into the deep structure of things. In
fact the peril may be so deep and slow-moving that, focusing as we do on
what is momentarily noticeable, it might scarcely seem noteworthy. As with
diseases in our physical bodies, so with the body politic—the gravest threats
are likely to have a sinister hiddenness to them. Authentically great dangers
entail a disintegration that takes time, or as Emily Dickinson put it, "Crum-
bling is not an instant's Act . . ."[1]

The great danger this chapter discusses is an organized decay that I will
call the corruption of democratic leadership. Given the political scandals
recurring in the daily news, this phrase immediately invites a very natural
misunderstanding. So we should begin by emphasizing that the corruption
under discussion here is not about politicians being "on the take." The
bribery and similar vices found among political leaders—as among the rest
of us—are important and certain worthy of correction, but these do not
rise to the level of greatness. As a danger, venality is all too commonplace
and seems part of our normal functioning.

In the following account, *corruption* is to be understood in the sense
that would have been familiar to our Founding Fathers. Dr. Samuel Johnson's eighteenth-century dictionary tells us that corruption is first defined
as the principle by which bodies tend to the separation of their parts. Corruption is a loss of wholeness, a falling apart from the inside. And from this
disintegration of what should be complete in its parts, comes rottenness.
Thus in the following discussion I am speaking of corruption and loss of
integrity, not as a character flaw in venal people, but as the decomposition
of a healthy, integrated state of wholeness.

Likewise, it helps if we scrape away modern incrustations from the term
democratic leadership. In the following account, leadership is not referring

to a role or personal quality of people who are somehow in charge. Here too, eighteenth-century terminology can offer a clearer understanding of the subject. Discussions and arguments leading up to the adoption of the U.S. Constitution said very little about democratic leadership as such. This is because America's political Founders sought to create, not a democratic, but a republican form of government. This "republicanism" meant that while the government derived all its powers (directly or indirectly) from the great body of the people, the governing would be done by a small number of citizens chosen (again, directly or indirectly) by the people.[2]

On this issue the Founders did have a great deal to say because they saw leadership in republican government as a problematic, complex—indeed fateful—transaction between the people and their representatives. Both elected "leaders" and electing "followers" were citizens engaged in a deliberative transaction of mutual consent, both guiding and being guided by each other over the long term. Republican self-government would be not just a top-down eliciting of consent or a bottom-up instructing of leaders, but a bottom-up/top-down transaction of reciprocal influence spread over time. The result would be to produce the governmental rules/decisions/policies by which everyone has to live. Stripped to its essentials, this reciprocating type of republican leadership is what I think America's Founding Fathers hoped for and tried to design with their daring experiment in self-government.

Thus in what follows, the phrase *corruption of democratic leadership* means this: a disintegration—loss of healthy wholeness—in the republican leadership transaction between the body of citizens and their governing representatives. It is not democratic leadership that is being corrupted. It is the modern system of democratic leadership that is doing the corrupting of republican self-government.

The Stakes of Republican Leadership

We should take very seriously the Founders' abiding fear that failure in the republican leadership transaction posed a great, indeed mortal, danger for America. They were not without hope. If the system of mutual consent and guidance in republican self-government worked properly, the rules/decisions/policies would serve the shared long-term interests of all citizens in such a political society.[3] However, it is accurate to say that the American Founders' fears far outweighed their hopes. If republican leadership did not work properly, the result would be not just an unfortunate shortfall in pursuit of the common good. The downside danger was utterly disproportionate. It was the wreck of the republic.

The controversies surrounding adoption of the U.S. Constitution have been called "one of the most extensive public debates on constitutionalism and on political principles ever recorded." According to the leading expert on this literature, this debate's one dominant theme was fear.[4] Contrary fears seemed to bracket every political argument. There was the fear of tyranny if a more centralized government power were created and fear of anarchy if it were not. Populist majorities posed an alarming threat to minority rights; minority cabals were an alarming threat to popular liberties. A government reflecting all the diverse interests of the people was a fearful picture of a chaotic struggle of all against all; a government failing to reflect all the diverse interests of the people was a fearful antirepublican conspiracy.

However, such fears were mainly derivative from a deeper worry. It was the fear that the Founding generation could scarcely speak in public, lest one appear a monarchist or offer encouragement to the enemies of republicanism. The nub of the matter was this: nothing about the new nation could succeed if the people and their representatives were incapable of relating to each other in a basically wise and virtuous way. From doubts about this capacity—the healthy transaction of republican leadership and popular consent—sprang the specific fears about too much or too little power in this or that part of the new constitutional machinery.

At first, the political class in the colonies had had the luxury of considering the problem of republican leadership in abstract philosophical terms. Could a republican form of government overcome the demagoguery that had brought ruin to both Athenian democracy and the Roman republic? Since ordinary people had trouble running their own lives well, how could one expect them to govern themselves collectively and be anything more than a mobocracy? Real-world political events after 1775 brought such philosophical speculations down to earth. The experience of trying to manage the Revolutionary War through the people's representatives in the states and Continental Congress for five years was close to disastrous. Then with independence won, republican self-government at both state and national levels fell into what seemed an ever-deepening political chaos during the 1780s. For observers like James Madison, it was obvious that both elected representatives and popular majorities were failing to act responsibly in pursuit of their own real interests and for the common good. That failure threatened the very premise of republican government. Instead, citizens and their representatives were governing in parochial, fickle, and unjust ways, reinforced by the demagoguery of "the courtiers of popularity."[5] Evidence indicated it was the scum rather than the cream that tended to rise to the top in popular government.

Precisely because the authors of the Constitution considered republican leadership a fateful problem, they devoted enormous thought and energy to designing government machinery to cope with it. What sort of machinery? First and most obvious was creation of a truly national government. With the power to enact, execute, and adjudicate its own laws over the extended republic, representative government on such a scale would do a much better job of safeguarding private rights and the public good. Unlike the prevailing disorder, such a large, national republic would filter and enlarge the quality of both the political representatives and popular majorities.[6] The Founders claimed that on this national republican scale, diverse parochial interests would more likely thwart each other; a genuine government would have the power to deal with national problems; men of talent would be attracted to seek representative office in such a government; and the consent of popular majorities would now have to be carefully constructed around truly common problems and just solutions.

Second, the new national government itself would be fitted with constitutional armature designed to promote deliberation among the representatives themselves. This armature is what today is regarded as most archaic about the original Constitution. It took the form of (1) a separate legislative chamber with representatives chosen by state legislatures for extremely long and staggered six-year terms (with this chamber alone to be consulted on matters of foreign policy and on judicial and other appointments to major national offices); (2) a separate, popularly elected legislative chamber made up of extraordinarily large districts to inhibit any narrow view of constituent representation; (3) a single national executive chosen, not by the people directly, but by state electors; (4) national judges with lifetime appointments; and (5) state control over voter qualifications, which was assumed to mean male property owners. While national representatives in the newly constituted republic would be accountable to the people in the long term, it would be an arm's-length relationship. National officeholders' work on the public's business would be insulated from shortsighted moods and the easy courting of popular opinion.

Structured in this way, the republican leadership transaction now would be both protected from its revealed vices and freed to give the careful attention required by national issues. One could then rest confident "on this great republican principle, that the people will have virtue and intelligence to select men of virtue and wisdom."[7] It seems fair to say that the Founders' ultimate faith—and the underpinning of our entire political order—was not in leaders or in the common people, but in their interaction under the constraints of the Constitution's design for ordered liberty.

The aim of the design was not to produce a deadlock of ambition countering ambition among representatives or a stalemate of diverse popular interests in the extended republic. Neither was the aim to govern by the will of the majority, since willfulness was just another name for tyranny (whether by a majority, an aristocratic minority, or a king). Instead, the aim of the constitutional design was to draw out the reasoned judgment of majorities.[8] It was a design to encourage the interactions and discussion by which representatives (among themselves) and the people (choosing among their would-be representatives) would have a chance to learn about and act on their common problems. Parsed by the constitutional design, both republican leadership and popular consent would have the opportunity to come to a truer view of their rights and the public good, rather than be enslaved to their narrow, short-sighted, and unrestrained interests.

The stakes were of the highest possible order. The Founders realized it was not merely a matter of producing good government or less bad government. Failure of the republican leadership transaction would mean representatives and the people hearing only what they want—rather than need—to hear and thus failing to learn about and act on their true interests. It would mean a self-governing people literally losing touch with reality. Such a people would systematically ignore or misjudge both their internal problems and their foreign threats. At that point Americans could not escape the destruction that had overtaken every other historical experiment in republican self-government. This was the deep taproot of the Founding Fathers' fear.

The New System of Democratic Leadership

There never was a golden age of republican leadership, not even among the Founders themselves. We need look no further than the bitter partisan battles racking Washington's and Adams's administrations (culminating in the gutter-politics of the 1800 election) to realize that the practice of republican leadership has always fallen well short of the constitutional ideals. The disastrous miscalculations that produced the War of 1812 appeared to confirm Founders' worst fears about a self-governing people losing touch with reality. Now fast forward through the whole course of American history and there is a surfeit of material chronicling one instance after another in which the hoped-for republican leadership transaction has failed in practice.

I would contend, however, that for most of American history such a chronicle points to failures that were less than systemic in nature. The crucial exception, of course, is the Civil War. Then it turned out that, despite heroic efforts to forestall the issue, only war could settle the conflict of national versus state sovereignty once slavery was engaged as a fundamentally moral problem. With that massive exception, the Founders' constitutional design for ongoing deliberation and consent did hold together even though the practice of fallible human beings often fell short. There is no point here trying to count the ways in which that practice fell short—on everything from managing the frontier and the corresponding treatment of Native Americans to managing the forces loosed by industrialization and the corresponding treatment of working people. Nonetheless, in all of this, the chronicle of failures in republican leadership amounts mostly to documenting the normal guile, ignorance, and perplexity of human beings—leaders and followers trying to cope with complex problems that no one really knew how to manage.

Since roughly the middle of the twentieth century the story is different. Something more systemic—Dickinson's "organized decay"—has been occurring to corrupt the republican leadership transaction. Living in its midst, we find it difficult to discern the overall shape of what has been happening. Those specializing in public affairs naturally focus on this or that development; and ordinary citizens, who are never more than intermittently interested in politics, naturally register only a vague sense of the results of what has been happening. What needs to be discerned are the emergent properties of a system that no one planned. Precedents for any given part of this system certainly can be found in American political history. However, taken as a whole it is a new way of doing politics. It is a system with its own differentiated structure and procedural routines of democratic leadership and followership. And it is a system fundamentally destructive of the deliberations hoped for in the republican leadership transaction.

Linear constraints of the printed page make it tempting to see simply a list of factors that add up to a given outcome. This is misleading because the organized decay we are dealing with is an emergent system. It has its own feedback loops, multipliers, gaming strategies, anticipated reactions, technological innovations, and other dynamic qualities. The various parts of the contemporary system of democratic leadership have been shaping and being shaped by each other for decades. This system reacts not only to its external environment but also to an inner environment of its own emerging creation. While leading political scientists seek for a dynamic theory about the interaction between the population and their governors,[9] political praxis has been creating just such a theory at ground level.

I know of no elegant way of encapsulating this new system of democratic leadership and so will simply break into it at a somewhat arbitrary point and look around at the interacting mechanism. It is a machine for the professional management of political power. Fueled by political money, it uses the modern media to give a semblance of democracy but gears its deeper machinations to ideological minorities active on policy issues. Since much work describing this system has been presented elsewhere,[10] the following discussion will briefly summarize its main features and then move on to the disastrous implications.

Professionalization of political communication. The beginning of all politics is the communicative act, the word, and so we might well start there. Borrowing marketing techniques honed in the private sector, political communication in the United States took a thoroughly professional turn after the Second World War.[11] The professionalization in question grew to cover the whole range of specialized services we now take for granted as the way of doing political business. These political management skills include scientific polling, focus group and other market research, campaign planning and management, media relations, fund-raising, opposition research, direct-mail and Internet marketing. All are now for hire and regarded as obligatory in running for and holding major public office. Development of this vast political machinery has been symbiotically related to the next feature.

New media. The channels for political communication changed radically after the 1940s. The new television medium emphasized the instantaneous visual image over the more leisurely spoken or printed word. Political events themselves became happenings made for television, and the medium soon became Americans' principal source of news as well as a pervasive presence in all facets of life. Within a generation, television itself became intertwined with new computer technology and the Internet. Communication became all but instantaneous and information ever more abundant and capable of being tailored to one's personal interests.

Issue activists.   These new professions and technologies of political communication could serve the needs of a new breed of political activists. Observers in the mid–twentieth century began noticing a change in the kinds of people devoted to political work. Old-style political party workers were being supplanted by issue activists more interested in using the two traditional party structures to promote particular ideological policy causes. The political turmoil of the 1960s dramatically affirmed this change with an accompanying greater ideological polarization in the Democratic and Republican parties. In the last half of the century the two parties became dominated by activists on the left and right wings of each party respectively. Leaders and would-be leaders now survived by appealing to their "base" of activists, rather than the broad middle mass of ordinary Americans. The effect has been to offer more polarized party images, policy options, media campaigns, and governing elites to a persistently unpolarized general voting public frustrated by the choices being offered.[12]

Procedural openness.   Activists pressed for, and achieved, a new participatory openness in American politics. This meant opening the political process to previously excluded voices—minorities, women, consumer advocates, and environmentalists to name a few. Equally important, it meant exposing the governing process to full public view. After the 1950s, and encouraged by abuses of power in the Vietnam War, Watergate, and other scandals, this shift to procedural openness swept through the institutional landscape. It changed the process of deliberation in Congress (public committee meetings, televised debates, recorded votes), the executive branch (freedom of information, disclosure and reporting requirements), the courts (expanded rules of standing and judicial review), the parties (control of nominations by primary elections rather than party leaders), and journalism (investigative reporting and competition for the next exposé). Deference to public officials and their internal negotiations and discussions became a thing of the past. In all this, it was not average citizens but political activists who were sufficiently motivated, organized, and funded to take advantage of the more open process.

Raised policy expectations.   At the same time, long-standing inhibitions about trying to use the national government to solve every type of social problem began dissolving. Education, health care, housing, transportation, urban development, environmental protection, civil rights, consumer affairs, gender relations, reproductive rights—virtually every domain of Americans' lives came to be seen as a legitimate topic on the national policy agenda. The government not only grew and stayed big. After the 1950s, the age-old question of whether the federal government had authority to act was replaced by a pervasive assumption that control of public policy constitutes the essence of politics. Whether Republicans or Democrats were in national office, this policy expectation became entrenched in the public mind. Not to believe in policy answers was an admission of political irrelevance. After the 1950s, conceptions of who we are as a people were increasingly translated into never-ending arguments about what policies Washington should or should not pursue.[13]

Interest groups.   The growth of federal government activism, policy expectations, and procedural openness was both cause and effect of a new mobilization of interest groups. New "public interest" and policy advocacy groups proliferated. They and older interest groups now encamped in Washington with permanent offices to protect and advance their influence over policymaking. Where once there had been several think tanks devoted so far as possible to objective research, there now grew a host of expert groups, all devoted primarily to policy advocacy over evenhanded research. Where a few large nationally federated interest groups had once organized active chapter members down to the level of congressional districts, a swarm of interest group elites now professionally managed the modern techniques of influencing public policy. This means seeking favorable decisions through the bureaucracies, courts, and congressional staffs, through fund-raising, lobbying coalitions, and targeted media campaigns. This can all be done with little need for active members, except when the experts at political influence might see a need to orchestrate the appearance of a "grassroots" uprising.[14]

Money.   Money has always played an important role in American politics. The new system of democratic leadership moves that role from importance to preeminence. This is because the entire system is built on a chain of commercial transactions demanding a continuous, immense flow of dollars.

Money is needed to pay for the specialists in polling, advertising, campaign management, public relations, and related services (including fund-raising). Money is needed for the well-paid professional staffs of political parties, lobbying organizations, issue advocacy groups. Above all, money is needed for the immensely expensive "media buys" that constitute the modern form of political communication. Thus anyone seeking or holding elective office must now expect to spend a major portion of his or her time fund-raising. The machinery of organized persuasion demands the nonstop mobilization of money rather than citizens, who are expected to be at most the passive, check-writing objects of that persuasion.

Our account in this section began with new political technologies and ended with citizens defined as consumers. Wherever one might have chosen to begin or end this listing, we still would be bracketing interlocking pieces of a single system of democratic leadership in contemporary American politics. It is a self-contained circle of nonstop professional political management, media strategies, ideological activism, single-issue policy advocacy, frenetic fund-raising, specialized access to decision-making, and fleeting moments of massive public exposure. The result of this system is a deep-seated and quietly advancing corruption of the republican leadership transaction that underlies our experiment in self-government.

Obviously there are very important issues that could be counted as dangers facing the nation. In recent years intelligent observers have tried to give the American public fair warning of the profound threats posed by, among other things, a mentality of American military empire, dependency on foreign oil, living on the edge of bankruptcy to foreign creditors, and a willingness to sacrifice civil liberties for the sake of security provided by the executive power.[15] However one assesses the pros and cons of such issues, the fact is that everything depends on the capacity of the underlying political system to deal with these or any other major issues. To return to the bodily analogy, the great danger does not lie in this or that infectious disease; it lies in a deficient immune system to deal with all such challenges.

Subverting Republican Self-Government

With a profound fear that self-government would self-destruct, the Founders created a constitutional system that they hoped would both protect and enhance the essential transactions of republican government. It was a transaction among citizens as leaders and citizens as followers—with the followers being ultimately sovereign in this form of government. They saw that the fate of the American people depended on this drawn-out, complex public conversation, safeguarded by such institutional arrangements and protections for civil liberties as the new political science could provide.

During the past two generations, roughly since World War II, we have created a fundamentally different system—an unwritten Anti-Constitution set against that constitutional design. This new system developed gradually, inadvertently, and without malice of forethought. Nevertheless, its central thrust is to subvert the deliberative transactions of republican leadership. It actively discourages the interactions and discussions by which representatives among themselves might learn about and act on the people's common problems. It deliberately intends that the people choosing among their would-be representatives will hear only what they want—rather than need—to hear about their true interests. It insists on constructing politics into a sell-job that works against eliciting the reasoned judgment of majorities. Consequently, it is a system predisposed to losing touch with reality.

Let us count the ways.

In the new regime, national representatives' work on the public's business is not insulated from shortsighted popular moods. On the contrary. The conduct of representative government is now continuously tuned into whatever transient and easily measured opinions are reported and/or can be professionally manufactured. In this environment, the courting of popular opinion is not an occasional lapse in representatives' deliberations. It is a full-time preoccupation of the permanent campaign that constitutes modern democratic leadership. These marketing campaigns without end are run out of the White House, congressional offices, interest group headquarters, policy advocacy groups, and political consulting firms.

This professionally scripted and strategically managed political communication has nothing to do with deliberation or learning through an open competition of ideas. By design, the modern system works at avoiding public interchanges that could lead anyone to a closer approximation of the truth of things. The dominant rules for "smart" politics are roughly as follows:

Assert only a very few simple themes (hence remaining silent about a complex understanding of anything).

Always stay on message (thus effectively disengaging from anything else being said).

Deflect rather than try to answer difficult questions (thereby avoiding the possibility of correcting error in your position).

Never acknowledge strong points in any opposing position (hence preventing development of any balanced view of things).

Never admit uncertainty or ignorance (thus covering up the most realistic thing to appreciate about any difficult issue).

Of course, clever politicians have always tried to do many of these same things. But heretofore they always did so in an amateur, hit-and-miss way. Today such rules of political communication have been thoroughly systematized and disciplined into a regime of nondialogue. I should emphasize that this is not a matter of bad leaders doing evil things; it is a matter of what rationality in the context requires.[16] The competitive constraints of the system itself select for these strategies and against anybody who would try to behave otherwise (i.e., explain complexities, acknowledge costs, honestly engage opposing views, and admit one's own fallibility). In this way our professionally managed system of talking-to-win drives out talking that could teach people about the reality of their common problems.[17] Two carefully scripted distortions meeting in public combat are not likely to produce a closer approximation to the truth. At best, they produce a third, hybrid distortion.

Meanwhile, in the shadows of this noisy public nonconversation, the politically active class can exploit the system to full advantage.[18] Those who are organized to feed the political spending machine have a major influence over who can plausibly run for office. They have privileged and continual access to their favored causes in the labyrinth of Washington policymaking. Contrary to what James Madison could have imagined, self-serving factions find it easy rather than difficult to combine and take advantage of the modern "participatory" system that is open in a very unpublic way.

And what of ordinary citizens, the people who are presumptively both followers and ultimate sovereigns in the leadership transaction? Self-government is not threatened by the mere fact that only a minority of citizens are politically active. A moment's reflection should tell us that a democratic society with a majority of the population constantly mobilized in full-blown political activism is bound to be an overheated, chaotic society in crisis.

The great danger lies in the modern system's pervasive disconnection between those in the political class who do politics and the mass of ordinary citizens who have politics done to them. For reasons already given, this system directs activists' activity into behavior that is destructive for government by discussion and public deliberation. On the other hand, the system shapes the rest of the people into a lumpen-citizenry. Public approval is courted by trying to tell this passive population of spectator-customers what they want to hear. Such disconnectedness, an inner lack of wholeness and integrity between leaders and followers, we have defined as corruption.

Rather than a transaction of republican leadership, the system of democratic leadership provides a political technology of imagery and salesmanship that teaches ordinary citizens to understand their political world in certain ways. These ways are hostile to civic judgment. Imagery draws viewers' attention into a continuous flow of quick-cutting, fragmentary, fast-paced information without pauses for reflection. Language is formatted into shorthand, staccato catch-phrases to produce the same effect. Supreme value is put on the immediate delivery of the latest information rather than on understanding context and historical development. This present-minded information is in turn framed into episodic story lines of conflict and drama designed to appeal to powerful emotions rather than reason. It is an oddly passive vitalism that is encouraged to be indifferent to everything that has made possible its own existence.

Technology now brings in everyone at all levels of literacy as observers of public problems. The generally inattentive members of this mass public are primed to use small scraps of low-cost information in making political decisions.[19] They can, for example, be easily brought to rally round an emotive patriotism in presidential war-making, but are also easily disillusioned and fickle if success is not achieved easily and quickly.[20] The mass consumers of information about the political world are not only discouraged from undertaking sustained, complex thinking with historical perspective. They are actively tutored in the opposite direction.

Whatever might have been the case in the earlier twentieth century, by no means is the mass-man of the information age simply part of a crowd herded by propagandists. That may be what the political class of the new system has hoped for, but what they have actually produced is something just as uncivic. The modern system of democratic leadership encourages citizen-customers to adopt strategies for coping with the attempted manipulation to which they are constantly subjected. For members of the younger generation who have had to grow up in this system, the obvious choice is simply to tune out, and they generally have.[21] The most prominent other coping mechanisms are distrust, cynicism, and withdrawal into comfort zones of personal bias.

Long-term historical data is lacking, but it appears clear that a general decline in the public's trust in government and politics (though not in the Constitution itself) began in the 1960s. Since then, trust has remained at low levels while a growing proportion of the population has considered government to be run by people and groups who are simply looking out for themselves. This is a plausible conclusion. Ordinary Americans do experience politics as something that is done to them, not by them. The new system of democratic leadership does treat people as customers and clients rather than citizens expressing common interests through collective political action. Citizenship does seem to amount to being the target of political marketing paid for by elites who are able to seek their policy aims without the need to mobilize popular constituencies.[22]

In such a world of democratic leadership, ordinary citizens learn that being politically knowledgeable consists of being able to unmask the sales pitches to which they are permanently subjected. Civic intelligence can then be perceived as nothing more than being a savvy—that is, cynical—political consumer. The media encourages this self-conception by reporting not so much what political representatives say and do but the strategies and gamesmanship that lies behind their words and deeds.

At the same time, working Americans are deluged with sensory input from modern technology and report the most troubling thing about it all is a sheer lack of focus. One can feel simultaneously that there is simply too much information, and that there is no real information at all. The result is that it makes ever more sense to screen out conflicting messages in order to create a personal comfort zone in the media. This strongly reinforces the preexisting human impulse to what psychologists call "naive realism," the inclination to believe that you see the world objectively and anyone who sees things differently is an ideologically biased extremist. The intensifying media competition for scarce public attention may well increase the amount of slanted information and niche-marketing rather than clear up the confusion. Readers and viewers claim to want accuracy, but "accuracy" typically means information confirming what they already believe.[23]

When today's political system teaches ordinary people to distrust everything and everyone that is not like-minded, Americans are being alienated not only from politics. They are being alienated from themselves as citizens.

On a Note of Caution

False alarms can be worse than no alarms at all, and so pointing to something as a great danger ought to be done with great carefulness. However, dismissing a diagnosis as too pessimistic can itself be a kind of false alarm. To acknowledge bad news from a cancer screening is not being pessimistic. It is plain good sense.

The diagnosis of our modern system of democratic leadership brings much bad news. It is a system whose prevailing tendencies work against constructive deliberation on the public's business. In the crucial transactions between and among the people and their representatives, there are forces systematically opposed to bringing the participants to a better understanding of reality. Like a spoiled child, political leadership produced by the modern system is both desperate for approval and preoccupied with getting its own way. For ordinary citizens, the wholeness of a relationship between representatives and the people is disconnected into a seller/buyer transaction where most customers think they are being had. The name for all of this is corruption, and its putridness hails from the grave of republics.

There are many constructive things that can be done. Internet blogs have opened new opportunities for fact-checking and citizen journalism, especially with younger citizens. Champions of good government continue to press for real campaign finance and lobbying reform. There is no point here in trying to multiply such examples. We may not notice them, but there many people in and at the fringes of politics trying to get beyond the gamesmanship and address the yearning for a more honest, honorable politics.

The hopeful fact is that since its very first days, the American experiment in self-government has never required majority support in order to succeed. If we date those first days to the independence struggle of 1775–77 the historical record should offer any contemporary American much encouragement. A close account of George Washington's experience in leading this struggle indicates that most of the officers, militia, national politicians, state politicians, and civilian residents with whom he had to deal were not up to the effort.[24] Cowardice, selfishness, shortsightedness, incompetence, disloyalty, indifference were the recurring themes. For the American cause, it sufficed that a determined minority in each category had, as Madison put it, the necessary "virtue and wisdom." That was enough to keep the experiment going.

Even so, we should recognize that it is a *system* that is in question. Unfortunately, it takes a crisis to change a system, and I am sorry to report that this is what one needs to be prepared for. Only then will we see how many Americans succumb to populist simplicities to wreck the republic and how many behave like the grown-up citizens our Founders hoped for in order to keep the experiment going. I am one of those who think that, while the Founders may have overestimated the potential wisdom of the people, today's political class greatly underestimates that same mental and spiritual capacity of Americans.[25]

The first requirement is pay attention—to become truly aware of what has been happening to us. To paraphrase Emily Dickinson, no man or nation has failed in an instant. We crash by slipping.

NOTES

1. Poem 997, written circa 1865.

2. On the republican form of government, the most relevant of *Federalist* papers are 10, 39, and 57.

3. As Madison or Hamilton put it at the beginning of *Federalist* 57:

The aim of every political constitution is, or ought to be, first to obtain for rulers men who possess most wisdom to discern, and most virtue to pursue, the common good of the society; and in the next place, to take the most effectual precautions for keeping them virtuous whilst they continue to hold their public trust. The elective mode of obtaining rulers is the characteristic policy of republican government. The means relied on in this form of government for preventing their degeneracy are numerous and various. The most effectual one is such a limitation of the term of appointments as will maintain a proper responsibility to the people.

4. Bernard Bailyn, *To Begin the World Anew* (New York: Knopf, 2003), 107–8.

5. Jack N. Rakove, *Original Meanings: Politics and Ideas in the Making of the Constitution* (New York: Knopf, 1996), 48, and 40–56 passim. Chapter 8 is especially informative on the issue of deliberative representation. Without going into detail here, it should be noted that contemporary political theorists have attempted to recapture and extend these basic ideas by developing "discourse theories" of "deliberative democracy." Prominent examples are Jürgen Habermas, *Between Facts and Norms: Contributions to a Discourse Theory of Law and Democracy* (Cambridge: MIT Press, 1995); John Rawls, *Political Liberalism* (New York: Columbia University Press, 1993); Amy Gutmann and Dennis Thompson, *Democracy and Disagreement* (Cambridge: Harvard University Press, 1996).

6. *Federalist* 10 and 51.

7. James Madison's speech before the Virginia Constitutional ratifying convention, June 20, 1788. Quoted in James T. Kloppenberg, "The Virtues of Liberalism: Christianity, Republicanism, and Ethics in Early American Political Discourse," *Journal of American*

History 74 (June 1987): 9–34. The same idea is expressed by Alexander Hamilton in *Federalist* 76.

8. I believe the most perceptive and learned discussion is still John Hallowell, *The Moral Foundation of Democracy* (Chicago: University of Chicago Press, 1954), chap. 6.

9. Margaret Levi, "Why We Need a New Theory of Government: Presidential Address to the American Political Science Association," *Perspectives on Politics* 4, no. 1 (2006): 6.

10. Hugh Heclo, "Campaigning and Governing: A Conspectus," in *The Permanent Campaign and Its Future,* ed. Norman Ornstein and Thomas Mann (Washington, D.C.: AEI Press, 2000); James Q. Wilson, "New Politics, New Elites, Old Publics," in *The New Politics of Public Policy,* ed. Marc C. Landy and Martin A. Levin (Baltimore: Johns Hopkins University Press, 1995).

11. Among early adopters were young congressman Richard Nixon's use of public relations experts in his 1950 California Senate race and the America Medical Association's campaign against national health insurance ("socialized medicine") amid a growing anti-Communist hysteria. Stanley Kelly, *Professional Public Relations and Political Power* (Baltimore: Johns Hopkins University Press, 1966).

12. Morris P. Fiorina, *Culture War? The Myth of a Polarized America,* 2nd ed. (New York: Pearson Longman, 2006).

13. These developments are chronicled in the chapters "Sixties Civics" and "From Tax and Spend to Mandate and Sue" in Sidney M. Milkis and Jerome M. Mileur, *The Great Society and the High Tide of Liberalism* (Amherst: University of Massachusetts Press, 2005).

14. Andrew Rich, *Think Tanks, Public Policy, and the Politics of Expertise* (New York: Cambridge University Press, 2004); Theda Skocpol, *Diminished Democracy: From Membership to Management in American Civic Life* (Norman: University of Oklahoma Press, 2003).

15. Chalmers Johnson, *The Sorrows of Empire: Militarism, Secrecy, and the End of the Republic* (New York: Metropolitan Books, 2004); Kevin Phillips, *American Theocracy* (New York: Viking, 2006).

16. As a call to republican leadership, one could hardly do better than Secretary of Defense Donald Rumsfeld's March 2001 memo to President Bush on the requirements for U.S. foreign military action:

> Finally—honesty: U.S. leadership must be brutally honest with itself, the Congress, the public and coalition partners. Do not make the effort sound even marginally easier or less costly than it could become. Preserving U.S. credibility requires that we promise less, or no more, than we are sure we can deliver. (Bob Woodward, *Bush at War,* quoted in the *Washington Post,* May 23, 2004)

Two years later, what was deemed necessary for publicly selling the war in Iraq rushed past such flashing warning signals.

17. Unfortunately, the same dynamic of the system applies to the array of Washington think tanks. Here too policy advocacy and media strategies have grown to overshadow objective and high-quality policy research. Rich, *Think Tanks.*

18. Task Force on Inequality and American Democracy, *American Democracy in an Age of Rising Inequality* (Washington, D.C.: American Political Science Association, 2004). A popularized account is Charles Lewis's *The Buying of the President 2004* (New York: Harper, 2004).

19. On this important issue, others have offered far more optimistic interpretations. See Samuel Popkin, *The Reasoning Voter* (Chicago: University of Chicago Press, 1991); Benjamin I. Page and Robert Y. Shapiro, *The Rational Public* (Chicago: University of Chicago Press, 1992); Arthur Lupia and Mathew D. McCubbins, *The Democratic Dilemma* (Cambridge: Cambridge University Press, 1998). On the coherence and responsiveness of aggregated public opinion in interaction with public policy and political events, see James A. Stimson, *Tides of Consent: How Public Opinion Shapes American Politics* (Cambridge: Cambridge University Press, 2004).

20. Matthew A. Baum, *Soft News Goes to War: Public Opinion and American Foreign Policy in the New Media Age* (Princeton: Princeton University Press, 2003).

21. David T. Z. Mindich, *Tuned Out: Why Americans under 40 Don't Follow the News* (New York: Oxford University Press, 2004).

22. Joseph Nye, Philip D. Zelikow, and David C. King, *Why People Don't Trust Government* (Cambridge: Harvard University Press, 1997); Matthew A. Crenson and Benjamin Ginsberg, *Downsizing Democracy: How America Sidelined Its Citizens and Privatized Its Public* (Baltimore: Johns Hopkins University Press, 2002).

23. On American workers' reported concerns about lack of focus, see *Overwork in America: When the Way We Work Becomes Too Much* (New York: Families and Work Institute, March 2005). Naive realism, and the tendency to perceive opponents as more extreme than they are, are discussed in John R. Chambers, Robert S. Baron, and Mary L. Inman, "Misperceptions in Intergroup Conflict," *Psychological Science* 17, no. 1 (2006): 38. On media competition and incentives for bias, see Andrei Shleifer and Sendhil Mullainathan, "The Market for News," *American Economic Review* 95, no. 4 (2005): 1031–53.

24. Douglas Southall Freeman, *George Washington: A Biography,* vol. 4, *Leader of the Revolution* (New York: Charles Scribner, 1951).

25. On this theme, see John Lukacs, *Democracy and Populism: Fear and Hatred* (New Haven: Yale University Press, 2005).

Contributors

Traci Burch holds appointments as Assistant Professor in Political Science at Northwestern University and Research Fellow at the American Bar Foundation. Her recent dissertation, "Punishment and Participation: How Criminal Convictions Threaten American Democracy" won the Robert Noxon Toppan Prize "for the best dissertation presented on a subject in political science" at Harvard University. Her research interests include criminal justice policy, race and ethnic politics, and political behavior.

James W. Ceaser is Professor of Politics at the University of Virginia, where he has taught since 1976. He has written several books on American politics and American political thought, including *Presidential Selection, Liberal Democracy and Political Science, Reconstructing America,* and *Nature and History in American Political Development.* He is a frequent contributor to the popular press.

Robert Faulkner is Professor of Political Science at Boston College, teaching mostly political philosophy. His most recent book is *The Case for Greatness: Honorable Ambition and Its Critics;* others are *Francis Bacon and the Project of Progress, Richard Hooker and the Politics of a Christian England,* and *The Jurisprudence of John Marshall.* He coedited Marshall's one-volume *Life of George Washington* and Alexandras Shtromas's *Totalitarianism and the Prospect of World Order.*

Niall Ferguson is Laurence A. Tisch Professor of History and William Ziegler Professor of Business Administration at Harvard, as well as being a Senior Research Fellow at Jesus College, Oxford University, and a Senior Fellow at the Hoover Institution, Stanford University. He is the author of many recent books, including *The Pity of War: Explaining World War One;*

The Cash Nexus: Money and Power in the Modern World, 1700–2000; Empire: The Rise and Demise of the British World Order and the Lessons for Global Power; Colossus: The Rise and Fall of the American Empire; and *The War of the World: Twentieth-century Conflict and the Descent of the West.*

William A. Galston is Senior Fellow in Governance Studies at the Brookings Institution and College Park Professor at the University of Maryland. He is the author of numerous works on political philosophy, American politics, and public policy. His most recent books include *Liberal Pluralism, The Practice of Liberal Pluralism,* and *Public Matters.* From 2003 through 2005 he was Deputy Assistant to President Clinton. His board memberships include the Council for Excellence in Governance and the National Endowment for Democracy.

Hugh Heclo is Robinson Professor of Public Affairs at George Mason University, a former Professor of Government at Harvard University, and prior to that a Senior Fellow at the Brookings Institution in Washington. Most recently he is author of *Christianity and American Democracy.* He currently serves on the twelve-member Scholars' Council advising the Librarian of Congress and in 2002 was honored by the American Political Science Association with the John Gaus Award for lifetime achievement in the fields of political science and public administration. For the past twenty-five years, he, his wife and daughter have operated a Christmas tree farm in the northern Shenandoah Valley.

Pierre Manent, born 1949 in Toulouse (France), was assistant to Raymond Aron, and now teaches the history of political philosophy at the École des Hautes Études en Sciences Sociales (Paris); in recent years he has been a Visiting Scholar at Boston College. Among his many books are those translated as *An Intellectual History of Liberalism, Tocqueville and the Nature of Democracy, The City of Man,* and *Modern Liberty and Its Discontents.* His most recent book is *A World beyond Politics? A Defense of the Nation-State.*

Harvey C. Mansfield, the William R. Kenan, Jr., Professor of Government at Harvard University, studies and teaches political philosophy. He has written on Edmund Burke and the nature of political parties, on Machiavelli and the invention of indirect government, in defense of a defensible liberalism, and in favor of a constitutional American political science. He has also written on the discovery and development of the theory of executive power, and is a translator of Machiavelli and Tocqueville. He just completed a book on manliness. In 2004 he received the National Humanities Medal from the President.

Peter Rodriguez is Associate Professor at the Darden Graduate School of Business at the University of Virginia, where he teaches classes on global economies and markets. He is an economist and specializes in the study of international business, trade, development, and government corruption. His research publications range from theoretical explorations of international trade policies and firm behavior to empirical and practice-based studies of issues in international business. Rodriguez worked as an associate in the Global Energy Group at JP Morgan Chase.

Kay Lehman Schlozman is J. Joseph Moakley Endowed Professor of Political Science at Boston College, where she teaches American politics. She has written numerous articles in professional journals and is coauthor of *Injury to Insult: Unemployment, Class and Political Response; Organized Interests and American Democracy, Voice and Equality: Civic Voluntarism in American Politics;* and *The Private Roots of Public Action.* She is the winner of the American Political Science Association's 2004 Rowman and Littlefield Award for Innovative Teaching in Political Science and the 2006 Frank J. Goodnow Award for Distinguished Service to the Profession of Political Science.

Susan Shell is Professor of Political Science at Boston College. Her publications include *The Rights of Reason: A Study of Kant's Philosophy and Politics; The Embodiment of Reason: Kant on Generation, Spirit, and Community;* and "The Liberal Critique of Gay Marriage" (*The Public Interest,* 2004). She has received fellowships from the National Endowment for the Humanities, the American Council of Learned Societies, the Radcliffe Institute, and the Earhart Foundation. She is currently completing a book on Kant and the limits of autonomy.

Peter Skerry is Professor of Political Science at Boston College and a non-resident senior fellow at the Brookings Institution. His book *Mexican Americans: The Ambivalent Minority* was awarded the Los Angeles Times Book Prize. He has written about race, religion, ethnicity, and immigration for a variety of publications including the *New York Times, New Republic,*

Foreign Policy, Washington Post, and *Time.* His most recent book was on the politics of the U.S. census, *Counting on the Census? Race, Group Identity, and the Evasion of Politics.* He is currently working on a book about Arabs and Muslims in the United States.

James Q. Wilson was a professor of government at Harvard for twenty-six years, then taught at UCLA for twelve. He is now a professor at Pepperdine University. Among his books are *The Moral Sense, The Marriage Problem, On Character,* and *American Government* (with John DiIulio). His essay in this volume was first delivered as the Tanner Lecture at Harvard. Wilson is a recipient of the Presidential Medal of Freedom.

Alan Wolfe is Professor of Political Science and Director of the Boisi Center for Religion and American Public Life at Boston College. His most recent books include *Does American Democracy Still Work? Return to Greatness: How America Lost Its Sense of Purpose and What It Needs to Do to Recover It; The Transformation of American Religion: How We Actually Live Our Faith;* and *An Intellectual in Public.* He is the author or editor of more than ten other books including *One Nation, After All* and *Moral Freedom: The Search for Virtue in a World of Choice,* which were both selected as New York Times Notable Books of the Year.

Index

Rawls, John, 69, 75, 76, 89, 91
Reagan, Ronald, 17, 21, 30, 97, 111, 174
Relativism, 68, 89, 243
Religion, 60, 66–67, 70–71, 76, 80, 87, 90, 92, 130–31, 193–214
Representation, 58, 72, 140–73, 196, 197–98, 247–48, 249–66
Rice, Condoleezza, 21
Rousseau, Jean Jacques, 28, 117, 126–29
Rumsfeld, Donald, 15, 21, 32, 47, 104–7

Savings, 217–37
Schmitt, Carl, 62–63, 72
September 11, 2001, 22–23, 31, 35, 46, 47, 58, 103–5, 109
Shays's Rebellion, 141
Social Security, 42, 134, 178, 220
Special interests. *See* Organized interests/ Special interests
State of nature. *See* Natural law
Strauss, Leo, 58, 60–61, 85–86, 99

Taxes, 40, 42, 100–102, 143, 160, 161, 163, 218, 223–24; and immigrants, 177–78; and religion, 200

Terrorism, 16, 23–24, 78, 103–5, 175
Tocqueville, Alexis de, 119–21, 126, 128, 131, 140, 198, 203, 208
Tolerance, 76, 90, 92, 122, 141, 199. *See also* Intolerance
Toleration, 66–67, 125, 208
Trade deficit, 42, 220, 225–29
Truman, Harry, 97, 111
Tyranny, 27, 36, 46, 57, 61, 68, 90, 91, 251, 253

U.S. Constitution, 38, 64, 109, 111, 140, 198, 203, 250–54, 258–59, 262, 264
United Nations, 48, 104

Vietnam War, 22, 30, 43, 50, 106, 107, 194, 256
Virtue, 20, 62, 70, 81, 99, 128, 238–48, 253, 263, 264 n. 3
Voluntary associations, 7, 8, 37, 156–57, 162

Washington, George, 121, 253, 263
Weber, Max, 87
Welfare, 100, 141, 159, 161, 178, 197
Williamson, Jeffrey G., 175, 182

Text design by Paula Newcomb

Typesetting by Delmastype, Ann Arbor, Michigan

Text font: Minion

Minion is a 1990 Adobe Originals typeface by Robert Slimbach. Minion is inspired by classical, old style typefaces of the late Renaissance, a period of elegant, beautiful, and highly readable type designs. Created primarily for text setting, Minion combines the aesthetic and functional qualities that make text type highly readable with the versatility of digital technology.

—*courtesy* adobe.com